D1761214

CW
4/12

DR 12/1)

1 5 APR 2014

Council

Cultural Sociology

Series Editors: Jeffrey C. Alexander, Ron Eyerman, David Inglis, and Philip Smith

Cultural sociology is widely acknowledged as one of the most vibrant areas of inquiry in the social sciences across the world today. The Palgrave Macmillan Series in Cultural Sociology is dedicated to the proposition that deep meanings make a profound difference in social life. Culture is not simply the glue that holds society together, a crutch for the weak, or a mystifying ideology that conceals power. Nor is it just practical knowledge, dry schemas, or knowhow. The series demonstrates how shared and circulating patterns of meaning actively and inescapably penetrate the social. Through codes and myths, narratives and icons, rituals and representations, these culture structures drive human action, inspire social movements, direct and build institutions, and so come to shape history. The series takes its lead from the cultural turn in the humanities, but insists on rigorous social science methods and aims at empirical explanations. Contributions engage in thick interpretations but also account for behavioral outcomes. They develop cultural theory but also deploy middle-range tools to challenge reductionist understandings of how the world actually works. In so doing, the books in this series embody the spirit of cultural sociology as an intellectual enterprise.

Jeffrey C. Alexander is the Lillian Chavenson Saden Professor of Sociology and Co-Director of the Center for Cultural Sociology at Yale University. From 1995–2010, he edited (with Steven Seidman) the *Cambridge Series on Cultural Social Studies* and from 2004–2009 (with Julia Adams, Ron Eyerman, and Philip Gorski) *Sociological Theory*. Among his recent books are *The Civil Sphere* and *The Performance of Politics: Obama's Victory and the Democratic Struggle for Power*.

Ron Eyerman is Professor of Sociology and Co-Director of the Center for Cultural Sociology at Yale University. His areas of research include social theory, trauma, and memory, and he has taught undergraduate and graduate courses on these topics. He is the author of *The Assassination of Theo van Gogh: From Social Drama to Cultural Trauma*.

David Inglis is Professor of Sociology at the University of Aberdeen. He is founding editor of the journal *Cultural Sociology*, published by Sage. His recent books include *The Globalization of Food* and *Cosmopolitanism*.

Philip Smith is Professor and Co-Director of the Yale Center for Cultural Sociology. His recent books include *Why War?*, *Punishment and Culture*, and *Incivility: The Rude Stranger in Everyday Life* (co-authored) among others.

Interpreting Clifford Geertz
Edited by Jeffrey C. Alexander
Philip Smith, and Matthew Norton

The Cultural Sociology of Political Assassination
Ron Eyerman

THE CULTURAL SOCIOLOGY OF POLITICAL ASSASSINATION

FROM MLK AND RFK TO FORTUYN AND VAN GOGH

RON EYERMAN

palgrave
macmillan

First published in 2011 by
PALGRAVE MACMILLAN®
in the United States—a division of St. Martin's Press LLC,
175 Fifth Avenue, New York, NY 10010.

Where this book is distributed in the UK, Europe and the rest of the world,
this is by Palgrave Macmillan, a division of Macmillan Publishers Limited,
registered in England, company number 785998, of Houndmills,
Basingstoke, Hampshire RG21 6XS.

Palgrave Macmillan is the global academic imprint of the above companies
and has companies and representatives throughout the world.

Palgrave® and Macmillan® are registered trademarks in the United States,
the United Kingdom, Europe and other countries.

ISBN: 978–0–230–11822–5 (hardcover)
ISBN: 978–0–230–11823–2 (paperback)

Library of Congress Cataloging-in-Publication Data

Eyerman, Ron.
    The cultural sociology of political assassination : from MLK and RFK to
Fortuyn and Van Gogh / by Ron Eyerman.
        p. cm.—(Cultural sociology)
    ISBN 978–0–230–11822–5—ISBN 978–0–230–11823–2
    1. Assassination—Political aspects. 2. King, Martin Luther, Jr.,
1929–1968. 3. Kennedy, Robert F., 1925–1968. 4. Palme, Olof,
1927–1986. I. Title.
HV6278.E94 2011
364.152′4—dc22   2011011765

A catalogue record of the book is available from the British Library.

Design by Newgen Imaging Systems (P) Ltd., Chennai, India.

First edition: October 2011

10 9 8 7 6 5 4 3 2 1

Printed in the United States of America.

Previous Publications

Narrating Trauma: On the Impact of Collective Suffering (edited with Jeffrey C. Alexander and Elizabeth Butler Breese), 2011.

The Assassination of Theo van Gogh: Social Drama and Cultural Trauma, 2008.

Myth, Meaning and Performance (edited with Lisa McCormick), 2006.

Cultural Trauma, Slavery, and the Formation of African American Identity, 2001.

CONTENTS

SERIES EDITORS' FOREWORD

POLITICAL ASSASSINATIONS ARE ALWAYS TERRIBLE AND SHOCKING EVENTS. In his cultural sociology of such horrendous occurrences, Ron Eyerman provides a new explanation as to why they are so shocking, and how the shock can vary in its depth and breadth. It is because political figures can be regarded as symbolic representations of their nations that their murder is shocking, for it is not only the individual but the entire collectivity that has been attacked. The extra-legal and violent character of the murder, moreover, and its root-edness in ethnic, racial, or racial prejudice, can call into question the demo-cratic and civil identity of a nation and initiate a long soul-searching, which may not only destabilize morale, but undermine the capacity for optimism and reform. Offering detailed, theoretically controlled case studies of news media, carrier groups, social performances, and emotions, Eyerman shows how political assassinations did create deep and ongoing cultural wounds in the United States and the Netherlands, and how they did not create such cultural trauma in the Swedish cases.

This volume deepens cultural–sociological understanding in fundamental ways. Carefully comparing variable affects across time and space, it produces new theoretical understandings of the key elements of the trauma process. It breaks new empirical ground by reconstructing compelling portraits of six different events across three different national contexts. Political assassina-tion thus becomes a new and revealing topic for sociological study.

ACKNOWLEDGMENTS

THIS BOOK IS IN MANY WAYS A CONTINUATION OF MY PREVIOUS WORK on the assassination of Theo van Gogh. Many of those who helped me with that project will be acknowledged again. My good friend and colleague Jeffrey Alexander, as he usually does, provided not only insightful comments but also through his rich theoretical imagination opened a number of windows that allowed a fresh perspective. Other colleagues at Yale, especially those associated with our Center for Cultural Sociology, must also be acknowledged; in addition to our students and faculty, visitors to the Center, Anna Lund, Vered Vinitzky-Seroussi, and Volker Heins read parts of the manuscript. Participants at presentations I made at Haverford College, Konstanz University, Lund University, and New York University helped me clarify my ideas. Nothing can compare, however, to our weekly Yale workshops where threads and themes from our conversations can be found knitted in the texture of my argument. At the NYU presentation the two discussants, Jan Gross and Ophelia Deroy, were outstanding in their constructive comments. Participants in my seminar Social Theory, Trauma, and Memory were relentless in their criticism and advice, most particularly Mira Debs and Yasushi Tanaka-Gutiez.

I would like to especially thank Karianne Esseveld, Isabel Jijon, Marc de Leeuw, and Jensen Sass for their help in gathering data and for providing insightful comments in the process. Bernadette Nadya Jaworsky read through the entire manuscript and not only did the editorial fine tuning, but helped to focus and clarify my argument. She also suggested some of the diagrams found in the text. Volker Heins, too, was very helpful in this regard. Nadine Amalfi helped me prepare the final version and offered advice about layout and design. Thank you all!

PROLOGUE

ON SATURDAY MORNING JANUARY 8, 2011, Arizona Congresswoman Gabrielle Giffords and 18 others were shot at a public rally outside a supermarket in Tucson, Arizona. As I write, Congresswoman Giffords, who was at first mistakenly reported killed, is in critical condition in hospital after being shot through the head. She has since made a remarkable recovery. Six others are dead, including a federal judge and a nine-year-old girl who were attending the event. The perpetrator, a 22-year-old white male named Jared Lee Loughner, is in police custody, having been apprehended at the scene by bystanders who tackled and disarmed him as he tried to escape. He has been arrested and formally charged. The criminal complaint filed in District Court lists five counts of "intent and attempt to kill," whereas the "Statement of Probable Cause" filed by a special agent for the Federal Bureau of Investigation (FBI) calls the complaint against Loughner the "Attempted Assassination of a Member of Congress; in violation of Title 18, United States Code Section 35" (http://documents.nytimes.com/criminal-complaint-against-jared-lee-loughner).

In the intense media coverage of this incident the word "assassination" was at first reluctantly and then readily applied, especially after it was used in the official charges brought against the perpetrator. Assassination, even in its formal and legal usage, is an emotionally powerful term because it opens collective memory to a long history of shocking and dramatic occurrences. As the horror unfolded through the mass media, the American public was given a confusing and often contentious account. The facts soon became clear enough and the storyline soon became established. However, the issue of the killer's motives—was he politically motivated and what contribution, if any, did local and national politics play in the context of the crime— became central points of debate over airwaves and through the Internet. Given that formal charges called this crime an assassination and not a murder, the discussion was pushed in a particular direction—one that would distinguish between assassination(as in the attempt on the life of an elected public official) and *political* assassination, which would add to that political motivation on the part of the perpetrator. This led to a ferocious debate, following largely along the political lines of liberal versus conservative, as to what exactly the politics of the alleged assassin were, on the one hand, and what effect the contentiously polarized political discourse of the current United States might have had on his behavior, on the other. In addition, media accounts have called attention to the background and mental state of the perpetrator, who was being portrayed as a loner with a history of erratic behavior, and the personalities and family histories of his victims. The fact that among those killed was a nine-year-old girl who happened to have been born on September 11, 2001 or 9/11, a very significant date in the American collective memory, has been highlighted. So too was the fact that the congresswoman was the wife of an American astronaut, as well as the proud owner of a gun of similar type to the one that was used to shoot her. All these details have provided twists and turns to the emerging narrative about the killing spree and its meaning.

Unlike murders, assassinations don't just happen; they must be designated, told, and established. Their meaning and significance is something hotly contested, especially in a contentious political context. This is because political assassinations engage and affect communities, including some and excluding others. The murder—or in this case, attempted murder—of a public figure arouses feelings of identification, empathy, and loss among groups of people, even if they are not part of any political constituency in the narrow sense. An assassination can thus create a community, at least in the associative sense, as much as it can threaten or destroy one. Because of their evocative emotive power, assassinations give rise to contentious actions and debate, such as the blame and name-calling that followed in the immediate wake of the attack on Congresswoman Giffords. They can also provide occasion for collective reflection and reconciliation. In a nationally televised speech at a memorial service for the victims of what was termed the Tucson Tragedy, American president Barack Obama called for "a new era of civility," and for an end to political "point-scoring and pettiness" (*New York Times,* January 13, 2011: p.1). Arizona governor Janet Brewer, embroiled in a contentious political struggle over illegal immigration, also took the occasion to call for collective healing. Brewer made reference to the city of Tucson and the state of Arizona in her remarks about loss, grief, and healing. Tucson, she said, would never be able to replace its loss. On this and other occasions Brewer has set out to repair the image of her state, which is described by some as a violent and hateful place. Such remarks reveal how assassinations can affect as well as engage community in a multiplicity of senses. They can shatter, they can unify, and they can leave an indelible mark on a people and a locality. The city of Dallas and the state of Texas will always be associated with the assassination of John Kennedy. Governor Brewer was perhaps referring to the same possibility with regard to Tucson and Arizona. Public representatives like Barack Obama and Janet Brewer follow a familiar script in the public performances after a shocking incident like an assassination. Those in authority are expected to perform the role of unifier, to call for calm and offer condolence in the public grieving following such an occurrence. Such persons become symbols of the collective will, as well as of collective suffering. How well leaders perform their authority is a key factor in determining how quickly and how successfully processes of collective repair are set in motion. Mass media accounts are another important factor. In the following chapters I analyze six political assassinations through the lens of the theory of cultural trauma with the aim of revealing all the factors that condition, contain, or catalyze cultural trauma. As I will explain in detail, by cultural trauma I mean a deep-going public discourse on the foundations of collective identity. In the Tucson shooting there remains a potential for cultural trauma at several levels of collective identity, the city, the state and the nation, and various groupings in between. Whether or not this occurs is not simply a matter of time, but a function of how well authorities perform; the success of various efforts at collective repair, including the judicial system; how the mass media narrate and interpret what occurred; and the power of various carrier groups, such as family members, political representatives, various interest groups such as the gun lobby, and so on. All these issues will be discussed in detail in what follows with reference to six assassinations.

CHAPTER 1

THE PRIMAL SCENE

ON NOVEMBER 22, 1963, JOHN FITZGERALD KENNEDY, thirty-fifth president of the United States, was shot while riding in an open motor vehicle on the streets of Dallas, Texas. Kennedy was sitting in a specially designed six-seat limousine, waving at cheering crowds when three shots rang out.[1] The first shot missed the vehicle entirely. The second hit Kennedy in the upper back, just below the shoulder, passing through his body and entering the back of Texas governor John Connelly, who was sitting front of the president. At the sound of the third shot, Jacqueline Kennedy turned instinctively toward her husband to see him slump forward as the bullet exploded in the back of his skull. On the frenzied race to the hospital, she held his shattered head in her lap, repeating over and over again, "Jack, Jack, what have they done to you" (Bugliosi 2007:67). Though there was a frantic effort to save his life, John Kennedy was essentially dead on arrival at the hospital. The news of the American president's death sent shock waves across the nation and around the world. An outpouring of grief followed the initial disbelief. People cried openly in the streets, and crowds of strangers gathered to discuss what had happened. Time appeared to stop as all attention turned to what was occurring in Dallas.

Although much of the Kennedy motorcade—from the arrival at Love Field through the streets of the city—was broadcast on television, there were no live pictures of the murder itself. Because television broadcasting was limited by the weight and cost of its equipment for this event, bulky stationary cameras were arranged at set locations along the route. None was in the vicinity of the murder scene. The first mediated broadcast of the shooting went out over radio and telegraph systems just four minutes after the occurrence and spread to newspaper offices around the country over the telephone and teletype. Journalists on the scene, as well as law enforcement authorities, contacted their superiors from landline telephones. There were so many phone calls into the nation's capital that day that the entire system collapsed. "Most of the nearly one and a half million telephones in service in the Washington metropolitan area on November 22 were used during the first half hour [of the murder]" (Bugliosi 2007:221). It would take almost half a day for service to return to normal. Something similar occurred in New York City and other urban centers across the country.

Minutes after the shooting, radio and television programs were interrupted by news flashes. Early reports announced that Vice President Lyndon Johnson had also been wounded. It was reported that two assassins, a man and a woman, had been seen shooting from the ledge of a building. Then came reports of arrested suspects: a black man, a white man in a business suit, and finally the breathless announcement that a suspect with a gun was being pursued at a local movie house. This man, later identified as Lee Harvey Oswald, was being sought in the shooting of a Dallas police officer, with a possible connection to the Kennedy assassination. A shifting of television cameras permitted live reporting from outside Dallas's Parkland Hospital, where anxious crowds had gathered awaiting news of the president's condition. The cameras outside the building captured a live interview with a Catholic priest who had just left the president's bedside; it was he who informed the world that the president was dead. This news spread across the nation via the Associated Press wire service. Then came the official announcement, with a live broadcast of reactions from the gathered crowd. TV audiences were taken across the airwaves and into the Dallas Trade Mart, where hundreds had been waiting to be addressed by the president; instead, they received a declaration of his death.

Through the eyes of television, the nation was made witness not to the actual murder, but to the sorrow and grief of thousands of fellow citizens. In this visualized collective reaction, the American nation was constituted as it never had been before. People stayed glued to their television screens for four days that November, from the shooting in Dallas to the funeral procession and burial in the nation's capital. As the *New York Times* put it, "The medium of television which played such a major part in the career of President Kennedy, is the instrument that is making the tragedy of his death such a deeply personal experience in millions of homes over this long weekend. In hushed living rooms everywhere, the uninterrupted coverage provided by the three national networks and their affiliated stations is holding families indoors to share in history's grim unfolding, the home screen for the first time fulfilling the heart rending function of giving a new dimension to grief" (quoted in Bugliosi 338:9).

The first images of the actual murder appeared in the form of still photographs taken from the now-famous Zapruder tape. Abraham Zapruder, a local Dallas business owner, was filming the presidential motorcade with a small handheld camera when the shots rang out.His film represents the only visual record of the actual occurrence. Zapruder appeared on the Dallas station WFAATV a little more than an hour and a half after the shooting to report what he had seen through his viewfinder: "I saw his head practically open up, all blood and everything, and I kept on shooting. That's about all, I'm just sick, I can't...," at which point the announcer broke in: "I think that pretty well expresses the entire feelings of the whole world" (transcript reprinted in *Newseum* 2003:102). Zapruder's film was in much demand, not least by law enforcement officials, who immediately sent a copy off to Washington. Against fierce competition, *Life Magazine* purchased all rights to the film from Zapruder for $150,000 within hours of its being developed. The same magazine provided free room and board for Oswald's wife and mother in the hope of getting an exclusive story.

The next day, November 24, the prime suspect in the assassination was himself assassinated—shot by an assailant in a basement walkway as he was being transferred from the Dallas city jail. This, unlike the actual killing of Kennedy, was televised and became the first murder to be broadcast live over the airwaves. Simultaneously, news of Oswald's death interrupted television broadcasts of the ceremonial removal of John F. Kennedy's body from the White House to the Capitol building in Washington, D.C., where it would lie in state. The body of the slain president had already created several controversies. The first occurred when federal authorities sought to move the body from the Dallas hospital to Washington. Since the murder of a president was not then a federal crime, all jurisdiction lay with local authority. The Dallas medical examiner refused to have the body moved. Eventually, his decision was forcefully overruled and the body of the dead president was secreted to the airport and hurriedly loaded onto Air Force One, the official presidential airplane. Finding a suitable place on the plane also provided a bit of a quandary, as there were no special provisions for such an eventuality. Two rows of seats in the rear section of the aircraft were removed to accommodate the casket containing the body. On the plane were also Jacqueline Kennedy and the newly sworn in Lyndon Johnson and his wife. A second—and much more openly resolved controversy—concerned the president's final burial place. Would it be his family's home territory in Massachusetts or the nation's political and spiritual center, Washington, D.C.? Here as well, the issue concerned who held rights to the body of a slain leader—the state or the family (Kantorowicz 1957, Wagner- Pacifici 1986, Verdery 2000).

The murder of the prime suspect in the killing of the president was devastating not only because it happened, and because it happened on television, but also because it denied the nation the ritual cleansing process of a public and publicized trial. The *New York Times* placed ultimate blame for this on the Dallas authorities and what it considered complicit mass media: "The shame all America must bear for the spirit of madness and hate that struck down President John F. Kennedy is multiplied by the monstrous murder of his accused assassin...The Dallas authorities, abetted and encouraged by the newspaper, TV, and radio press, trampled on every principle of justice in their handling of Lee H. Oswald...It was an outrageous breach of police responsibility—no matter what the demands of reporters and cameramen may have been—to move Oswald in public under circumstances in which he could so easily have been the victim of attack...Now there can never be a trial that will determine Oswald's guilt or innocence by the standards of impartial justice that are one of the proudest adornments of our democracy" (*New York Times,* November 24, 1963, reprinted in *Four Days in November* 2003:445–6). The lack of cleansing by trial was probably the most likely cause for the rise and forcefulness of the many conspiracy theories that have emerged regarding this case, though this process would not have been any guarantee against them, as is evident from some of the cases discussed in this book.

Words like shame, tragedy, shock, and trauma were common throughout media reportage of the assassination of John F. Kennedy. The assassination of an American president by itself would have been cause for a massive outpouring of sorrow and grief and would have surely been considered a great tragedy for the nation and a source of shame in that, as one person quoted by the *Times* put it: "It could happen here, where we are supposed to be civilized." But the assassination of the assassin was cause for escalated shock and shame. The death of a president in office is anticipated by the principle of political succession, and the quick installation of the vice president was meant to calm all fears and to quash potential political exploitation. It provided a sense of order at a moment when disorder threatened. The murder, in full public view of the probable perpetrator, added insult to injury in that the systematic workings of retribution and justice were denied. This vital ritual process of civic repair is meant to not only find and convict the guilty but also to provide the broader public with the performed representation of the workings of a civilized society. But the pinnacle of the "civilized" world had revealed another side of itself through the events of those four fateful days. As the *New York Times* again put it, with reference to the televised juxtaposition of the victim's grieving widow and the violent end of the probable perpetrator: "The American people saw two scenes on the television today that illustrate the dualism of American life, the nobility and tenderness on the one hand, and the brutality on the other" (*Four Days in November* 2003:44). The first was a reference to the noble bearing of Jacqueline Kennedy and the rest of the Kennedy family and the second to the violent underbelly of American society that would only become more visible and escalate in the years ahead.

The assassination of John F. Kennedy represents a precursor to all of the assassinations discussed in this book. It provides both a reference point as well as a backdrop. As point of reference, the Kennedy assassination has been recalled and drawn upon by law enforcement authorities responsible for political leaders, by those leaders themselves, and by the publics affected by those assassinations. Pim Fortuyn was referred to as the "Dutch Kennedy," both before and after his own assassination. After Olof Palme was killed in 1986, the connection between his and the Kennedy assassination was immediately drawn—by the Swedish police looking for the killer, by mass media, and by ordinary Swedes in expressing their grief and sorrow. In one of those quirks of history, Palme had represented the Swedish government at Kennedy's funeral. The choreography of Kennedy's funeral also provided a referential model for that of Palme, as well as for that of Robert Kennedy in 1968. The unprecedented media coverage of the Kennedy assassination, most particularly the role of television, would also become a model for constructing and mediating the reportage of later political assassinations.

As both news and media event (Dayan and Katz 1992), the Kennedy assassination became a template for future coverage (Zelizer 2000). It provided a frame through which a mass audience could not only view, but also interpret the meaning of this occurrence. By focusing on particular aspects of the occurrence and reactions to it, media coverage could highlight certain features and use narratives to construct and offer a coded or "preferred reading" (Hall 1980) of what was happening. With headlines like "The Nation Mourns" and "Grieving Throngs View Kennedy Bier," daily newspapers reinforced broadcast images of shocked and grief-stricken family members and anonymous citizens alike. These fostered not only instant identification, but also imprinted lasting memories that would endure and be available for recall during seemingly similar occurrences. Who will ever forget the image of Jacqueline Kennedy's grieving face or that of her young son John John, saluting his dead father as the casket wheeled past? Such images created a sense of solidarity, a feeling of community, among broad and geographically wide-ranging affected publics, which coalesced into a largely anonymous group stretching far beyond national borders. Its members would forever identify with each other through that highly charged emotional moment, a moment that even years later could be recalled in a heartbeat and re-experienced through the prompting of reproduced images. The impact of this sort of recollection extends far beyond the images, however, as powerful as they may be. Even for those who may not have seen such images, the assassination of John F. Kennedy became an emotional reference point for articulating the experience of political assassination as such. It is an assassination that has become part of global collective memory.

It can be useful in an American context to ask why not Abraham Lincoln? He was the first U.S. president to be assassinated, and his death had a devastating impact on the newly mending nation, occurring as it did in the midst of celebrations marking the end of the Civil War and the victory of the Northern armies in 1865. Barry Schwartz (2000) has shown how Lincoln's assassination has affected American collective memory, which even the distance of time and the contentious context of its occurrence have not diminished. The opening paragraph of Schwartz's book reveals its relevance nearly a century later:

> "Moments after President John F. Kennedy was buried in Arlington National Cemetery, a black limousine pulled up to the Lincoln Memorial. The two people inside sat silently for ten minutes, gazing at the memorial and thinking about the image inside. Scanning the past for images to make sense of their grief, Bobby and Jackie Kennedy had found Abraham Lincoln." (Schwartz 2000:ix)

This poignant image reminds us that Lincoln's memory is still very much alive in the American imagination. John F. Kennedy's body rested on a replica of the catafalque that had supported Lincoln's, and the planners of the Kennedy funeral procession had consulted those drawn up by their predecessors a hundred years ago.

There is no denying this importance to collective memory. The difference between the impact of the two assassinations lies in the role of television and the power of visual mass media generally. The Kennedy assassination occurred at a time when the notion of celebrity was being transformed and when a new audience for its representation was emerging. Television was becoming the main vehicle of a moving image based celebrity consciousness, which more than complemented one that had already been established during the 1930s and 1940s through photo-based magazines like *Life* and *Look* and the motion picture. At the same time, the Kennedys were the subject of unprecedented media attention and identification. Here was a successful young and handsome man, with a beautiful wife and two young children who, with the aid of visual media, had captured the aspirations of a new, postwar generation and in the process changed the way the country looked at its political leaders. Now this rising star, a true hero in the military, civil, and family sense, was dead. With the circumstances of his death immediately broadcast and diffused throughout the nation and world, reaction could be both immediate and simultaneous, in other words, shared as a collective. I believe this context makes for a substantial difference in the ways in which the shared memory of John Fitzgerald Kennedy has been constructed and perpetuated.

Mass media have altered the meaning of political assassination dramatically since Abraham Lincoln's death. Mass media create coherency, a media *event*. Employing word and image, they provide a narrative frame through which chaos makes sense. This frame is then disseminated far and wide to an anonymous multilayered audience, providing it with a common point of reference. In the process, an occurrence is transformed into a social drama with many layers of meaning and affect (Eyerman 2008). The sphere of the media also acts as a central vehicle that drives a process I will identify as cultural trauma, a public discourse that touches the very foundations of collective identity. In saying this, I am not making any claims here about necessary and sufficient conditions for a political assassination to become a cultural trauma, that is, cultural traumas only occur in societies where there is a well-developed mass media and a celebrity culture. Abraham Lincoln's assassination was a traumatic occurrence, which contributed to an already ongoing public discourse on the foundations of collective identity. Because it occurred at the very end of a devastating civil war, this discourse was bound to be partisan and polarized, with each side having its own version of who the perpetrators and victims were. This makes this assassination and its relation to cultural trauma different from the ones I study here.

CHAPTER 2

POLITICAL ASSASSINATION, TRAUMA, AND NARRATION

MY CONCERN IN THIS BOOK IS WITH POLITICAL ASSASSINATION as a form of traumatic event, and how, with the aid of mass-mediated representation, the murder of an important public person can set in motion a process of cultural trauma. My primary case studies are Martin Luther King, Jr., and Robert F. Kennedy in the United States. Abraham Lincoln and John F. Kennedy will also be discussed, as they provide historical reference points concerning the meaning and responses to assassination in the United States. Olof Palme and Anna Lindh in Sweden and Pim Fortuyn and Theo van Gogh in the Netherlands round out my study, providing a nation-based, comparative dimension. With the aid of these examples, I elaborate and develop the theory of cultural trauma as I map the process from "traumatic occurrence" to "significant event" over the historical course of these assassinations. Selecting cases is not an easy task, not least because writing about events that are close-at-hand and near to heart is difficult, but also because the number of assassinations in recent times has increased dramatically. Writing in 1985, Franklin Ford could remark on what he described as "the unprecedented rise in the number of assassinations attempted.... Their incidence increased roughly tenfold between the nineteenth century and what has elapsed of the twentieth. More ominous still, the rate of increase has been steepest during the last three decades" (1985:299).

THINGS HAVE ONLY GOTTEN WORSE

I chose the examples above for several reasons. As such, they were all political assassinations of a different type that occurred in relatively close temporal proximity in three different national contexts. They offer the opportunity to reflect on the historicity and cultural variation of political assassination in stable modern democracies. The fact that both Sweden and the Netherlands are constitutional monarchies adds an interesting dimension. These examples also provide an opportunity to elaborate on the theory of cultural trauma— understood here as a mediated public discourse in which fundamental notions grounding collective identity are brought into play—and its relation to traumatic occurrence. All my examples were traumatic in the traditional meaning of the term—shocking occurrences that left long-standing afteref- fects for both the individual and the nation. Though the nation-state will be my primary level of analysis, several of my cases had powerful resonat- ing effects beyond national boundaries. Comparing them will permit me to more clearly specify the conditions that are conducive to transforming a traumatic occurrence into a cultural trauma, and in the process, provide grounds for the further development of that theory.

There are other reasons for choosing these examples. Directly after the murder of Robert Kennedy in June 1968, President Lyndon Johnson ordered the establishment of the U.S. National Commission on the Causes and Prevention of Violence (hereafter referred to as "the Commission"), primarily composed of social scientists, to investigate "the causes and prevention of violence" (Kirkham, Levy, and Crotty, 2002[1969]). In its published report, the Commissionfound the occurrence of political assassination to be closely correlated with national levels of political violence. They also found that whereas political violence and assassination were relatively common in the United States, they were relatively uncommon in both Sweden and the Netherlands. During one of the main periods of the Commission's concern (1948–1967), there were no assassination events (successful/unsuccessful attempts or conspiratorial plots) in either the Netherlands or Sweden, whereas the United States experienced 16 such events (Kirkham et al. 2002[1969], 120–123). The same study ranked the United States fifth among the 86 nations surveyed—the highest amongst the "developed" countries. Based on the Commission's report, no one would have predicted that in the follow- ing decades Sweden and the Netherlands, two of the most politically stable, economically developed, and culturally tolerant nations in the world, would each experience not one but two successful and successive political assassina- tions. Why this happened is one of the concerns of this book.

Are there any broader lessons beyond corrective policy issues to be learned from analyzing political assassinations? Like natural disasters, political assassinations provide an occasion for collectivities to reflect on themselves. Hurricane Katrina in 2005 revealed aspects of the United States that were well hidden from many of its citizens. That poor people existed and that many of them were black was probably well known, but the powerful winds that battered New Orleans and pierced its levees, causing millions to flee their homes, exposed this reality in an unprecedented way. Who will forget the images of families stranded on rooftops and on highway overpasses wait-ing for days for help to arrive? Not only did this mediated event bring the issue of race and poverty forcefully to collective awareness, but the victims—who they were, how they should be labeled (as refugees?), and how they were treated—became cause for national debate. This public discourse raised not only the issue of responsibility, but also the broader question, "What type of society are we, in which such a tragedy could happen?" Political assassina-tions are similar in that they bring to the surface aspects of a society that normally lie deeply hidden, making them a potential catalyst for broad pub-lic debate. One major difference between political assassination and natural disaster is that between a so-called force of nature and the human hand (see White 2008 for a related discussion concerning "event" and "fact"). The issue of human responsibility arose in regard to Hurricane Katrina, both in relation to the construction of the levee system that was meant to protect the city of New Orleans and in the response of political authorities to the disaster. But the main cause, the forceful winds, was largely seen as lying outside human control. I say "largely," because an argument can be made that some of the blame for that extraordinarily powerful hurricane may lie in what has been called global warming, the causes of which lie in human actions and decisions.

In the shock they evoke, natural disasters and political assassinations raise the question, "Why has this happened to us?" They have the capacity to awaken a sense of collective belonging, to create a "we," while at the same time raising questions about the grounds upon which that collectivity rests. Such occurrences raise the issue not only of why this happened to us, but also of who or what was responsible. The religious might see an act of God, a sign or a punishment, in such an occurrence. For the secular, natural disasters are just that, natural, something inflicted by forces outside human control. From this perspective, although we might be able to track their path or even make predictions about their likely occurrence, natural phenomena, such as hurricanes and earthquakes, are not interpreted as the direct result of human action. Political assassinations, on the other hand, are the result of human actions—there is no one and nothing else to blame. The question, "Why has this happened to us?" which implies a collectivity, an "us," also involves the search for those responsible. It is here that traumatic occurrences align with cultural trauma. Attributing blame and settling on who is responsible is a central part of the process of cultural trauma, and in political assas-sination, as opposed to natural disasters, the responsible party is a human agent. The process of re-forming a collectivity, of bringing it to conscious-ness, and of naming the outside other that is responsible is a political process. What would more likely turn such a traumatic occurrence into a cultural trauma for example would be the fact that the responsible party was someone inside the collective. All these issues will be subjects for further discussion in later chapters. The point I wish to make here is that for the analyst, political assassinations provide unique opportunities to study the foundations of collective identity as well as those of collective memory; both are intimately intertwined. This has been a central issue in sociological thought since its origins in the nineteenth century.

CRISIS, TRAUMA, AND NARRATION

What makes a trauma a *cultural* trauma? To begin to define this concept, it is useful to first examine how its emergence and evolution differ from other ways of thinking about intense and shocking occurrences, such as crisis and traditional notions of trauma. Jürgen Habermas opens *Legitimation Crisis* (1975) with a discussion of the concept of "crisis," making clear the difference between the term's medical and social scientific uses. In its medical usage, he associates crisis with the "idea of an objective force that deprives a subject of some part of his normal sovereignty...in classical aesthetics...crisis signifies the turning point in a fateful process that, despite all objectivity, does not simply impose itself from outside and does not remain external to the identity of the persons caught up in it" (Habermas 1975:1–2). Habermas then goes on to develop a social scientific notion of crisis, which takes its starting point in systems theory, where "crisis states assume the form of a disintegration of social institutions" and threaten collective identity. He makes the claim that "social systems too have identities and can lose them" (Habermas 1975: 3), creating conditions in which a complex process of unfolding can spiral and threaten a social system to its core. Looked at in this sophisticated sense, and of course as common sense, crisis may well be a term that could be applied to the aftermath of political assassinations. Indeed, there are similarities in Habermas's use of the term in reference to legitimation crisis and my use of cultural trauma. Against the more objective notion of crisis used in the medical sciences, which is similar to the medical use of trauma, Habermas argues that crises must be interpreted and understood as such. They must, in other words, be narrated in order to be understood as crises. For Habermas, a legitimation crisis occurs when the self-image of a nation is threatened. This is also characteristic of cultural trauma, which can be defined as a discursive response to a tear in the social fabric, where the foundations of an established collective identity are shaken by a traumatic occurrence and are in need of renarration and repair. Both concepts make reference to a shattering of everyday routine and the taken-for-granted assumptions that guide them. Cultural trauma is a form of identity crisis in which a collectivity loses the secure sense of itself and seems to be adrift, existing in that liminal space Durkheim called anomie. But cultural trauma differs from crisis not only in that it affects the foundations of a collective identity, thus engaging the social whole and not merely one or several institutions (Smelser 2004), but also with regard to longevity and long-term effects. Cultural traumas are foundational identity crises.

Cultural traumas can be passed across generations, with their effects preserved in individual and collective memory, only to emerge in later generations via what could be called postcrisis symptoms. The deeply felt sense of crisis analyzed by Habermas might also evoke strong emotional response; such emotional content is absent, however, or rarely mentioned in his account. The economic crises of the 1930s left deep scars and had long-term effects, such as the mistrust in banks and in the credit system, on the generation that experienced it. Narrated as the "Great Depression," an economic crisis became a cultural trauma, affecting the way individual citizens and national leaders would react to seemingly similar crises, where deeply hidden anxieties could trigger seemingly irrational or impulse responses as well as rational reflection and contextual comparison. Consider, for example, the world financial crisis of 2008, where immediate comparisons to the Great Depression were drawn or denied.

Crises can develop into cultural traumas through a meaning struggle and a form of narration in which perpetrators and victims are named and asymmetrically positioned. Trauma requires narration of a specific kind, one in which neither irony nor humor is possible: the shock to the system is experienced as too great. Like crises, traumas produce a loss of confidence in the world and in the individual—and for the nation, a loss of confidence. The assassinations of King and Kennedy helped produced such a loss in the United States, which came to final fruition when the Vietnam War ended. The reaction to 9/11 can perhaps be understood with reference to these historical moments, as an acting out of repressed traumatic memory. The same might be said of the collective reactions to the more recent assassination of Osama Bin Laden, the alleged mastermind of the September 11 attacks. Cultural traumas are as much about acting out as working through, two key notions in the classical notion of trauma.

In its classical interpretation, to be discussed below, trauma disrupts narrative (Caruth 1996, LaCapra 2001), in the sense that it ruptures the flow of everyday experience. Here, trauma lies outside existing narrative, awaiting its formal representation. For cultural trauma theory, trauma emerges through narrative, which gives form to its emotional content. Trauma has been linked to modernity (Kaplan 2005) and to the modern experience of time. The modern experience of time is that of a constant and continual flow moving irrevocably forward, as in the expressions "time moves on" and "time heals all wounds." Trauma, according to this classical view, is out of time, a break in this flow, and is at once symptom and cause. Trauma presupposes this view of time in order for it to be experienced as interrupted, broken, and shattered. Trauma here is experienced through symptoms, the involuntary reactions to a past event, an acting out that requires working through. In this sense, trauma is always already there, awaiting representation. Cultural trauma implies something different; trauma emerges through narration rather than existing prior to it. The acts of narration make visible, articulate, and give meaning and words to what is strongly felt but not grasped. The trauma is named and given voice through the ongoing public dialogue or meaning struggle; it does not exist as a thing-in-itself, but only comes to be through dialogue and narration. This process, or what has been termed the "trauma drama" (Alexander 2004), is simultaneously an acting out (reacting) as well as a working through (attempts to name and heal). It is also a process in which the mass media and other carrier groups play a leading role, both in terms of articulating and representing and in the healing and working through. The media can orchestrate, being a prime and self-interested agent and a force in the process of social repair.

POLITICAL ASSASSINATION

What constitutes political assassination?[1] The U.S. Commission referred to earlier defines assassination as a particular type of murder where three elements are interwoven: "(1) a target that is a prominent political figure; (2) a political motive for the killing; (3) the potential political impact of the death or escape from death, as the case may be" (Kirkham et al. 2002[1969]:1). Is the murder or attempted murder of a political figure sufficient to call perpetrators political assassins? According to Murray Havens, "Assassination is the deliberate, extra legal killing of an individual for political purposes" (cited in Wilkinson 1976:3). What is it that makes a murder an assassination and a murderer an assassin in the sense implied above? Has the meaning and effect of political assassination changed over time, or has it remained relatively the same? The politically motivated murder of public figures and the common-sense meaning of political assassination have been well studied. There exist hundreds of books on the topic, mostly about individual cases, but also some general and generalizing theoretical analyses (for example, Kirkham et al. 1969, Horowitz 1972, Ford 1985, Bell 2005). In addition to fictional accounts, which in the form of thrillers and crime novels are a popular genre, there seems to be a fascination with true-crime stories, among which political assassination would be one subfield. The topic is also of great interest to academics, historians, psychologists, and political scientists. Sociologists have concerned themselves with analyzing and explaining the phenomenon, an interest the Commission report reflects.

From the perspective of what can be called police theorizing, political murders are analyzed—like all other such crimes—in terms of means, motive, and opportunity. Here the term "assassin" is important only in the legal prosecution of the crime. In its investigation of the murder of Robert Kennedy, for example, the Los Angeles police department became convinced that Sirhan Sirhan was the killer only after establishing without doubt that he had the means, an eight-shot 22-caliber pistol; the motivation; incriminating evidence that he hated and had stalked his victim; that he had the opportunity; and finally, that he was present in the crowd surrounding the victim as he was pushed through the pantry of L.A.'s Ambassador Hotel on the night of June 5, 1968. A central point of contention during Sirhan's trial, however, concerned distinguishing the act of murder from assassination. In their attempt to save their client from the gas chamber, Sirhan's attorneys (against his own expressed wishes) based their case on the concept of "diminished capacity," meaning that he was not in full control of himself when he shot his victim. Neither the murderer nor the murder was under dispute, only the perpetrator's mental state during the act. Their client had murdered a politician and thus could be called an assassin, but because he was not in full control of his mental state at the time of the occurrence, he was not a political assassin from a legal point of view.

James Earl Ray was arrested in connection with the murder of Martin Luther King. Jr. Because a plea bargain allowed him to avoid execution and receive a life sentence, there was only the shadow of a public trial. While conspiracy theories continue to flourish—and according to opinion polls, many Americans continue to believe them—Ray appears to have acted alone, and the issue of his motivation still remains a puzzle (see Ayton 2005 and Sides 2010 for that latest attempts to resolve the issue). Is the murder of a public figure by a petty criminal a political assassination? Two days after King's death on April 7, 1968, police in Oakland, California, riddled the 18-year-old body of Black Panther leader Bobby Hutton with a barrage of bullets; many, though not of course the authorities, called that a political assassination. When James Earl Ray was apprehended by British police in London in June 1968, the issue of whether or not he was the perpetrator of a political assassination was of paramount importance. British law was restrictive with regard to the extradition of those accused of political offences, but less so regarding assassination. The attorney arguing on Ray's behalf attempted to prevent his extradition by claiming that because MLK was the leader of a political movement to which the murderer was opposed, the motivation must have been political, thus exempting him from extradition. Those arguing for the government of the United States countered by claiming that the motives were personal, for private, rather than political purposes. The latter arguments won out, and Ray was eventually extradited (Ayton 2005:213).

For our purposes, that which marks political assassination and distinguishes assassination from murder is the collectivity that the act of killing engages. A political assassination is a murder that engages a political community:the American nation, in the case of Robert Kennedy and Martin Luther King; the Swedish nation, with Olof Palme and Anna Lindh; and the Dutch nation, in the case of Pim Fortyn and Theo van Gogh. Even though Van Gogh was not an elected official, he was nonetheless murdered as a representative figure. As I argue elsewhere, to his killer and those who publicly protested his death, Theo van Gogh represented the Dutch nation (Eyerman 2008).

WHY DO POLITICAL ASSASSINATIONS OCCUR?

From the sociological perspective of rational choice theory, a political murder could also be looked at in terms of opportunity, means, and motive, but more with consideration to the potential gain for the perpetrator. The Commission found not only a high level of political violence in the United States, but also that such violence "paid off." As a general rule applied to many social and political movements in the United States, the tactical use of violence has paid off, it claimed, in that it led to a situation where " the values supported by violence were ultimately adopted by the majority involved" (Kirkham et al. 2002 [1969]: 235). From this perspective, political violence, even assassination, might appear rational in the calculative sense as a means toward achieving desired ends. However, the Commission also found that the assassination of major political figures in the United States was not a common tool of those seeking social change. Rather, the many attempts to assassinate American presidents were judged (with one possible exception) to be the act of mentally disturbed lone assassins and thus not rational in the calculative sense of the term. How, then, does one explain their occurrence? One can treat them as individual occurrences, as the Commission does, while at the same time historicizing them, seeing each example as unique to its time and place, without necessarily exploring the specific interactions between the individual and the social context. Success or failure could then be evaluated in terms of potential gain to the individual or collective perpetrator. Similarly, the occurrence itself could be explained according to the intentions of the perpetrator as circumscribed by the opportunities provided, with the conclusion that political assassinations are more likely to occur when circumstances make them meaningful to rational actors.

Though there is a concern with context, the prime focus in this approach lies with the assassin, especially if prediction and prevention are major considerations.[2] Thus the Commission, as well as modern police work, attempts to construct a "profile" of the typical assassin and to specify the social conditions that may have spawned him. The masculine pronoun is appropriate in this case, as they write:

[W]e could predict after President Kennedy's assassination that the next assassin would probably be short and slight of build, foreign born, and from a broken family—most probably with the father either absent or unresponsive to the child. He would be a loner, unmarried, with no steady female friends, and have a history of good work terminated from one to three years before the assassination attempt by a seeming listlessness and irascibility. He would identify with a political or religious movement, with the assassination triggered by a specific issue that relates to the principles of the cause of the movement. Although identifying with the cause, the assassin would not in fact be part of or able to contribute to the movement. (Kirkham et al. 2002 [1969]: 65–66)

Such a profile exactly fit Sirhan Sirhan (on whom it was partially based), the killer of Robert Kennedy, and, in many of its aspects, the killers of Martin Luther King, Jr., Anna Lindh, and Theo van Gogh.

The most common motive attached to these lone assassins is that of attempting to overcome a sense of alienation through a dramatic act that will bring immediate public recognition. Thus, the police official in charge of investigating the murder of Anna Lindh writes about her killer: "He wanted to pay back the society he felt did not understand him. The knife attack on Anna Lindh was his way of acting out his inner frustration" (Jennekvist 2005:196, my translation). Although Jennekvist goes on to call this a "political" motivation, the gain for the perpetrator is not political in the sense of having one's values accepted by the majority, in the notion that the murder of a particular political figure would lead to some extensive political change. Here the motivation was more personal, the hope of gaining recognition as a meaningful person, of being seen as someone else than might appear to be the case on first glance, that is, the disturbed, marginalized misfit.[3] A distinctly political motivation may in this case be added on or attributed either by the person themselves or by outsiders. The fact that Sirhan Sirhan was a Palestinian refugee who had experienced childhood trauma was useful to his defense attorneys, some of whom joined the case primarily to publicize what they saw as the Palestinian cause. However, as in James Earl Ray's extradition, making such "political" claims threatened their argument for "diminished capacity." On the other side of the political spectrum, one later commentator, Mel Ayton (2007), goes so far as to call Sirhan "the forgotten terrorist," a precursor of the later acts of the Palestine Liberation Organization (PLO). However that may be, rather than being a politically motivated "terrorist" act, Sirhan's murder of Robert Kennedy may have been an impulsive, opportunistic act, as appears to have been the case in the murder of Anna Lindh and perhaps also of Olof Palme (see note 1, this chapter). A case can be made for this based on the fact that no one knew until the last minute which exit route Kennedy would take through the Ambassador Hotel, and that Sirhan claimed to have his pistol in his pocket mainly because he was afraid it would be stolen if he left it in his car.

What distinguishes my investigation from those just discussed is my concern with the effects of political assassination, rather than with the actual event itself. This follows from the application of the theory of cultural trauma. Cultural trauma highlights not only the meaning struggle that follows a shocking occurrence like a political assassination, but also the long- and short-term effects it might have for a collective. In addition, this book seeks to provide a wider historical understanding to the meaning of political assassination by asking whether or not the phenomenon has the same meaning today as it had in the past. If one thinks about the impact of the assassination of Archduke Ferdinand (often cited as one of the prime causes of the First World War) and compares it, for example, to the assassinations of those mentioned above, the impact of the former will be found to have far exceeded that of the latter. This might be explained as in rational choice theory by arguing that in the type of democracy represented by the United States, the impact of murdering a leader is generally much less than in a monarchy of the type Austria Hungary was in 1914. This would mean looking at impact through the narrow lens of political systems guided by a restricted view of politics. Taking a broader historical and cultural view, one could argue that political assassination itself has changed character, and that the murder of individual leaders or representative figures—such as Ferdinand and John Kennedy—has declined in direct political significance, although its cultural significance, its meaning in collective memory, cannot be denied. In the contemporary mass-media-driven world of representation, the murder of faceless masses, randomly selected collections of individuals, has seemingly as much impact when filtered through the global media. Any discussion of political assassination must take into account the transformation brought about through the globalization of mass communications, and how this has affected its meaning, in terms of form (how and where it is carried out) and content (its impact). This allows one to highlight and analyze the role of the media, art, film, and the Internet in shaping meaning and representation. It also opens the possibility of bringing in cultural trauma theory, the struggle for meaning, the trauma drama, and the importance of political murder in relation to collective as well as individual identity—the last being the main focus of police and rational choice theory.

CLASSICAL TRAUMA THEORY

Trauma stems from the ancient Greek word meaning "wound." However, in contemporary medical and psychiatric literature, writes Cathy Caruth (1996:3–4), "the term trauma is understood as a wound inflicted not upon the body but upon the mind." The wound is inflicted by a shock so powerful that it breaches "the mind's experience of time, self and the world," eventually manifesting itself in dreams and flashbacks. Geoffrey Hartman (1996:159) defines trauma as "events or states of feeling that threaten" the limits of experience and which "puncture lived time and exist only as phantasms," while for Dominick LaCapra, "trauma is a shattering experience that distorts memory...and may render it particularly vulnerable and fallible in the reporting of events" (2004:61). In this conception, an occurrence is traumatic not simply because it is forceful, but because it is unthinkable, in that it "resists simple comprehension" (Caruth 1996:6) and cannot be easily assimilated into already established frameworks of understanding. From this perspective, trauma is an experience so powerful that it cannot be understood as it occurs, but must be recalled and reconstructed from the deep recesses of memory. When describing their real-time experience of the murder of Anna Lindh, both the country's prime minister and the chief investigating officer said that it felt "unreal" (*overklig*). Sirhan Sirhan, a perpetrator, not a victim, claimed to have a memory blackout during the shooting of Robert Kennedy (apparently not unusual in violent crimes), and witnesses to that occurrence reported that things seemed to move in slow motion and be out of time.

The perceived unreality of an occurrence is part of what is meant by shock, a numbing of the senses and an inability to accept or take in what has in fact happened. There is also a probable mixing of "this has not happened" and "this cannot happen," as well as "this cannot happen here." The latter was part of the collective shock experienced in both Sweden and the Netherlands, where political murder and violence were rare. Such experience is usually relatively short-lived, as the possibility of denial fades and "reality" forces itself onto consciousness. However, for some victims, the aftereffects never fade and experience continues to haunt their consciousness. Newspaper accounts following the murders of Robert Kennedy and Olof Palme report a "stunned" nation, and the banner headline of the *San Francisco Chronicle* following the murder of the city's mayor and Harvey Milk, to cite another well-known political assassination, proclaimed, "The City Weeps." Such collective attributions may be difficult to scientifically maintain, but they are easy to understand and accept. Public opinion surveys taken after both these occurrences confirm this. A survey of contemporary reactions to the JFK assassination reports: 79 percent of those interviewed felt they had lost a dear and close friend; 73 percent said they were angry

that such a thing could happen; 83 percent felt ashamed that such a thing
could happen in the United States; 53 percent acknowledged that they had
cried at the news; and 97 percent reported that they thought about the hurt
inflicted on the victim's family (data provided by R.S. Sigel in Sigel (ed).
Learning About Politics 1970, cited in Åsard 2006, 103–4; see also Bonjean
et al. 1965). Public reaction to the Palme murder was comparable: 90 percent
reported feeling upset that such a thing could happen in Sweden; 84 percent
could not believe it; 82 percent felt angry that such a thing could happen
in Sweden; 80 percent thought of the hurt inflicted on the family; and as
many felt sad. Forty-two percent felt as if they had lost a close friend (Åsard
2006: 170). Although these reactions and figures might not represent 'the
nation', they do reflect a collective sense of shock. Erikson (1978) reports
similar collective shock in his study of the aftermath of the flood at Buffalo
Creek, for which he uses the term 'collective trauma,' and later proposes that
"trauma can create community" just as a shocking occurrence can destroy
it (Erikson 1995:185).

According to Fassin and Rechtman (2009:30), it was London doctors
treating the effects of railroad accidents in the late 1860s who "opened the
path to trauma psychiatry." A little later, Freud and Breuer first associated
trauma with sexual fantasy and what they labeled hysteric response, restrict-
ing its application to women. Freud later expanded this notion to the effects
of industrial and transportation accidents and elaborated these reflections
in connection with the treatment of the victims of trench warfare during
the First World War. In the latter, trauma makes reference to a real occurrence; a physical blow that overwhelms the senses and against which the
mind and body must defend itself. In addition to numbness, a condition
in which the capacity to feel pain is temporarily suspended, amnesia is a
defense mechanism of the mind. The victim simply forgets or denies that
anything has occurred. In developing a dynamic model, Freud called this
the period of latency, where in this state of denial or forgetting, the trauma
victim can appear quite normal in carrying out everyday routines. There
is no exact time frame for this period—it could last for days or years—but
the experience will at some point remerge and manifest itself, according to
this theory, either in nightmares or some otherwise inexplicable abnormal
behavior. Freud's notion of trauma thus builds around the direct experience
of an actual occurrence and clearly identifiable victims. For later theorists
in this tradition, Auschwitz and Hiroshima fully disclosed the catastrophic
potential of modernity, and trauma and modernity became intimately
linked in a much more general and abstract way (Bauman 1989, Caruth
1996, Horkheimer and Adorno 2002, LaCapra 2004, and Kaplan 2005).[4]
From this perspective, one of the manifestations of a catastrophic age is
taken to be the insufficiency of word and narrative to capture the effect of

traumatic experience. Insufficient or even illegitimate as it may be, there has been an array of theoretical reflection around the idea of traumatic experience and traumatic memory (LaCapra 2001 and White 2008, for example).

Contemporary revisions of the classical notion of trauma focus on two aspects: first, the traumatic effects on the victim—the recurrent unwanted intrusion of memory and its effect on behavior ; and second, on the possibility, or rather, as Caruth (1995) expresses it, "impossibility," of memory—the opening up through trauma of a specific kind of experience that becomes available not only to the therapist but also to the theorist. Trauma opens up another world to the observer, and thus, in a tragic sense, creates an opportunity to see what would otherwise have remained deeply hidden. In this sense, trauma at the individual level resembles crisis at the societal level. A crisis, such as a severe economic depression, is a shocking occurrence that can cause a breakdown in daily routines and expose at the same time the largely taken-for- granted values that guide them; crises in this sense reveals to a collective the grounds of its collective identity (Habermas 1975). Like individual trauma, a societal crisis is both a shock and an opportunity to see what otherwise remains deeply hidden. At the collective level, such trauma can be inclusive as well as exclusive; old collectivities can be reaffirmed and new ones created. Thus, the murder of Theo van Gogh provided the opportunity to readdress the very idea of "Dutchness" and the issue of whether or not Muslim immigrants would be included.

What is a traumatic occurrence? A traumatic occurrence is one that leaves those who experience it, directly or indirectly, with long-standing memory traces, which affects not only their emotional life, but also their behavior in unexpected and uncontrollable ways. More importantly in our context is that a traumatic occurrence creates a biographical and historical watershed, a sense of before and after, that can shape what Mannheim referred to as generational consciousness. One can distinguish gradations and levels with respect to traumatic occurrences, according to nearness to the actual situation—for example, being in the pantry room at the Ambassador Hotel during RFK's shooting left very deep impressions on those at the scene. Closeness with the victim would also affect the force of the trauma, even if one were not actually present. Göran Persson, the Swedish prime minister, was a close friend of Anna Lindh, so close that five years later, he reported still having her phone number prerecorded in his cell phone. Although not actually present at the scene of her murder, he remains deeply affected by her death. Similarly, one of the state prosecutors involved in the Lindh investigation reported feelings of great uneasiness when meeting the press, feelings she traced back to her work on the Palme investigation; the memory of that failure had set itself in her body. A third category could be identification with the person or with what the person represented. Upon hearing the announcement of Lindh's death, members of the working press and police corps wept openly. Photographer Bill Eppridge (2008) reports that he had tears running down his face while taking pictures of mourners as the funeral train carrying the body of RFK moved slowly from New York to Washington, D.C. He and a colleague were so moved by Kennedy's murder that they refused to take a photograph of his casket being lowered into the ground—as if they could not, and would not accept what had happened.

The reactions of these professionals to political assassination point to different types of shock and trauma, for individuals and collectivities, and to a range of possible reasons why this might be the case. Robert Kennedy and Anna Lindh were similar in the sense that both were representative political figures, but not (yet) heads of their respective nations. Both were, perhaps, on their way to this position, and their deaths were similarly shocking in that respect. Reactions to their assassinations evoked great collective sadness as well as shock, a sense of loss, and thoughts about what could have become, had they lived. These strong emotions left long-standing memory traces—at least we can say that with surety with reference to RFK as 40 years have passed, and the effects are still present and discussed. At the time, however, collective emotional reaction to their respective deaths varied. Though some feared that violence would erupt in the wake of Kennedy's death, none did. No one expected violence in the aftermath of Lindh's death. Great waves of violence erupted after the announcement of Martin Luther King's death and, on a lesser scale, that of Theo van Gogh. Though neither was an elected official, both King and Van Gogh were representative public figures and both were identified with partisan constituencies, though of entirely different sorts and scales. The death of Pim Fortuyn evoked strong displays of collective emotion, as his supporters blamed both the opposing political parties and the mass media for his murder. Immediately following his death, there were massive demonstrations, but few incidents of violence. Fortuyn was the leader of an opposition party, an anti-establishment movement, and even though he might very well have been elected prime minister in the coming election, he did not represent the nation and its promise—if not its formal political authority—in the same way as did Lindh or Robert Kennedy. The outcome of a traumatic occurrence is not fixed or determined; rather, outcomes are contingent and complex, and their analysis requires thick, multilayered interpretation.

TRAUMATIC OCCURRENCES VERSUS TRAUMATIC EVENTS

In addressing the meaning of political assassination, I will apply trauma theory, both in its traditional psychoanalytic meaning and in its contemporary

literary and cultural forms. For example, I will distinguish traumatic occurrences from traumatic events, where the former takes a more traditional—
that is to say, Freudian—notion of trauma and the latter a cultural one. From
there, I will discuss the meaning of significant events (Abrams 1982, Sewell
1992, White 2008), such as the assassinations of MLK and RFK, in the
re-ordering of U.S. society and the world at large. According to Alexander
and Breese (in Eyerman et al 2011), events become traumatic as they are
mediated and diffused,and our contemporary, mass-media-saturated world
is more prone to this type of traumatic event than the world of the past. The
political assassinations I investigate here were much more than media-created
events. However, they were events that had an impact upon—and affected
greatly—the social ordering of the societies in which they occurred. I will
also look at how these assassinations are remembered and memorialized.

In a previous book (Eyerman 2008), I made the distinction between occurrence and event in order to highlight the real-time unfolding of action and
its representation and dissemination in the mass media. Just as the assassination of the Dutch filmmaker Theo van Gogh can be reconstructed through
the real-time experience of the victim and the perpetrator, the murders of
King, Kennedy, Palme, Lindh, and Fortuyn can also be similarly described.
For those who were present, these occurrences were indeed traumatic, in
the term's traditional meaning. As shocking as they were for those present,
the murders of MLK and RFK evoked shock and dramatic response as the
news was reported and spread throughout the nation and the world, transforming the occurrences into events. The murder of King evoked a range
of collective responses that ranged from mass displays of mourning—more
than 200,000 marched through the streets of Atlanta at his funeral—to acts
of violence—between 75–125 ghetto areas "went up in flames" at the same
time as Georgia Governor Lester Maddox called King "an enemy of our
country" (Perlstein 2008: 256–7, see also Risen 2009). News of the murder
of Robert Kennedy (in the midst of an increasingly successful political campaign and just two months after that of King) evoked no violence (although
it had been feared)—only sorrow and despair. The loss of these two representative figures in close conjunction led to a period of national reflection on
the collective foundations of American society in a climate of polarization
and violence. Beyond the attempt to uncover who was responsible and why,
these events generated great public discussion on the meaning and direction
of American society and pointed to a fundamental turn in American political
culture. This discursive process is what I mean by cultural trauma.

CULTURAL TRAUMA

In an insightful discussion of the difference between psychological and cultural trauma, Neil Smelser (2004) emphasizes one essential distinction in

the fact that cultural traumas are made, not born. He goes on to define a cultural trauma as "an invasive and overwhelming event that is believed to undermine or overwhelm one or several essential ingredients of a culture or the culture as a whole" (Smelser in Alexander et al. 2004:38). Though acknowledging the discursive aspect of cultural trauma, Smelser grounds the process in an event. I think, however, that the key phrase here is "believed to undermine," a notion that undercuts any idea that an event could be traumatic in itself. This opens up two vital questions that underpin the analyses set forth in this book: (1) can any occurrence or event be made traumatic, so that it is "believed to undermine" an established collective identity? and (2) if not, what is it that permits some occurrences to become traumatic in this sense and not other seemingly equally powerful or shocking occurrences? The first question points to the power to create belief. A radical social constructivist might argue that given the ultimate power to persuade, one could turn any occurrence into a "trauma."[5] This would be to push the idea "traumas are made not born," to its limits. At the other extreme, a strong naturalist or lay trauma account (Alexander 2004) would make the claim that certain events are traumatic in themselves, that is, they are the direct cause of traumatic effect. In previous books (Eyerman 2001, 2008), I have tried to make the case for a middle position, which argues that certain occurrences—in our current case, political assassinations—may create conditions conducive to setting in motion a process of cultural trauma without being traumatic in themselves. This will not happen without the aid of meaning-making forces, such as mass media, and certain carrier groups (Alexander 2004), such as intellectuals, who influence the formation and direction of a process of cultural trauma.[6] However, not all or any interpretative frame will "fit" or make sense; there must be some relation, real or perceived, to some referent—an occurrence, experience, or event, which itself appears to be "always there."

Cultural traumas are not things, but processes of meaning making and attribution, a contentious contest in which various individuals and groups struggle to define a situation and to manage and control it. I would add that these forces are unlikely to create a trauma out of nothing; there is likely to be some powerful, shocking occurrence that creates the possibility, providing the opportunity to mobilize opinions and emotions. There are thus two sides to a cultural trauma—an emotional experience and an interpretative reaction. Shocks arouse emotion by breaking everyday routines (behaviors as well as cognitive frameworks) and, as such, they demand interpretation, opening a discursive field where well-placed individuals can play a determinate role. In modern societies, access to mass media is significant in this process. The polarity between perpetrator and victim is what distinguishes cultural trauma as discourse. In this sense, cultural trauma is a contentious discursive process framed by a dichotomy between perpetrator and victim, which is spurred by a powerful, unforgettable occurrence. What also characterizes cultural trauma as discourse is that an established collective identity is shaken and its foundations called into question. It is a discursive process where the emotions that are triggered by a traumatic occurrence are worked through, and an attempt is made to heal the collective wound (Erikson 1995).

Yet, cultural traumas are more than a struggle between competing actors to define a situation, to distinguish perpetrator and victim, and to identify the nature of the pain. That would limit the process to instrumental or strategic interaction. Cultural traumas are also a response to deeply felt emotions, which are publicly expressed and represented in this very same process, which implies an expressive and communicative aspect,[7] making claims to authenticity and sincerity connected to collective identity and memory. Anything connected to identity falls within the realm of the sacred (Giesen 2004) and, as such, is bound up with powerful emotions. There are deeply rooted emotions and scripted identities to be drawn upon in such situations. I am thinking here of ethnic or national identities, which may lie under the surface, but can be mobilized in the face of a shocking occurrence such as a political assassination. This was the case with the assassination of Archduke Ferdinand, and the process catalyzed by this occurrence spiraled into a world war that fundamentally altered the political geography of Europe. In this sense, a cultural trauma is a narrative emerging out of a traumatic occurrence, where collective identities are at stake. This turns our attention to the question of how narratives, as well as beliefs and identities, are shaped, issues I will return to shortly.

Smelser (2004:37–38) makes another distinction that will be useful in this discussion of political assassination—that between social and cultural trauma. While a cultural trauma invokes public discourse on the fundaments of collective identity at its broadest level—that of a nation, for example—social trauma refers to "strains on institutions" and "disruptions of social life." Smelser's example of cultural trauma is the Protestant Reformation, which posed a successful "fundamental threat to the dominant Catholic world view" (2004:38). Social trauma refers to a process similar in form to cultural trauma, but more delimited to particular institutions or groups in a society rather than to the social whole. His example is the Great Depression, which affected the lives of most Americans but never threatened their fundamental values or beliefs, though there were organizations and movements that sought to make this happen. There is thus an element of success and failure in the relationship between a social and a cultural trauma in Smelser's account. Shocking events such as political assassinations may appear to shake an entire nation, but their long-term traumatic effects may be more strongly felt in specific institutions or by particular groups. Two examples illustrate this. The murder of Olof Palme in Sweden shocked the nation in a powerful way, but its long-term effects appear to be most strongly felt in the Social Democratic Party and in the police corps. The murder and its representation also affected journalism and the mass media. In fact, Swedish journalism, which includes radio as a central feature, was fundamentally altered after the Palme murder, and this event remains as a prime reference point in the education of journalists.[8] The murder of King in the United States was shocking, but was most powerfully felt among African Americans. Whether or not it is also possible to speak of a cultural trauma in these cases will be something discussed later in this book.

We can now return to the question of how it is that a collective comes to believe that an occurrence "overwhelms" their already established collective identity. Collective identities are rooted in beliefs that are maintained in everyday life through routine practices. Routines provide confirmation and security in that they allow beliefs to be taken for granted, to be—in a sense—forgotten. An example may help illustrate what I mean. One of the first public statements made by the Swedish prime minister after the death of Anna Lindh was, "This is an attack on our democratic society." That Sweden is a democratic society is a fundamental belief and value grounding modern Swedish collective identity. This belief is not only taught in schools, but is also bound up with routine practices, such as voting every three years to elect the government. The fact that Sweden is a "democracy" is normally taken for granted. The murder of Anna Lindh was shocking not only because she was a well-known member of the collective, but also because she was a political figure—a representative of that democratic process. At least for the prime minister, another representative figure, her murder presented a threat to that fundamental value/identity, as well as to the political process that underpins it. It was thus important—for the security and the stability of that identity—not only that the murderer be caught, which was a police matter, but also that the rules and procedures of the political system that would guarantee stability were immediately put on display. This was even clearer in the murder of Prime Minister Olof Palme, where the same radio bulletin that announced the murder to the public also confirmed that the government was already meeting to ensure the succession of his replacement. Since shocking events such as political assassinations break everyday routines and can call into question fundamental taken-for-granted beliefs that ground individual and collective identity, it is important that those in positions of authority act quickly to reaffirm those basic identities. To act in this manner is one way of assuring, or attempting to ensure, that the shock caused by political assassination will be contained and limited to an institution or set of institutions—in this case, that of politics and law enforcement—and not involve the society at large. If quick action is not taken, or if such performances of authority fail, there is an extended risk that a social trauma will become a cultural trauma.

This allows us to make use of one more idea in Smelser's discussion of cultural trauma—that of shocking occurrences as being "potentially" traumatic, which must be successfully "endowed with negative affect" in order to be fully realized. Central to the meaning struggle, and thus to the making of a cultural trauma, is the successful attribution of terms such as "national tragedy," "national shame," and "national catastrophe" or even "national trauma"—and their acceptance by a significant part of the collective. This is what is meant by the phrase "come to believe to undermine"—that a significant number of members of a collective,(who can say how many?)—have come to believe that the shock is a "national tragedy" that has undermined the fundamental beliefs defining the collective. This is what turns or transforms a shock into a cultural trauma and leads to Smelser's more formal definition: "A cultural trauma is a memory accepted or given credence by a relevant membership group and evoking an event or situation which is a) laden with negative affect, b) represented as indelible, and c) regarded as threatening a society's existence or violating one or more of its fundamental cultural pre-suppositions" (Smelser 2004:44).

THE ROLE OF CARRIER GROUPS

Even when speaking of a collective, however, one must ask, "trauma for whom?" (Giesen 2004, Eyerman 2008). Imaginary collectivities, like nations or ethnic groups, are rarely unified or univocal. One effect of a traumatic occurrence can be to provide a sense of coherence and collectivity, even if this is also imaginary and temporary. The attack on New York's World Trade Center in 2001 appeared to unify the American nation into an emotional collective, producing ritual practices that helped sustain it, just as the phrase "9/11" is meant to evoke and signify shared experience and collective understanding. But digging beneath that ephemeral surface, in large part facilitated through mass-mediated representations, one would undoubtedly find individuals and even groups dissenting in that feeling. In this sense, a traumatic occurrence has the potential to both unify and divide; to create insiders and outsiders. This potential must, however, be realized, and it is here that what Alexander (2004:11), following Max Weber, called "carrier groups" play an important role. Such groups articulate and represent trauma, making it available for communication and shared understanding. They help transform emotional response into words and images that can be dispersed and remembered. Artists, writers, journalists and political and religious leaders are important social categories in this articulation, playing a key role in the trauma process. Howeverthe idea of carrier groups is broader than these professional categories. Carrier groups can be pre-existing or can emerge in response to a particular traumatic occurrence, whereas professional categories—such as those mentioned—may well be significant agents within them. For example, the murder of Pim Fortuyn was clearly traumatic for his followers, and this group played an important role in turning that occurrence into a national event. However, the media in general and journalists in particular also played an indispensable role in that process, whatever their feelings toward Fortuyn were. Many have noted that both the rise and fall of Fortuyn were strongly influenced by the mass media. In fact, at the mass demonstrations that followed his death, one of the slogans repeated over and over by his supporters was that he was, in fact, murdered by the mass media, even if the actual killer was a lone individual already in custody.

Not only are carrier groups central to the making of cultural trauma, they are also important in its continued effect. Carrier groups are bearers of memory. As mentioned, the groups most affected over the long term by the murder of Olof Palme were the Swedish Social Democratic Party and the Swedish police corps. The murder of Anna Lindh 17 years later bought the memory of Palme's murder directly to life for both groups. The reactions of the police to Lindh's murder were determined to a great extent by their sense of failure regarding Palme's murder, and the Social Democratic Party was viscerally reminded of the loss of their exulted leader when Foreign Minister Anna Lindh, also a party member, died. Cultural trauma in this sense refers to a process through which collectivities are articulated, formed, and re-formed in the light of traumatic occurrences such as political assassinations. Shocking occurrences and traumatic events need not have only negative outcomes for all concerned. The failed assassination attempt on American president Ronald Reagan on March 30, 1981—just 69 days into his presidency—actually served to strengthen his public image and gave him greater political capital. He was able to push through his political platform with greater ease. The same could be said for George W. Bush in the aftermath of 9/11.

Carrier groups include such collective actors placed under broad umbrella concepts such as the "mass media." In a remarkable passage written soon after the assassination of JFK, Theodore White, an American journalist responsible for a series of firsthand accounts of "the making of the president," described the power of television in helping to create a sense of collective belonging that would become part of the myth and legend of collective memory:

> The spectacle of the next three days is so new to memory that to retell it falls impossibly short of still-fresh emotions. What will be difficult for historians to grasp, however, was that the ceremonies that followed were more than spectacle—they were a political and psychological event of measureless

dimension. And in this event, the chief servant was American television, performing duties of journalism with supreme excellence. Within minutes of the shot, American television was already mobilizing. In half an hour, all commercial programs had been wiped from the air, and thereafter, abandoning all cost accounting, television proceeded to unify the nation...The political result of this participation, of this national lament, as a psychological event which no practical politician will ever be able to ignore...The drama gave all people a sense of identification and translated the majesty of leadership into an intimate simplicity of Biblical nature. There was in the drama of the four days all things to bind men—a hero, slain; a sorrowing wife; a stricken mother and family; and two enchanting children. So broad was the emotional span, embracing every member of every family from schoolchild to grandparent, that it made the grief of the Kennedy's a common grief. (1965:13–14)

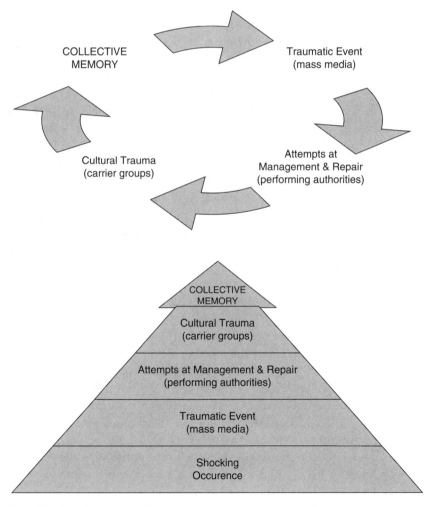

Figure 2.1   From Occurrence to Memory.

Deeply hidden in collective memory, collective representation, stories, myths and symbols were drawn upon as a sense of belonging was created through mass-mediated trauma, and in the process collective memory was itself reconstituted.

An attempt at a schematic diagram would look like this (see figure 2.1).

THE IMPORTANCE OF MORAL FRAMEWORKS

As previously mentioned, cultural trauma is a historically bound and produced discursive process, in which the positions of perpetrator and victim are central. It emerges in the context of a shocking occurrence and carries the notion that "we are not the same" after such an occurrence. Accordingly, periodization—as a sense of before and after—is as central to the trauma process as are perpetrators and victims. In political assassinations, there are at least two victims, the murdered individual and the collective that associates itself with that individual. Carrier groups articulate the significance of this occurrence for the collective, and to the extent that they are successful, the occurrence becomes a vital part of that group's collective memory. More than this, however, the polarity between perpetrator and victim is encased within a culturally specific normative framework where, for example, perpetrators may be represented as evil and tainted and victims as good and innocent. In some cases, such as that of Anna Lindh, perpetrators can also be represented as victims as we will see. The framing of victim and perpetrator is part of the meaning struggle in the trauma process. The specific content of this normative framework varies according to the historical narratives that define the parameters of national identity. In the Netherlands, for example, the Second World War marked a significant turning point in defining what it meant to be Dutch (Eyerman 2008). The surprisingly quick defeat of the Dutch army and the occupation of the country by the Germans provided a newly refined moral framework for what was good and evil, with good being associated with a rather ambiguous loyalty to the exiled House of Orange and evil being associated with the ideology of the occupier—Nazism in particular and fascism more generally. This framework helped shape public discourse both before and after the murders of Pim Fortuyn and Theo van Gogh, and it provided—to an extent at least—the framework through which the murders were interpreted. For those on the political left, as the charismatic leader of a social movement, Fortuyn represented a revitalized fascism, while Theo van Gogh heard the thumping of black boots when he looked at Muslims. Both these victims of assassination claimed to be defending the innocent Dutch (nation) from impending evil. The portrayal of the perpetrator in each case varied significantly. Although it was not difficult to paint the killer of Theo van Gogh as the epitome of evil, it was more difficult in the case of the solidly Dutch individual who murdered Fortuyn. Another "root narrative" (Wagner-Pacifici 1986) through which these occurrences were filtered, was that of the right to free speech and expression, a discourse that had taken new form in the 1960s. As representative figures of that expressive and self-centered generation, Van Gogh and Fortuyn both claimed the right to publicly say what they felt and to live their lives accordingly, no matter what others might think or do. The right to free expression and to choose one's "lifestyle" provided a principled standpoint around which many diverse individuals could collectively rally in the aftermath of these murders. Their respective killers also interpreted their actions through a normative moral framework. Volkert van der Graaf viewed his victim as representing an evil that threatened the foundations of a just and caring Dutch society, just as Mohammed B. saw in Theo van Gogh all the evil that was Western civilization. From the point of view of the established order, one dimension of the cultural trauma process is the potential rupture and the attempts to maintain and repair such a moral framework. If the killer of Pim Fortuyn had turned out to be the Muslim extremist, as many had anticipated, this would have confirmed and reinforced the established notions of good and evil. When it turned out that the killer was a rather ordinary Dutchman, the effect was confusion and the search for an explanation. That he could be labeled an "animal-rights activist" provided some consolation. This labeling of the perpetrator as an extremist also reaffirmed the claim that this was a political assassination, something that became a centerpiece at the trial.

It is possible to construct a schematic such as the following (figure 2.2), where the two crossing lines define a field of traumatic and nontraumatic political assassinations.

As defined by an assumed national consensus, the persons killed in this study all fall within the space where victims are represented as "good" and the perpetrators inhabit the "evil" realm. One can think of other cases where the opposite was the case, such as that of the Black Panther Bobby Hutton mentioned earlier—he represents an evil victim and the person that brought him to "justice" is thus good. This labeling would presumably play a role in any trauma process and shape the possibility of an emergent cultural trauma.

Utilizing a moral framework highlights the cultural aspects that may or may not condition the emergence of cultural trauma. By asking the question, "Under what conditions does a traumatic occurrence like political assassination evolve

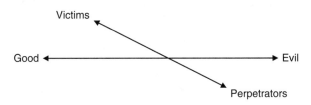

Figure 2.2   Moral framework.

into cultural trauma?" employing concepts like "carrier groups," and exploring how well legitimate authority defines and manages the situation, one follows a well-established explanatory path best laid out by Max Weber in his compara- tive studies around the emergence of capitalism. Adding a moral framework lends a specifically cultural dimension to this explanation. The factors—or, to use traditional language, variables—at play in determining what does or does not become a cultural trauma are the specific cultural structures, the moral framework defining good and evil, and the grounding myths of the nation that are present in a society at any given time. These help to define what is under- stood as a threat to the collective and to give political assassinations some of their force. This is another way of saying that our emotional reactions—even those to shocking occurrences—are necessarily filtered through an already existing and readily available cultural framework or discourse. This includes reactions to assassinations. One of the central cultural discourses grounding the self-understanding of modern democracies (such as those in this study) is that of being civilized, not primitive, with reactions to acts of violence—even those that may threaten their stability. Assassinations and assassins must thus be treated in a way that conforms to this ideal, which explains why one of the acts of established authority is to call for a calm and "reasoned" response.

Political assassinations are almost all, by definition, traumatic beyond the experience of those present. However, if the perpetrator can be defined as a mentally unstable, lone individual, some of the force of that potential is mitigated. The event can then be stabilized and contained as shocking and traumatic for a time and even included in the collective memory, but will not have the long-term negative impact of a cultural trauma. Cultural traumas can only be known and studied retrospectively. It is only after the passing of time—how much exactly is uncertain—that we can know if the effects of a traumatic occurrence are still felt, still alive. In this sense, cultural trauma resembles the trauma experienced by individuals; its effects remain under the surface and become visible, are revealed, long after the fact.

In the chapters that follow, I will apply the theory of cultural trauma ret- rospectively to map a discursive process and, at the same time, to provide a framework for comparing my six cases. Here the theory becomes a framework through which one can organize historical and empirical material in a struc- tured and coherent way, allowing one to make sense of seemingly disparate occurrences. As a framework for analysis, cultural trauma allows one to study the struggle, to come to grips with these assassinations and traumatic occur- rences, to locate the central actors in this meaning struggle, and to trace the process over long periods of time. The framework also permits one to locate and map the political and cultural changes that followed from these traumatic occurrences. After the detailed descriptions of the six cases presented in these chapters, the concluding chapter will return more directly to these theoretical issues, elaborating on them through a comparison of the cases.

CHAPTER 3

REMEMBERING THE 1960s: THE ASSASSINATIONS OF MARTIN LUTHER KING JR. AND ROBERT KENNEDY

"My cause, my race, is worth dying for."

Martin Luther King Jr.

"Spiro Agnew is my insurance policy, because no assassin in his right mind would kill me."

Richard Nixon

(When asked why the much-disliked Agnew was his choice for vice president in 1972)

"One out of every five Presidents since 1865 has been assassinated."

President Lyndon Johnson June 10, 1968

"Violence is as American as cherry pie."

H. Rap Brown

DURING THE 2008 AMERICAN PRESIDENTIAL PRIMARIES, the *New York Times* reported that "a daughter persuaded her mother to still vote for Senator Obama, even though the mother feared that winning would put him in danger."[1] During that campaign, and after, many expressed fear that Barack Obama, as the country's first African American president, would become the object of violence or even assassination. This possibility was even voiced by a rival, Senator Hillary Clinton, as part of her own bid for the nomination. The memory of the assassinations of John and Robert Kennedy and, most especially, Martin Luther King, weigh so heavily on American collective memory that there exists anticipation that someone extraordinary, in the sense of being special or in some way different, would be a target, should he or she attain or even seek national office. Studies of anticipation/ memory reveal two sides of a coin; on the one side, memories of disturbing emotional events are more vivid and deeply imprinted in the brain, and on the other, the expectation of an emotional event plays a role in how that event will be remembered. In our case, the former is the most interesting. While concentrating on the assassinations of Martin Luther King and Robert Kennedy, this chapter is about the decade of the 1960s, a decade that imprinted trauma onto the nation's collective memory. Although these assassinations were traumatic in the traditional, psychoanalytic sense, both singularly and cumulatively, the decade was, above all, marked by cultural trauma. The 1960s began with the fanfare of an election and ended with the sorrow of assassination.

It has been suggested that in the United States, the 1960s ended on November 22, 1963, the day JFK was murdered in Dallas (Pete Hamill 2008). The intention here is symbolic, of course, but there is a deeper meaning that is worth considering. Rather than marking out a period of time, "the sixties" has come to represent an era characterized by idealistic social change or by violent and disorderly conflict. How one views or remembers the 1960s has much to do with political positioning. For American liberals like Hamill, the election of the Democratic candidate JFK and the corresponding defeat of Republican Richard Nixon in 1960 marked the dawning of a new era, one filled with the hope of progressive social reform; Kennedy's assassination signaled the end of that hope. From a similar though more radial perspective, one could extend the 1960s to 1968 when the "Great Society" programs put in place by Kennedy's replacement Lyndon Johnson began to unravel in the face of urban disorder and the escalation of the Vietnam War and its opposition, a process that culminated in the deaths of MLK and RFK. From the other side of the political spectrum, the 1960s might be remembered as a time of excess, when a postwar generation raised in a permissive culture ran rampant, distorting and misusing fundamental American values. From this vantage point, the deaths of Martin Luther King and Robert Kennedy could be seen as the logical outcome of lawlessness. Both of these perspectives on the 1960s have been codified and diffused into American popular memory through all forms of mass media and popular culture. In the film *Forrest Gump* (1994), for example, as Edward P. Morgan puts it,

> the representation of this bygone era dichotomizes the past into a "good" and a "bad" sixties—the triumphant southern civil rights movement and a hopeful young president on the one hand; on the other, a stereotyped Black Panther, a war in which Americans suffer at the hands of invisible Vietnamese, an abusive Students for a Democratic Society...and an excessively self-indulgent counter-culture that deteriorates into hard drugs.... (2006:137)

In the United States, political assassination marked the 1960s, and regardless of one's political perspective, the assassinations of MLK and RFK signaled a turning point—they represent a yardstick in American collective memory.[2] This is especially true with reference to MLK, whose birthday is now a national holiday—a commemoration during which the same question is posed annually—"How far have we come since his death?" Martin Luther King went from being one of the most hated men in the nation to becoming a hallowed icon and a universal symbol of the dream for racial equality. Robert Kennedy's fate, on the other hand, seems almost entirely entwined with his family rather than with any political philosophy or moral position. Yet the memory of his tragic death, especially when experienced and interpreted in sequential relation to those of John F. Kennedy and Martin Luther King, constituted the last stage in a cumulative series of shocks in a trauma process and was openly manifested as a cultural trauma. Seen through the successive dramas of assassination, from JFK to MLK and RFK, the 1960s is a period of cultural trauma during which the foundations of American collective identity were opened up for reflection and debate. What kind of society was this in which young and vibrant political leaders could be killed? What were the causes, and who were the perpetrators? What could possibly be next? This process of national self-reflection occurred in various arenas—throughout mass media, houses of government, on the streets, and around the table in private homes. It had racial, gendered, and generational, as well as political, dimensions, only aspects of which will be taken up here.

While not as divisive as the Civil War, the 1960s represent a period of rupture out of which competing memory frames emerged. Such "emblematic memories"—socially constructed frameworks, "which impart . . . broad interpretive meaning and criteria of selection to personal memory" (Stern 2004:105)—have developed into competing master narratives that give meaning to particular events. Thus, for liberal Americans, the 1960s are framed through an emancipatory narrative, in which one fondly attaches excitement and optimism to the early years of the civil rights and antiwar movements. The phrase connotes the end of stifling Cold War conservatism, an outbreak of social experimentation and sexual liberation, and colorful displays of human creativity against a background of pulsating music. This emancipatory narrative is countered by one of salvation and redemption, which views the 1960s as an aberration, a period when America lost its soul and its moral compass. Within this frame, these assassinations, though tragic, ushered in a welcome return to normalcy—to the fundamental values of God, nation, and family, "which made the country great." However remembered, the assassinations of Martin Luther King and Robert Kennedy evoked horror and a sense of collective shame, as they exacerbated existing wounds and added new fuel to debates about the meaning and direction of

American society. They marked a watershed after which nothing appeared the same.

The murder of Martin Luther King sparked civil disorder at a level not experienced since the Civil War. Black Panther chairperson Elaine Brown called this response "the most massive uprising of black people in the history of America" (1992:130). However exaggerated this might have been, along with the escalating opposition to the Vietnam War, urban disorder contributed greatly to Lyndon Johnson's decision not to seek reelection in 1968, a decision he announced to a stunned public just days before the murder of MLK. The political disarray his decision engendered within the Democratic Party only enhanced the opportunities for a new "law and order" conservatism that crossed party lines. This vague, yet emotionally charged, ideological frame focused on domestic issues such as public welfare, a "permissive" culture, and urban violence. After King's death, the chasm between blacks and whites, young and old, and left and right only widened. For many Americans, the one political leader capable of bridging this gap, while at the same time restoring respect for the law, was JFK's younger brother, the former crime-fighting attorney general and current liberal senator from New York, Robert F. Kennedy. Kennedy's assassination on June 4, 1968, in Los Angeles, after having won one of the biggest political victories of his career, extinguished that hope—and the social and political polarization escalated. American political culture was on the cusp of a radical shift to the right, and the effects would be long-standing.

A SHIFT TO THE RIGHT

The political consequences, however, were immediate. The 1968 Democratic convention held in Chicago nominated Hubert Humphrey as its candidate. Humphrey was the current vice president, and his nomination signaled political continuity. Outside the convention hall, violent clashes between police—using what Connecticut senator and convention delegate Abraham Ribicoff termed "Gestapo tactics"—and antiwar protestors were broadcast around the world. Next to the *New York Times's* front-page photograph of a smiling Hubert Humphrey (flanked by his wife and his running mate Edwin Muskie and his wife) was a story headlined, "Thousands March, Scores Arrested, Some Delegates—Tear gas used."[3] According to the story, "[M]ore than 150 people, including nine convention delegates, were arrested after National Guardsmen halted 3,000 persons marching towards the International Amphitheater," where the convention was being held. These events led to the well-publicized trial of the "Chicago Seven," in which protest leaders were convicted of conspiracy, only to have that judgment overturned by a higher court. Domestic turmoil continued to escalate at pace with the war in Vietnam. In November, Richard Nixon—who was vice president under Dwight David Eisenhower in the 1950s before losing the election to JFK in 1960—defeated Humphrey by a narrow margin (43.42 percent to 42.72 percent, with 13.53 percent of the popular vote going to George Wallace, a right-wing third-party candidate), and the political circle was complete: American politics was rewound to 1960 and was being replayed with new characters.

California governor Ronald Reagan, who had risen to political prominence as a "law and order" politician, was a Republican candidate in the presidential primaries in 1968. As was the case when Reagan was running for governor, his campaign centered on fierce opposition to antiwar protestors and the "black extremists" who stirred up trouble in urban ghettos. Though unsuccessful in both 1968 and 1976, Reagan would be elected president in 1980. Once in the White House, Richard Nixon, who in his inaugural address promised to bring Americans together and to end the war in Vietnam, continued the Cold War policy of containing Communism that marked his early political career.[4] Divisions within the country only grew greater up to Nixon's forced resignation in August 1974 in the wake of the Watergate scandal and the threat of impeachment. Nixon was replaced by his vice president, Gerald Ford, who eventually pardoned the former president. The Vietnam War ended in the defeat of American forces, with stark images of their hasty withdrawal after the fall of Saigon in 1975 was broadcast into American homes and around the world. The effects of this humiliating defeat would be felt for decades, most especially within the military itself, giving rise to public discussion where phrases like "national trauma" and "national disgrace" were common.

In speculating on what could have been different had Robert Kennedy not been killed and had gone on to win the Democratic nomination and the presidency in 1968, Thurston Clarke (2008:9–10) writes,

> ...He would have negotiated a settlement to the Vietnam War soon after his inauguration, saving the lives of the two million Vietnamese and twenty thousand American servicemen killed during the Nixon Administration. Because he would not have bombed Cambodia, America would have escaped the trauma of Kent State and Jackson State, and Cambodia would have escaped the murderous Pol Pot regime. The Watergate would be just another apartment building, and America would have avoided the disillusionment and cynicism following that scandal."

Of course, we will never know how much of this would really have happened; what we do know is that the murder of Robert Kennedy, in the wake of the murder of Martin Luther King Jr., profoundly affected American society, evoking a wide-ranging public discourse that touched the collective foundations of the nation.

Martin Luther King Jr. was shot by James Earl Ray on April 3, 1968, while standing on a balcony walkway of the Lorraine Motel in Memphis, Tennessee. He was 39 years old. King came to Memphis to lead a march in support of striking sanitation workers and was joking with colleagues in the courtyard below when the shot rang out.[5] The shooter lay in wait about 200 feet away, by the window of a hall toilet in the boarding house where he had rented a room. That window offered Ray a direct line of fire, and he killed King with a single shot from a high-powered hunting rifle. As the news spread, rioting broke out in American cities: in Washington, D.C., 10 persons died; and in Newark 600 were left homeless by the approximately 200 fires started. As Perlstein (2008:256, see also Risen 2009) recounts, "Seventy-five ghettos went up in flames by one count, 125 by another: Baltimore, Cincinnati, Kansas City, Pittsburgh, Detroit—again." The final tally of the damage from the rioting after Martin Luther King's murder put the number of the dead at 39, with "more than 2,600...injured, and 21,000...arrested" (Risen 2009:4). Damages amounted to what would be around $385 million at current rates. Federal troops occupied three major cites (Baltimore, Washington, and Chicago) and the National Guard was deployed in a dozen more, with violence erupting in more than 120 cities across the country (Risen 2009:4). There were at least two major effects of these occurrences; they gave conservative politicians emotional fodder in their political campaigns, as calls for "law and order" were added to those against the communist threat. This helped Richard Nixon gain the necessary margin of votes to win the presidential election in November 1968. Second, the televised images of rebellious blacks transformed the way African Americans were perceived by white Americans. From being victims, they now became perpetrators. White sympathy and support for the civil rights movement, which had already fallen from its highest point of 42 percent favorable in 1965, to 82 percent unfavorable in the summer of 1967, now reached a new low (Risen 2009: 7).

RFK SPEAKS OUT

Robert Kennedy was one of the first national political leaders to address King's death. In an impromptu and intimate manner, Kennedy announced the murder to a crowd assembled in Indianapolis, Indiana, to hear him make a campaign speech. In an appeal for calm, Kennedy drew a comparison with his own anguish when told of his brother's assassination. It was the first time he had spoken publicly of his own feelings about the assassination of JFK, and it was clear that he experienced King's death through that of his brother. The *Chicago Sun-Times* reporter following Kennedy's campaign recalled, "It was unbearable to watch him [and] to know that he was thinking about his brother" (quoted in Clarke 2008:89). Addressing the shocked and angry crowd, Kennedy said, "For those of you who are black and are tempted to be filled with hatred and mistrust of the injustice of such an act, against all white people, I would only say that I can also feel in my own heart the same kind of feeling. I had a member of my family killed, but he was killed by a white man. But we have to make an effort in the United States, we have to make an effort to understand, to get beyond, or go beyond these rather difficult times" (Clarke 2008: 96).

The next day in Cleveland, Kennedy returned to the murder of MLK in a prepared speech. Rather than condemning the individuals involved, he shifted focus to the nation and its collective identity:

> Whenever any American's life is taken by another American unnecessarily— whether it is done in the name of the law or in the defiance of law, by one man or a gang, in cold blood or in passion, in an attack of violence or in response to violence—whenever we tear at the fabric of life which another man has painfully and clumsily woven for himself and his children, the whole nation is degraded. (quoted in Risen 2009:142–43)

The murder of an American by an American was here described as a national shame, by a representative of that collectivity, the negative attribution Smelser (2004) identified as essential in constructing a cultural trauma. A fundamental principle of American life had been breached, Kennedy declared, and he went on to speak about institutional violence: "There is another kind of violence, the violence of institutions; indifference and inaction and slow decay." What was needed, he thought, was a renewed sense of collective mission, in the name of civic repair: "Surely, we can learn, at least, to look at those around us as fellow men and surely we can begin to work a little harder to bind up the wounds among us and to become in our hearts brothers and countrymen once again" (quoted in Risen 2009:143). As a representative figure, Robert Kennedy articulated a cultural trauma, a tear in the social fabric that linked the individual and collective, at the same time as he sought to repair it.

In his speech to the nation broadcast live a few hours after the murder of Martin Luther King, President Lyndon Johnson, in another attempt at civil repair, also appealed for calm and for Americans to work together toward a more equal and just society. Johnson declared April 9 a national day of mourning, and 200,000 marched through the Atlanta streets at King's funeral. As we will see in more detail later, not everyone agreed. Georgia governor Lester Maddox threatened to raise the state flag from its ordered half-mast position, declaring King "an enemy of our country." *The Thunderbolt,* a right-wing newspaper supporting the presidential candidacy of George

Wallace, declared: "The man who shot King was actually upholding the law of the land...He should be given the Congressional Medal and a large annual pension, plus a Presidential pardon" (cited in Ford 1985:220). The Imperial Wizard of the KKK was quoted as saying (in *Muhammad Speaks,* the newspaper of the Nation of Islam) "The nigger got what he deserved." J. B. Stoner, founder of the National States Rights Party and editor of the *Thunderbolt,* cited above, proudly recalled for readers of *Muhammad Speaks* the cheering reactions of the crowd to his announcement of King's death that evening of April 4, 1968. "King's a good nigger now," he said (cited in Chappell chapter 2:). James Earl Ray later attempted to hire Stoner as his defense attorney in his failed attempt to reverse his own guilty plea (Watters 1969:15). Less extreme, conservatives such as California governor and presidential candidate Ronald Reagan called King's death a "great tragedy," while claiming that its cause lay in the lack of law and order in the country: He said the murder of MLK began "with our first acceptance of compromise with the laws of the land" (*Los Angeles Times* April 6, 1968:3). William F. Buckley also blamed the victim, as well as the culture, at the same time as he denounced the murderer, in his syndicated column (April 9, 1968): "The cretin who leveled his rifle on the head of King may have absorbed the talk, so freely available, about the supremacy of the individual conscience, such talk as Martin Luther King, God rest his troubled soul, had so widely and so indiscriminately made" (cited by Chappell unpublished manuscript).

The murder of Martin Luther King was a shocking occurrence, which sparked off not only strong individual and collective reaction, but also a struggle to define its meaning for American society as a whole. Richard Nixon called the assassination a tragedy for the nation and called on Americans "to redeem this terrible act" (*Chicago Tribune* April 5, 1968:23). Stokely Carmichael, former chairman of the Student Nonviolent Coordinating Committee (SNCC), identified as a "black power advocate" by the *Chicago Tribune* (April 6, 1968:N9), said King's death must be avenged: "When white America killed Dr. King, it declared war on us...We have to retaliate for the execution of Dr. King." King's death was featured in every form of mass media, and many of those in a position of authority were called upon to react. The *Los Angeles Times* called it a national tragedy and the *New York Times* a national disaster. Every citizen was called upon to take a stand, to have an opinion. One central aspect of this meaning struggle concerned not only who was to blame, but also what deeper forces might be responsible. The *Chicago Tribune* joined the chorus blaming the "permissive culture" in an editorial; the nation, the editors declared, should mourn for King, but also because

"moral values are at the lowest level since the decadence in Rome..." If you are black, so goes the convention, you are right, and you must be indulged in every wish. Why, sure, break the window and make off with the color TV set, the case of liquor, the beer, the dress, the coat and the shoes. We won't shoot you. That would be police brutality…If you are white, you are wrong. Feel guilty about it. Assume the collective guilt of all your progenitors, even if neither you or anyone you know is a descendent of slave owners." (cited in Perlstein (2008:258))

Senator Robert Byrd of West Virginia thought King brought the murder on himself: "One cannot preach nonviolence and at the same time advocate defiance of the law…For to defy the law is to invite violence, especially in a tense atmosphere" (quoted in Chappell). This view was shared by Elijah Muhammad, leader of the Nation of Islam, who called King "an enemy of his own people" who "got what he preached for" (quoted in Chappell).

The *Kerner Report*, commissioned by President Lyndon Johnson in 1967 to investigate the causes of urban disorder, published its results one month before King's murder. It warned, "Our nation is moving toward two societies, one black, one white, separate and unequal."[6] Martin Luther King's murder helped make even more visible the racial aspect of the widening breech in the national collective. Assigning blame for the murder would be essential in any attempt at repair. The *Chicago Tribune* editorial writers knew this, and in the same editorial cited above wrote, "The murder of Dr. King was a crime and the sin of an individual," while "the rest of us [were] not contributory…" (April 9, 1968, quoted in Perlstein 2008:258). If responsibility could be squarely placed in the hands of a lone assassin, then the "rest of us," that is, the American nation—or at least its white majority—could continue on as normal after an appropriate amount of mourning. This, after all, is clearly a function of such ritual acts as public funerals and other forms of commemoration in recognizing the passing of an important person. However, if there were more than one killer, a conspiracy, or some collective responsibility, then returning to normal, everyday life would not be as easy. In blaming King's death on a permissive culture, or on black aggressiveness, as Reagan and the more ambivalent *Tribune* editorialists did, something more needed doing than prosecuting a guilty party. To this day, suspicions of conspiracy, including the involvement of federal police authorities and organized crime, continue to haunt the memory of Martin Luther King's death. Jesse Jackson, one of King's associates, who was also present at the Memphis motel that evening, went so far as to write a foreword in James Earl Ray's own account of the murder in which he claims his own innocence and the involvement of powerful mysterious others (Ray 1992). Jackson writes, "I have never accepted the 'one crazy man' theory of political assassinations. I certainly do not accept such a theory with regard to James Earl Ray and Dr. Martin Luther King Jr. I have always believed that there was a conspiracy involved in

Dr. King's assassination. I have always believed that the government was part of a conspiracy, either directly or indirectly, to assassinate him" (Jackson in Ray 1992:5).[7] After RFK's murder, the issue would be raised again, but from a different point of view, by the National Commission among many others. As for Ray himself, he claimed to have been duped by a mysterious French-Canadian seaman named Raoul, who had himself actually carried out the murder (Ray 1992).

THE MURDER

We have a clear record of the shooting of Martin Luther King; it was observed and recorded firsthand by local and national police authorities and the mass media. There were more than 40 law enforcement officers tracking King's every move from the moment he arrived in Memphis to the time when he was shot. Martin Luther King's hotel room was under constant surveillance, and as he stood on the motel balcony the evening of April 4, a pair of police binoculars was trained on him from a firehouse across the street. As the shot rang out, the observing police officer recorded what he saw: "Dr. King falling backward, his hands shooting up as if to grab his head, then landing heavily on his back" (quoted in Frank 1972:84; it was a fireman who had momentarily borrowed the binoculars who made this observation according to Sides 2010). A representative of the Justice Department, James Laue, "knelt down and pressed a towel against the wound in King's right cheek." As he did so, he was thinking, "Kennedy...Kennedy...Kennedy" (Clarke 2008: 88). Responding to the police officer's shouts, Fire Captain Carthel Weeden called an ambulance. At the same moment, members of the tactical police on duty in the fire station ran toward the motel. The ambulance arrived four minutes later to take King to a nearby hospital. Shot through the jaw, the bullet severing his spinal cord, Martin Luther King died on the operating table, though he was essentially dead on arrival. His close friend and associate Ralph Abernathy made the announcement to the assembled mass media at 7:25 P.M.[8] All this was conveyed directly as it occurred to the attorney general of the United States, Ramsay Clark, who would soon be ordered to Memphis by President Johnson to head the investigation, who also closely followed the unfolding events.

Earl Caldwell, a *New York Times* reporter assigned to cover the Memphis strike story, was renting a room a floor below King in the Loraine Motel when he heard the shot. Caldwell ran to the second floor balcony and arrived to hear the Rev. James Bevel softly say, "It ended as it had to end. It was written that way." While phoning in his story to his New York editors from a pay phone in the motel courtyard, Caldwell thought to himself, "It's true, it's like a review you have read of a play and now you see the play..."

(quoted in Frank 1972:83). It was Caldwell's name that appeared on the byline of the front-page story about King's death that appeared in the *Times* the next morning, but no mention was made of his firsthand witnessing. *Life* magazine also had a photographer staying at the motel. Some of his photographs of the immediate aftermath of the murder, including those of a strategy meeting of King's associates following the shooting, were not released until April 2009, 41 years later, in part because they were thought so sensitive (Henry Groskinsky, cnn.com/2009/living/04/21/slideshow. MLK.Life/index.html/).

With the police so close at hand, the attempt to find the killer began immediately. Following the presumed trajectory of the bullet, police quickly located the rooming house window—and a palm print on the bathroom wall—from where the shot was fired. They also found a witness who had followed the comings and goings in the rooming house. The killer left a clear trail, having discarded his rifle in a nearby trash bin, and eyewitnesses not only saw him throw it there, but also observed his getaway. The first police alarm went out over their radio at 6:08 P.M., only minutes after the shooting. It announced a "Suspect described as a young white male, well-dressed, believed in late model white Mustang, going north on Main from scene of shooting" (quoted in Frank 1972:98; see also Sides (2010), who gives a detailed blow-by-blow account of the movements of King and Ray). Yet, despite what was termed "the greatest manhunt of our time," it took more than a month for the perpetrator to be captured. Using a series of aliases, James Earl Ray managed to avoid American authorities and to make his way to London via Canada. After some time in that city, Ray was apprehended at Heathrow Airport while boarding a flight to Brussels from where he hoped to fly to Rhodesia, seeking sanctuary in a country governed by white supremacists and employment in a mercenary army.

Notified of his arrest, the U.S. government immediately prepared for Ray's extradition and return to Memphis to stand trial. Ray was making his own preparations, having contracted, through his court-appointed British lawyer, what he thought was a sympathetic attorney in Alabama to defend him, should this occur. Ray was flown in the greatest secrecy between military bases in England and Tennessee on an Air Force jet, whose only passengers, in addition to the crew, were Ray, four members of the FBI, and a physician. Both the takeoff and the landing were made under the cover of darkness; all this was done with the memory of the murder of Lee Harvey Oswald in mind. The "fiasco" in Dallas was clearly etched into the institutional memory of American law enforcement officials. News of the arrest of a suspect in the murder of Martin Luther King reached the American public in the midst of the official mourning for Robert Kennedy. The televised broadcast of the funeral train carrying Kennedy's body to Washington on June 8, 1968, was interrupted with this news.

After changing defense attorneys at the last moment, James Earl Ray pleaded guilty to murdering Martin Luther King. He did so after being convinced that he would be found guilty and sentenced to death. Lawyers on both sides worried about the effects of this plea bargain, and before the deal was struck, prosecutors spoke with Coretta King and local black leaders. Ray at first resisted, claiming that he was innocent, a dupe of conspiratorial others, and appeared to believe that even if convicted, being seen as a hired gun would raise his status in the eyes of his reference group: the criminal world. Convinced by his own attorney that a trial could only lead to the death penalty, Ray finally consented to plead guilty in exchange for life imprisonment. Ray's "trial" officially lasted 2 hours and 37 minutes, as the prosecutors read their case to the jury. As noted, he would later try (unsuccessfully) to alter this plea.

MEANS, MOTIVE, AND OPPORTUNITY

Why did James Earl Ray kill Martin Luther King? Ray most likely decided to kill King early in 1968 during a stay in Los Angeles, when he was drifting around looking for something to give meaning to his life (Frank 1972:323). He set out from Los Angeles in March and began stalking his victim, traveling to Atlanta, then Birmingham and Selma, all the while carrying a handgun. Because King was under constant police protection, Ray apparently realized he would need a long-range rifle to carry out his plan. He followed King to Memphis, where the latter's every move, including the motel where he stayed, was announced in the local newspaper, with accompanying photographs to mark its location. Finding his target was not difficult, and with the police less visible (they had chosen to hide their presence), Ray seized the opportunity. He found a place with a clear view of King's living quarters to stay in and purchased a hunting rifle equipped with a telescopic sight. King proved an easy target, but Ray's escape was a matter of clumsy luck. The undercover police watching King were at Ray's rooming house within 45 seconds of the shot, yet he somehow escaped. As Ray ran toward his car, he caught sight of the onrushing police, which caused him to discard his unwieldy weapon where it would be immediately discovered. Ray was able to flee the city because no all-points bulletin was issued and no roadblocks set up. This was in part because Memphis police had been caught up in a false, yet mesmerizing, CB-radio report of a high-speed car chase involving the getaway vehicle (Sides 2010:195–7). By sheer luck and cunning, Ray managed to stay one step ahead of his pursuers.

According to Gerold Frank, law-enforcement authorities compiled a list of motives while they were preparing their prosecution: "Racism, anti-Communism, patriotism, the yearning for status of a man doomed from birth to be last on the totem pole, the resentment of such a man for a "Nigger" who had the arrogance of fame, the admiration of white women; the private rage always held in check, seeking an object, waiting for a moment of full, triumphant release…" (1972:364). James Earl Ray was a product of his time as much as he was of the more intimate social relations of family, schools, and local community. His personality was formed in the conservative values of the small midwestern town where he grew up, during the confrontational Cold War period. His attitudes toward blacks were shaped by the prejudices of that time and reinforced by his own experiences at the lower end of the social order, including the many years he had spent in prison. As an adult, Ray flirted with right-wing political organizations, such as the John Birch Society, which provided him with a vague, but clearly defensive ideology to further legitimate his basic prejudices: it was the Communists and the Jews who were responsible for his personal failings. When respected leaders such as FBI chief J. Edgar Hoover publicly accused Martin Luther King of being a Communist fellow traveler, this only reaffirmed the civil rights leader as a legitimate target of Ray's hate. The idea that killing King would offer immediate worldwide recognition and raise his status within the criminal world, in which he had spent much of his life, only added to this. To James Earl Ray, Martin Luther King represented all that he despised, and murdering him would, in addition, raise his status and give him the recognition he had never received. From a small-time petty crook, Ray would become an assassin, an object of fear and respect, rather than of ridicule. In need of recognition within the criminal status hierarchy, Ray could have murdered any visible public figure, but he chose Martin Luther King on the basis of his personal prejudices; he hated blacks, especially confident and successful ones. Many in his close environment, including his brothers, considered murdering King not merely legitimate but an extreme act of patriotism.[9] "In parts of America, I'm a national hero," Ray boasted (Sides 2010: 380).

The arrest and trial of James Earl Ray took on great significance in this period of social and political polarization. For those concerned with social repair, it was of prime importance to classify this deed as the act of a lone individual and, in the best case, an individual who was not politically motivated. Thus, whether or not this was a murder or an assassination was not simply a matter of semantics or strict legal argument. I've already mentioned the discussion that arose after Ray's arrest by the British police and the legal significance of the categorization; whether or not this was a political assassination would make his extradition either difficult or easy. Due to the peculiarities of British law, Ray's defense attorney claimed that Ray's act was political, something that, if true, could have delayed or even hindered entirely his extradition, while others representing the prosecution claimed the opposite for the same reason. This would later be modified when Ray was returned to the United States and the actual trial began. However, the importance of showing that this was the act of a lone individual, even if motivated by racial hatred, was important if the societal breech widened by the murder was to be repaired. A swift and speedy trial was essential. This was made even more the case by the memory of the murder of Lee Harvey Oswald, accused of killing JFK, before he could be brought to trial. This would also be in the minds of many after the murder of Robert Kennedy and the apprehension of Sirhan Sirhan his killer, as we will soon see. The fact that no trial occurred and that a deal was made caused an angry reaction on many sides, most notably amongst African Americans. Speaking with community leaders in Memphis one year after the murder, Watters writes,

> Black reaction to the handling of the Ray case, to the 'deal', was generally angry, said the Rev. Mr. Lawson and others. A lot of people, he said, felt that it was a cover-up...What it meant, said Mr. Lawson in his ability to articulate what probably most black Memphis people and others across the nation felt, was that 'the trial shows the power structure's inability to respond to human need—in this sense the legal power structure. The real need was to give facts, answer questions...A court that pushes through a case without all the facts crushes the dreams of black people that institutions respond to their needs...They feel that the racism of the nation killed Dr. King. (1969:16)

For Watters himself, the lack of a trial "failed...that function of justice most valuable to a society—catharsis and expiation" Watters (1969: 15).

In the murder of Martin Luther King, where there existed widely divergent positions and outbreaks of violence, swift resolution might have been a better solution from the point of view of collective repair than a long, drawn-out, and contentious trial. In the case where a minority leader was murdered, many in the majority might well prefer to close the issue as quickly as possible, with the thought that public memory is short, especially in the media age. The affected minority would have another view of this, of course, and the occurrence would surely become another powerful incident in the group's memory. In the case of the Martin Luther King, we could call this a racial memory, which is distinct from and lives alongside a national, collective memory. For the majority, however, plea bargain rather than public trial might appear a good solution, and this is precisely what occurred. One could also speak about the memory of a place, about how, for example, the image of Dallas was forever tainted and, in this case, that of the city of Memphis and the aftereffects of a traumatic occurrence. The mass media made much of the fact that King was killed there. After *Time* magazine in its reportage on the assassination referred to Memphis as a "decadent river town," the judge dealing with the sentencing of James Earl Ray (the proceedings of which were held in Memphis) remarked at the close of the case, "I submit that up to now, we have not done too badly for a "decadent river town" (Watters 1969:18). Watters also reports some of the positive outcomes of the assassination:

> One effect of the assassination was to stir this liberal element (of Memphis) into greater activity and into deeper involvement in the ordering of the society. Another was to expose, poor as well as affluent but mainly in the middle-class, to the ideas, the ideals, the plights, the articulate demands of black Memphis citizens, and even to win some of these whites, if not to complete sympathy, to sympathetic actions. (Watters 1969: 20)

"Memphis, writes Hampton Sides, "was reeling from the assassination in every possible way, rethinking itself, questioning its identity" (2010:307).

MEDIA REPORTAGE

The murder of Martin Luther King was the subject of extraordinary media coverage. Just as law enforcement authorities had been monitoring his every move, so the mass media followed Martin Luther King with great interest and intensity. The *New York Times* had a reporter living right beneath King at the Lorraine Motel, and other national news media were almost as observant. The local press in Memphis had their own intense coverage, which, as we have seen, was where his killer turned for information about his victim's whereabouts and schedule. As defined by the media, Martin Luther King was a celebrity, and his personal and public life was defined as newsworthy. Up to his death, King personified, in a mass media geared to personalities, one dominant element of the civil rights movement. His representation was determined by where that particular media venue stood in relation to the issues raised by that movement. This would change significantly after his death, when King became "the *only* leader worth mentioning in the civil rights movement" (Dyson 2008:146). If the civil rights movement was understood as a threat, then MLK was portrayed through that lens; if the movement was seen as a moral force for progressive social change, that too affected his representation. After King's death, there emerged a struggle over how he should be remembered and represented. As an iconic and heroic figure, King gave the movement a more sympathetic face than would be the case if he were remembered as an agitator. Except for a few extreme cases, such as the right-wing paper mentioned above, these various frameworks of interpretation did not significantly affect the first- hand coverage of his murder, though it did impact the events that followed. Editorial comment was another story, as the quotation from the Chicago paper above reveals. In 1968, the American news media could be easily divided along racial lines; there existed a black press and a white press, which could be further divided between liberal, conservative, and openly segregationist. The black press itself was divided between separatist and integrationist, as well as between the politically radical, such as the Black Panther Party, and the ultra-conservative nation of Islam. These divisions were reflected in editorial comments in the days following King's murder.

The first media reports went out immediately. Radio and television stations interrupted their regular broadcasting to make the announcement. The fact that the shooting occurred at around 6:00 P.M. meant that it was the beginning of prime time, when, at least on the East Coast, normal broadcasting included the evening news. Newspapers, then the most popular source of information, have another rhythm, and the news of the shooting and death of Martin Luther King made banner headlines in the morning papers of April 5. The weekly newsmagazines, with their own distinctive rhythm and readership, are a third source of information whose self-understood role is to provide meaning to the confusing flow of events reported in the daily papers.

Reportage of King's death assumed and reflected a racially and politically polarized nation. The *Washington Post* (April 7, 1968: B6) spoke of "the whole Negro community" and the "whole white community" when it considered reactions of the murder, while the *New York Times* (April 6, 1968: 38) warned of "extremists of both sides," and columnist James Reston (*New York Times* April 7, 1968:E12) identified the victim with "his people."

At the same time, the murder was considered as resulting from a long historical legacy stemming from slavery and thus reflecting the nation's past and threatening its present image. This was a "national tragedy," "an event of horror and shame to America and a shock to the world," which "underscores once more the tragedy of the divisions which rip and tear our society" (*Los Angeles Times* April 5, 1968: A4). Two days later the same paper spoke of "A Crossroads in U.S. History" (April 7, 1968:K6). In a similar vein, the *New York Times* (April 5, 1968:46) called King's murder "a national disaster," where "the bullet that extinguished the life of Dr. King has struck deep into the fabric of this country and has torn into the fiber of every American of every race, color and creed. Each of us has died a little with the death..." Who was to blame and "What can I do?" wondered *Time* (May 17, 1968). Assuming it was speaking to a white audience, the editors answered by turning the question around, "For today's white, the question is not, 'What can I do?' but 'What does the Negro want me to Do?'" The answer, in other words, was to recognize the problem and to "listen" to the other side. The *Wall Street Journal* did not agree that whites or the historical legacy of slavery bore some of the burden for the murder; they believed accusations of "collective guilt" were wrongly placed. The paper disagreed with anthropologist Ashley Montagu who "in a recent letter to the *New York Times*...contends that white Americans "are as responsible for the death of one of humanity's greatest leaders...as if we had pulled the trigger ourselves" (*Wall Street Journal* April 15, 1968:18). Rather than collective guilt, the *Journal* thought that blame should be placed on the individual responsible, not on race or nation. "If all are guilty, the one who did the deed is not more so...it does not help...for people, learned or otherwise, to prate nonsense about collective guilt." The meaning struggle in the immediate aftermath sought answers to the question of who the perpetrator was—a lone individual, a white man, a racist—and whether or not the nation, or some part of it, bore some of the responsibility for the deed. This was to continue through the pursuit, capture, and sentencing of James Earl Ray.

The views of the Black Panther Party can be gleaned from the writing and speeches of its leaders. Eldridge Cleaver (1968: 105), the Party's Minister of Information, considered King an "Uncle Tom," a racial appeaser in the tradition of Booker T. Washington, "the Martin Luther King of his day." Following a rhetorical path laid out by Malcolm X (who spoke of "Reverend Chicken Wing ,"one of America's "twentieth century uncle toms"), Cleaver had previously unfavorably compared King to the assassinated Malcolm X and others who had died for the racial cause. After King's own assassination, Cleaver was forced to retract some of this when he wrote that King's death was "a certainty," because it was based on a "self-deceiving doctrine" of nonviolence in the face of white suppression. (Chappell). Cleaver predicted, "America will be painted red. Dead bodies will litter the streets," and that after King's assassination "all black people in America have become Black Panthers in spirit." The days of being a victim were over, Cleaver wrote: "Now there is the gun and the bomb, dynamite and the knife, and they will be used liberally in America. America will bleed. America will suffer" (quoted in Chappell from *Ramparts* (May 1968 48–49 "The Death of Martin Luther King: Requiem for Nonviolence"). CORE's director Floyd McKissick and other more moderate black leaders agreed with Cleaver that "Dr. Martin Luther King was the last prince of nonviolence...nonviolence is a dead philosophy...it was the white people that killed nonviolence..." (*New York Times* April 5, 1968:26). While some black militants hoped King's death would be a catalyst for revolt or, at the very least, a radical change in strategy, notably segregationist newspaper editors and columnists became much more moderate, even respectful, in their tone when referring to the dead MLK. Writing in the *Richmond News Leader,* James K. Kirkpatrick said that King "was the bravest man I ever knew in public life...No white southerner ever matched a fraction of his courage. To watch one of his marches was to sense the awesome power of strong character combined with high purpose. This is the way it must have been, one reflected, when the early Christians braved the hate and ridicule of Rome" (quoted in Chappell:17). Thomas J. Waring of the *Charleston News & Courier,* on the other hand, wrote, "While we intend no disrespect to the dead or to those who venerate Dr. King, we cannot accept the accuracy of his own description of nonviolence...he left a trail of discontent that sooner or later flared into violence" (quoted in Chappell:18). Summing up his discussion, Chappell writes, "Many major southern dailies, including some with fiery segregationist histories, were indistinguishable from liberal northern papers (18).

There are clear themes that emerge out of media reportage in the days after the murder of Martin Luther King, some of which would be repeated a few months later when Robert Kennedy was killed. That the United States was a "sick society" prone to violence, where murder and assassination reflected a "moral breakdown" and a "loss of public order." The murder of MLK was a "national disgrace" and a "trauma" that greatly affected the way the country was viewed by others and altered its standing in the world.

> The murder of Dr. King should show us what we should have seen long ago. We are a sick society that has fallen far short of what we claim to be. Is it not time that every American opens his eyes?...A kind of mental and moral decay is eating out the vitals of this country. And for my part I do not see how the nation can ever recover the routine of the life that was—what used to be normality. (*Los Angeles Times* April 8, 1968)

The editors clearly thought, however, that something could be learned from this occurrence, if only Americans would open their eyes, while, at the same time, saying the country could never be the same. The *New York Times* pointedly identified the "sickness" (April 8, 1968). "It is not the particular individual—the assassin—who is responsible for the death of MLK. It is the ideas that exist within the American society that are responsible. These ideas—these untruths—will continue to produce acts of violence as long as the white people allow discrimination and prejudice."

The grounds of America's "sickness" would widen with the murder of RFK, and when the Soviet Union joined in pointing this out, President Lyndon Johnson felt compelled to respond: "It would be wrong to conclude from this act that our country is sick. Now is the time to prove it" (*Washington Post* June 8, 1968), to which the papers editors countered, "I mourn for a president who says that our country is not sick...Our society is sick." Billy Graham agreed, speaking in Australia; the evangelist, who at the time was popularly known as "America's pastor," said, "Tens of thousands of Americans are mentally deranged...it indicates the sickness of the American society" (*Chicago Tribune* April 5, 1968:23). After the murder of RFK the "sickness" was located in the nation's proneness to violence and unwillingness to act to combat its root causes—the lack of gun control and the violence on television and in Vietnam.

Time (April 19, 1968) offered its own summation of the nation's condition as reflected in the news media. "Grief," "shock," and "shame"—the words appeared over and over again in the nation's press after the assassination of Martin Luther King. "We are becoming in the eyes of the world, and to an alarming degree in fact," said the *Louisville-Courier-Journal*, "a violent nation of violent people, given to a disregard for life that must shame decent people here and throughout the world." *Time* editors declined to state their own opinion, preferring to quote others, including the *Wall Street Journal*, which claimed, "White America may have been more shocked than Black America at the assassination. To Negroes, the slaying of Dr. King, many observers suggest, was just another injustice, however horrific," and then "one Negro paper, the *Los Angeles Herald-Dispatch*, wrote " The American Caucasian has lost the best friend he ever had." This editorializing was followed by a call for a moratorium on editorial comment: "*The Herald-Dispatch* does not propose to discuss Dr. King and his activities in the wake of a $500 million funeral—a real Hollywood production. This production has created entirely too much emotion. When people are emotional, they are unable to think or reason. We plan to discuss it in three weeks, when our minds are less tense."[10] This was all wishful thinking in the aftermath of some of the worst collective violence in the nation's history and a few weeks before RFK would be assassinated in Los Angeles.

In a prophetic editorial published eight days after MLK's assassination, *Time* had called that death "a tragic finale to an American drama," while naming King a "transcendent symbol...if there were ever a transcendent Negro symbol, it was Martin Luther King" (*Time* April 12, 1968). While the magazine limited this transcendent symbolism to "Negroes," the legend of MLK has now moved beyond the confines of American race relations to become a universal symbol of equality between peoples. From being a "drum major" for civil rights legislation in the United States (as *Time* put it at the inaugural King holiday in 1986), by 1989, according to *U.S. News and World Report*, "people of all persuasions now have a sense that he challenges them to be at their best and that he's articulating principles they believe in that are larger than race" (cited in Morgan 2006:143). This was written when King had been dead for more than 20 years. Two processes were at work here; on the one hand, King's memory was, by this time, so domesticated that even those (such as *U.S. News*) who had opposed his actions when they were actually occurring could now see him as representing all that was best in America, and, on the other, King's image and message was being lifted from its context and universalized. King's image, as Morgan (2006:144) shows, was also being commercialized: "In 1999, with the approval of the Atlanta-based King Center, Apple Computer featured King in magazine and billboard ads as part of its 'think different' campaign, in effect translating determined political opposition into creative entrepreneurship. In 2001, against an image of King speaking (to an empty mall) from the steps of the Lincoln Memorial in 1963, a television voice-over suggested to viewers, 'Before you inspire, before you can touch, you must first connect. And the company that connects more of the world is Alcatel…' "

The symbolic transformation of King had been in preparation even before his death, most notably when he was awarded the Nobel Peace Prize in 1964. King was only 35 when he received the prize, the youngest man to do so at the time. *Ebony Magazine* provides a description:

> For nearly 45 minutes the young man sat stiffly in his black cutaway and gray and white cravat, nervously clasping and unclasping his hands, sometimes closing his eyes, often glancing at his wife who sat nearby. All this time speakers had praised the young man's work and the Norwegian Broadcasting Orchestra had played Mozart and Gershwin in his honor. Then the trumpets sounded. Someone nudged the young man, and he rose from his seat. As Norway's King Olav V, Crown Prince Harald, high government officials, the diplomatic corps and one of the largest crowds ever jammed into the Festival hall of Oslo University stood and applauded, the Rev. Dr. Martin Luther King Jr. stepped on stage to receive the Nobel Peace Prize for 1964. (findarticles.com/p/articles/m1077is_2_55/ai_58118335/)

During his five-minute acceptance speech, King made numerous references to the civil rights struggle in the United States and the condition of black Americans, but he also sought to transcend that immediate context. "Today I come to Oslo as a trustee, inspired and with renewed dedication to humanity. I accept this prize on behalf of all men who love peace and brotherhood" (Nobel Acceptance Speech). Prior to coming to Oslo, King stopped in London, where he preached to a packed St. Paul's Cathedral, and his visit was widely reported in the British press. "Responding to questions, he discussed British race relations, caste in India, world peace, called for Britain and the United States to put strong pressure on South Africa… (Sewell 1996:206). While in London, King met with the Indian prime minister as well as British officials. He also spoke to thousands at peace rallies and demonstrations. After Oslo, King visited Stockholm, where he was met with similar enthusiasm. Only exhaustion caused him to forgo similar engagements in Copenhagen and Paris. King was, in other words, a powerful symbolic and representative figure well beyond the United States even before his death. His death, especially the way he died, was the catalyst to his transfiguration. King died a martyr to a cause that was, by this time, universally acknowledged as just. He was, according to media reports, "a martyr for justice" (BBC) and "a martyr for peace" (oilempire.us/mlk/html). The story was summed up by the *Washington Post*: "As he lay dying, the popular beatification was already underway: Martin Luther King Jr., general and martyr to the greatest moral crusade on the nation's racial battlefield" (www.washingtonpost.com/wp-srv/national/longterm/mlk/legacy.htm).

COMMEMORATION AND MEANING

On Monday, April 8, four days after the assassination, Correta Scott King, in a black mourning gown, with two of her young children by her side, led a silent march of about 20,000 people through the streets of Memphis in support of the still-striking sanitation workers. Among the 20,000 were many celebrities, including actors and entertainers Sidney Poitier, Sammy Davis, Jr., Bill Cosby, and Dr. Benjamin Spock, the cause célèbre of the "permissive generation" (Sides 2010:269). The next day in Atlanta, over 150, 000 people gathered for the funeral of Martin Luther King, Jr. The funeral procession from Ebenezer Baptist Church to Morehouse College was carried live on national television and viewed by more than 120 million people around the world (Sides 2010: 277). The list of celebrities and dignitaries, which included Jackie Kennedy, but not Lyndon Johnson, was more than impressive. According to *Newsweek,* the two widows were seen "leaning toward each other like parentheses around the tragic half decade" (quoted in Sides 2010:278). James Earl Ray was watching the broadcast from his hideaway in Canada.

The conflict over how to remember and memorialize Martin Luther King began immediately after his death as a struggle between members of his own organization, the Southern Christian Leadership Conference (SCLC), and his family.[11] The SCLC favored increased social activism as a means of honoring King, while "Mrs. King placed more emphasis on establishing the King Center in Atlanta, Georgia, and favoring calls to establish a holiday in her husband's memory" (Alderman 2006:73). The groups also differed as to whether it was his birth or death that should be commemorated, with the activists favoring the day of his death and his family his birth. Commemorating King as the victim of assassination in the midst of a political struggle would mean commemorating his activism and would have to deal in some way with his violent death, while celebrating his birth would be much more neutral, personal, and private.[12] The latter would also more easily lend itself to the nonpartisan ideal of establishing a national holiday, celebrating a neutered representative of "American ideals." On another plane, this was also a struggle over whether to commemorate an individual, a racial or ethnic group, or a social movement.

The path toward commemorating MLK, though contentious, was made easier by the actions of those in positions of power and authority who had strongly opposed his activism during King's lifetime, namely, southern segregationists. While strong grassroots opposition existed, and continues to exist, many influential segregationists, such as the senators and newspaper editors mentioned earlier, remained relatively silent or changed their tone after King's death. This permitted his supporters more leeway and more public space to fight over how MLK should be commemorated, rather than if he should be. Such struggles occurred locally as well as nationally.

Memorials for Martin Luther King are numerous and varied. There are currently more than 730 places in the United States where roads are named after him. The vast majority of these are in the South (Alderman 2006, who sees this as part of a larger movement by African Americans to gain recognition). There are also numerous schools and other public buildings that bear his name. Already a "sight-seeing curiosity and shrine" (Watters 1969:15) immediately after the assassination, the Lorraine Motel and the rooming house from which Ray fired his fatal shot have been incorporated into the National Civil Rights Museum, which formally opened in 1991. Room 306, where King spent his last night, has been kept as it was when he stood on the balcony the evening of April 4, 1968, and the two automobiles that were then parked beneath have now been replaced by exact replicas. The process, which was more than 20 years in the making, was not without controversy. A woman who thought turning the site of King's death into a museum would dilute his political message camped outside for years in protest (Alderman 2006:75 provides a photo). The motel is the site of an annual ceremony, and during the presidential campaign in 2008, Republican senator and presidential aspirant John McCain showed up unexpectedly to make an impromptu speech in which he apologized for voting in 1983 against making King's birthday a national holiday. Among the surprised participants at the Lorraine that day was Jesse Jackson, who had been present at the motel in April 1968. The debate over the establishment of a national holiday commemorating MLK's birthday is revealing about both the contention surrounding his person and the debate over co-optation versus cultural change.

The Congressional Black Caucus (CBC) was a leading force in the debate surrounding the King holiday. One member, Representative John Conyers of Michigan, had introduced a bill calling for a national holiday four days after the assassination. This bill was voted down, as was the one Conyers introduced in 1979. In 1971, more than 1 million signatures were gathered and sent to Congress in support of the holiday, and between 1973–79, four states (Illinois, Massachusetts, Connecticut, and New Jersey) declared a King holiday. On January 15, 1981, (King's birthday), the groups sponsoring the attempt to create a national holiday organized a benefit concert where Stevie Wonder, a sponsor, sang "Happy Birthday," in a reggae-like melody containing the words "I've never understood how a man who was that good could not have a day set aside for his celebration." This was recorded along with excerpts from King's speeches and distributed as a vinyl LP. Two years later a new bill sponsored by Rep. Katie Hall of Indiana was introduced and passed the House by a vote of 338–90. It was then ratified by the Senate with a vote of 78–22, after a furious debate in which Senator Jesse Helms (R-NC) called Martin Luther King a "Communist," among other things, and had King's FBI files sent to each member of the Senate. Senator Daniel Patrick Moynihan (D-NY) famously stomped the files on the Senate floor, calling them "a packet of filth" (www.avoiceonline.org/mlk/history/html). The bill was signed into law by President Ronald Reagan in 1983. Reagan had first threatened to veto the bill and would later apologize for his opposition. In her final report, Rep. Hall wrote, "MLK, Jr. gave to this country a new understanding of equality and justice for all... This legislation will act as a national commitment to Dr. King's vision of an ideal America... The work and ideals of Dr. King must surface in the form of a national holiday whereby every American will be reminded of his great struggles and contribution to mankind" (www.avoiceonline.org/mlk/history/html). Here we can see some of the intentions behind commemoration, but also the lifting of King's memory from American race relations to a more universal level and from the nation to the world.

FROM NATIONAL TO UNIVERSAL SYMBOL

The transformation of MLK from political activist to national symbol, which culminated in the establishment of a nation holiday honoring the date of his birth, thus began immediately after his death. When delivering his official proclamation to lower the flags on government buildings and naval vessels to half-mast, President Lyndon Johnson opened his remarks by saying, "Once again the heart of America is heavy. The spirit of America weeps for a tragedy that denies the very meaning of our land. The life of a man who symbolized the freedom and faith of America has been taken" (reported in the *New York Times* April 6, 1968:23). *Life Magazine* put it this way: "King was a thoroughly good man who achieved greatness by showing forth the Negro cause at its best. His was the old American cause of equal rights for all men..." (*Life* April 12, 1968, cited in Daynes 1997:119). This association of MLK with national values was both narrowed and expanded by *Time* a few days later. Under the headline "Transcendent Symbol," the editors wrote,

> ... [I]f ever there were a transcendent Negro symbol, it was MLK. Bridging the void between black despair and white unconcern, he spoke so powerfully of and from the wretchedness of the Negro's condition that he became the moral guidon of civil rights not only to Americans but also the world beyond. If not the actual catalyst, he was the legitimizer of progress toward racial equality. (*Time*, April 12, 1968)

While *Time* delimited King's identity, it also raised his meaning to a global plane.

Such words were performative, in the sense that they were part of a transformative process that had real effects. MLK as "transcendent symbol" was differentiated from Martin Luther King the person, and this transfiguration affected not only how King was remembered, but also how people acted with reference to that memory. On the one hand, one could speak of a "domestication", a process where the more radical and contentious sides of King's actions and ideas are conveniently forgotten or downplayed; this is a claim made by Dyson, Morgan, and many others. The *New York Times* reflected on this in its January 15, 1993, editorial: "A disturbing revisionism threatens the memory of Dr. Martin Luther King, Jr., whose 64th birthday Americans celebrate today. In life, he was the passionate voice of a civil rights revolution, an apostle of civil disobedience, and a speaker of uncomfortable truths to power. In memory, some now cast him as the unthreatening 'Moderate Alternative,' an integrationist whose nonviolence can be favorably contrasted to more militant strategies of black empowerment" (cited in Daynes 1997:119). Memorializing King in this way would make it easy to fit him into the American pantheon as a crusader for "American values" and as a quintessential "American." Celebrating his birthday would then mean celebrating America and lend itself to the same type of ritualized patriotic acts and actions that are performed on other national holidays. Critics such as those mentioned earlier would see this commemoration through the negative light of co-optation, not only as distorting the "real" MLK, the agitator and activist, but also as molding his image for domestic use, as yet another symbol of the country's hegemonic power, its ability to absorb and co-opt all opposition and transform it to its own advantage. On the other hand, however, one could speak not of co-optation and domestication, but of a radical transformation, in a moral and cultural, if not political sense. From this perspective, the incorporation of MLK into the American pantheon and the transformation of his image represent a clear cultural shift, providing a new moral yardstick for gauging progress and also what being an American means. This too would have great effect, not only on how King is remembered, but also on how people act with regard to that memory. The issue of whether such a shift was "merely" symbolic or was a sign of substantial institutional change continues to this day, especially after the election of Barack Obama. Whatever one's position, it seems undeniable that the inclusion of Martin Luther King into the pantheon of American heroes marked a major shift in American perspectives on race and racism, something that helped make the presidency of Barack Obama possible.

THE ASSASSINATION OF ROBERT KENNEDY

At 12:15 A.M. on June 5, 1968, an assassin shot and mortally wounded Senator Robert F. Kennedy of New York in a narrow kitchen pantry of the Ambassador Hotel in Los Angeles. Just moments earlier, the forty-two-year-old Kennedy had left a ballroom celebration in the wake of winning the California Democratic presidential primary. No fewer that seventy-seven people were crowded in the pantry when twenty-four-year-old Palestinian immigrant Sirhan Bishara Sirhan, using an eight-shot .22-caliber revolver, opened fire on the senator. Kennedy was shot three times and died early the following day. Five other people were shot once, but all survived. (Moldea 1995:13)

In a last-minute decision, Kennedy followed the advice of a hotel employee to duck through the kitchen pantry in order to more quickly get to where a press conference had been organized in another part of the hotel. Sirhan Sirhan was in the same pantry in search of a cup of coffee to help sober him up for the drive home after attending several political campaign parties. As a precaution, because he was afraid that it would be stolen if left in his car, or because he felt he was being followed by enemies, Sirhan had a revolver in his pocket, one he had earlier used for target practice. There was little security at the hotel and even less in the pantry. In 1968, the secret service did not guard presidential aspirants, and the Kennedy campaign team did not want uniformed police officers to be seen in the vicinity of their candidate. The short, dark Sirhan blended easily with the crowd—he was mistaken for kitchen help, which was largely Latino.[13] Even the hotel's assistant maître d' leading Kennedy through the pantry thought as much. When Sirhan pushed forward toward the senator, those who saw him thought he wanted to shake his hand. According to his own account, the shots Sirhan fired came as a shock even to himself. Later, he would disclaim any memory of them. After shooting Kennedy, Sirhan emptied his gun into the surrounding room as he was pinned to a tabletop and the pistol wrestled from him. All around was chaos, as the victim lay dying on the pantry floor and the perpetrator was pummeled by a mass of distraught witnesses. Two LA police officers described the scene they encountered as they rushed into the hotel:

"We saw about five thousand hysterical people. They were going bananas...I didn't realize it was Kennedy who had been shot down—until I saw him lying on the floor. He was in shock and looked aged...we saw a guy on top of a table. Someone [Ambassador assistant maitre d' Karl Uecker] had him in a headlock. Rosey Grier [former football star and one of Kennedy's 'unofficial' bodyguards] was lying on his body, like a dead weight. I remember Rosey was crying...Jesse Unruh [the speaker of the California State Assembly] was on top of one of the tables with his knee in Sirhan's back, shouting 'We don't want another Dallas here!...This one's going to stand trial! He's going to pay! No one's going to kill him!' (quoted in Moldea 1995:47)

Another police officer thought that likely: "People were screaming, 'Lynch him!' and 'Kill him!'. This was not a good scene. We were in jeopardy just being with him. I had been in riot situations all through the sixties, and this was clearly a dangerous situation. Had we not arrived he would not have survived too much longer. And I don't think we would have either" (quoted in Moldea 1995: 48).

The chaos continued even after the perpetrator and victim had been removed. Kennedy was taken to a nearby hospital and Sirhan to the local Ramparts precinct house.[14] When officers arrived to secure the crime scene and gather evidence, they found shocked and hysterical people everywhere. One police sergeant recalled,

> ... [We moved out in the main ballroom, where Kennedy had been speaking. And then we moved out into the main lobby. And there was a fountain. And the hotel manager came through and asked us to assist them in getting the crowd out of the hotel. A real phenomena had occurred there. These people were in shock. You had people around that fountain who were actually kneeling and praying. They were dipping their hands in the water of that fountain and using it to cross themselves. (Moldea 1995:66–67)

The shadow and memory of the JFK assassination hung over the actions of all the authorities, from the police officers to the attending medical staff and the coroner who performed the autopsy, to the judge who presided over the trial and the news media that reported it all. Security around the still-unidentified suspect was extremely close and personal. At the crime scene one of the police officers in charge remarked: "The first thing we decided was that we didn't want what happened in Dallas to happen" (Moldea 1995:70); the interrogating officer at the Ramparts police station recalled, " We had Dallas on our minds. This guy [Kennedy] would have been the next president. I don't have a doubt in my mind. I tell you, as I was sitting there looking at this little guy [Sirhan], I thought, 'Man it just goes to show that we're all vulnerable'" (Moldea 1995:75), and the doctor performing the autopsy said, " I think all of us had learned from five years prior to that, with the death of President Kennedy, that the work on him had been done too fast under the circumstances...I said to myself, 'not again. Remember Dallas." (Moldea 1995:84). Later, when both the defense and the prosecution had agreed on a plea bargain in order to avoid a lengthy trial, the presiding judge invoked the memory of Dallas in his denial and told the attorneys: "I think you have got a very much interested public. I don't let the public influence me, but, at the same time, there are a lot of ramifications. And they continually point to the Oswald matter, and they just wonder what is going on, because that fellow wasn't tried...So we will just go through a trial" (quoted in Moldea 1995:120). Curiously, the assassination of Martin Luther King, much closer in time, was only rarely mentioned, though Sirhan Sirhan was reportedly "fascinated by the television coverage of the King assassination. Amazed that the assassin could kill and get away while he killed" (Kaiser 2008:141).

As the relaxed and playful perpetrator refused to identify himself, police were forced to trace his identity through the available evidence, his car keys, and the murder weapon: the history of the murder weapon led to Sirhan's brother, who had last purchased the gun. While they were speaking with Munir Sirhan and obtaining his permission to search his brother's room, another brother, having seen Sirhan's photograph in the morning newspaper, had already arrived at a local police station to identify the suspected killer. The room search led to the discovery of Sirhan's incriminating notebooks, which contained handwritten phrases like "RFK must be disposed of like his brother," "RFK must die...," "RFK must be assassinated," and "RFK must be assassinated before 5 June 68...," over and over (see Moldea 1995 and Kaiser 2008 for facsimiles).[15] These notebooks would become a major piece of evidence for the prosecution, and their admission in court was disputed (unsuccessfully) by the defense. Also at issue during the trial was Sirhan's childhood. One of the investigating police officers would note, "There was probably a tremendous amount of trauma when Sirhan was small. There were villages that were being wiped out. I could easily see why and how this hatred between the Arabs and Jews affected him" (Quoted in Moldea 1995:102). Memory and trauma were central actors in this unfolding drama, as was forgetting.

Sirhan Bishara Sirhan was born in 1944 to Christian parents in Jerusalem, Palestine, in the midst of bloody battles for control of that city. He grew up on a street that formed a dividing line between Arabs and Jews, and at the age of four, he was witness to battles that led to the establishment of the state of Israel.

> In the spring of 1948, St. Paul's Street is a mass of barbed wire. In the darkness of night, Zionist commandoes move in boldly on a British radio station above Sirhan's home. They dynamite the upper story and make the Sirhan bathroom into a machine gun nest...while the family cowers in the basement.... "Sirhan runs screaming to the family apartment with a water bucket half full of water. Members of the other families in the crowded compound pour out of their rooms to see what Sirhan is crying about. They find him in the hallway, staring down at a human hand floating on top of the water. Sirhan is quivering with fright"...After an explosion rocked his neighborhood, "young Sirhan clutches his private parts and shudders uncontrollably for hours. (All as reported by his mother and older brother to Robert Kaiser. (2008:131–32)

Under hypnosis, induced by a psychiatrist employed by the defense, Sirhan began weeping and moaning when "traumatized anew with a suggestion that he think about the war in Jerusalem" (Kaiser 2008: 275). As the defense explained to him when Sirhan questioned some of the testimony during the trial, they were attempting to "establish a bridge between your childhood traumas and your current feelings" (quoted in Kaiser 2008:267). At the trial, "It was testified that on several occasions after witnessing such events [child-hood traumas] he (Sirhan) lapsed into a trance, his body stiffened, his fists clenched, and his mouth became contorted...The defense contended that these experiences created a twisted mind which diminished Sirhan's capacity to premeditate murder" (Moldea 1995: 121).

After the failed attempt to avoid a trial through a plea bargain in which guilt was admitted, Sirhan's defense focused on his mental state during the murder, his "diminished capacity," which would in part be explained by Sirhan's traumatic childhood.[16] The concept of diminished capacity, which at this time was relatively well-established in the California legal system but has since been rescinded, is usually contrasted to claims of "not guilty for reasons of insanity," in which case a defendant could be freed. In cases of diminished capacity, the hoped- for outcome is not freedom but a lesser sentence. Thus, guilt is admitted, but complete control over one's actions is denied, imply-ing that mental functions are diminished or impaired, at least temporarily, during a violent act. Premeditation is possible under such a defense, but the person would lack "the capacity to "maturely and meaningfully reflect upon the gravity of his contemplated act" (Kaiser 2008:274). Thus even with the incriminating notebooks and evidence that Sirhan appeared to have stalked his victim, the fact that he was not in complete control of himself in that kitchen pantry could lead to a lesser sentence than the death penalty. In order to forcefully make this claim, the defense called an array of mental health professionals to testify. As the trial went on, Sirhan became more and more enraged, possibly embarrassed by the claims to his being mentally impaired. At one point, when Sirhan loudly protested his own attorney's claims about the aftereffects of his childhood experiences, he had to be restrained and the jury sent out of the courtroom. He stood up and declared, "I, at this time, sir, withdraw my original plea of not guilty and submit the plea of guilty as charged on all counts." He then asked that his attorneys remove themselves from the case and that he be executed (Moldea 1995:121). This was disal-lowed and the trial continued.

The trial itself, as represented through mass media, was more or less the-ater for the American public, since the outcome was never really in doubt. The only issue was whether or not the final judgment would be death or life in prison. What, after all, was the proper penalty for assassination? At the penalty hearing following the trial, the prosecution made the case for execution, without ever saying so explicitly. They claimed this was more than simple murder:

> Robert F. Kennedy [the prosecutor said] was struck down at a moment when he represented the hopes and ideas of an important segment of this nation. History may well record that, but for this defendant, Senator Kennedy might have succeeded to the highest honor and responsibility that the American democratic process can bestow. Beyond doubt, the tragedy that occurred in the early-morning hours of June 5, 1968, at the Ambassador Hotel was politically motivated. (quoted in Kaiser 2008:334–45)

After pointing out the arrogance of the defendant, the smirk on his face when his own attorney asked in court for America to pray for the Kennedy family, the fact that he would boast about having committed "the crime of the century," and that "we have lavishly expended our resources for the sake of a cold-blooded political assassin while content to send patriotic Americans to Vietnam with a $70 rifle and our best wishes," the proper penalty was obvious (Kaiser 2008:334–35 for a summation). In their counter, Sirhan's defense attorneys argued that killing one man did not bring back another, that violence only begets more violence, and that the United States needed to show the world that it was a civilized nation by sparing someone who had committed the most unthinkable of crimes. Defense attorneys called upon the memory of Robert Kennedy in their attempt to save Sirhan's life, quoting from RFK's speech the night after the assassination of MLK. They also read into the record a handwritten letter from Edward Kennedy, the senator's younger brother, who in his plea for mercy said that his brother would not condone an execution, even for the man responsible for his own death. In a final appeal before the judge levied sentence, Sirhan's attorneys compared their client with James Earl Ray. Sirhan, they argued, had never been in trouble with the law, was mentally ill, and was now to be executed, while Ray, a career criminal, would be serving life in prison. The same comparison was drawn in the mass media (Kaiser 2008:348).

On April 23, 1969, the jury found Sirhan Sirhan guilty of murder in the first degree and sentenced him to death; the judge concurred. However, California would later change its policy and outlaw execution; Sirhan Sirhan remains in prison, where his appeals for parole have consistently been denied.

Sirhan's family arrived in the United States in January 1957 as political refugees, when he was 12 years old. None would become citizens, and Sirhan Sirhan was formally a Jordanian when he shot Robert Kennedy. Yet, as Kaiser (2008:126) writes, America did represent something for him, "an escape from his hated condition as a Palestinian Arab, a member of a mini-minority." "When we become citizens, Mama," he once asked his mother, "will we get blond hair and blue eyes?" As a young boy in Pasadena, California, Sirhan made gestures toward being All-American, with a bicycle, a paper route, attendance at high school dances, and participation in the Cadets, a form of R.O.T.C. Yet, upon graduation, when asked by friends to sign their school yearbooks, he did so in Arabic. There was no hyphenated ethnic position Sirhan could adopt, no Arab-American community, real or imagined, to join. He was clearly ambiguous about his identity. It was not until he was in prison, when reading about himself in mass media, that he began to "see himself as a Arab patriot, [and] attained a new sense of himself..." (Kaiser 2008:129).

During and after his trial, Sirhan represented himself more and more as a Palestinian Arab and a political activist. He did not want to be portrayed as mentally ill, not even to save his own life. "I'm proud of being an Arab...And I'm ashamed of being an Arab—a second-class citizen—in western society," he told one of the psychiatrists working on his defense (Kaiser 2008:86). Added to his defense team during the trial was a group of attorneys associated with Arab causes, who sought as much as possible to make Middle-Eastern politics a focal point. They too were against any claims to psychological instability. Robert Kennedy's alleged support of Israel was seen as motivation for his murder, as was the influence of Black Power advocates, some of whom had apparently also "marked Kennedy for execution" (Kaiser 2008:371). A climate of violence and desperation on the part of those marginalized through American power, it was claimed, provided a context within which Sirhan interpreted and performed his deed. Kaiser (2008:371), who spent a great deal of time with Sirhan as part of his defense team, put it this way: "Sirhan heard the angry rhetoric of the Black Panthers in Oakland who called Bob Kennedy a fascist pig; and the words made him feel justified in having killed the pig." All this, however, was largely after the fact.

In prison as well Sirhan would gain status as an assassin—not your everyday criminal. In this sense, he was similar to James Earl Ray, whose "trial" was occurring simultaneously, fitting the profile of the typical assassin. Yet in his own mind, he was very different from Ray, whose arrest and legal battles Sirhan followed closely. In a television interview, Sirhan was asked to compare himself to Ray and Lee Harvey Oswald. He replied that there was no comparison. "They knew what they were doing. They used telescopic lenses, they both planned to get away" (Kaiser 2008:351). He, on the other hand, faced his victim and shot him at close range. When in an earlier interview he was asked why he had not shot Kennedy between the eyes, Sirhan had replied, "Because the son-of-a-bitch turned his head at the last second" (quoted in Kaiser 2008:366). In his eyes, this made him a real assassin. His killing was personal more than it was political; even if he hadn't used a knife, he was close enough to look his victim squarely in the face when he pulled the trigger.

MEDIA REPRESENTATION

As a presidential candidate and a man with near-celebrity status, Robert Kennedy was under constant media surveillance; television and newspaper reporters followed him everywhere during the campaign, including into the pantry of the Ambassador Hotel on June 4, 1968. The shots fired by Sirhan Sirhan were wedged between the arms of two newspaper photographers and a radio broadcaster was interviewing the senator as he walked through the pantry. The final moments are recorded: "Senator Kennedy has been shot! Senator Kennedy has been shot; is that possible? Is it possible, ladies and gentlemen... is it possible, he has. Not only Senator Kennedy. Oh my God, Senator Kennedy has been shot and another man, a Kennedy campaign manager and possible shot in the head. I am right here" (quoted in Kaiser 2008:11, see also Clarke 2008:274). The first bulletins over local radio (based on UPI (United Press International) reports) announced that the senator had been shot in the hip; minutes later, this was amended to say that one shot was fired at Kennedy and that five shots were "pumped into his assistant, a man tentatively identified as Jesse Grier" (Kaiser 2008:16). Television news reporters tried to piece together on camera what had happened at the same time as the law enforcement authorities were doing the same behind the scenes. One of the originating conspiracy theories stems from an on-camera interview directly after the shooting.[17] And in an indirect way, it was the media that set the stage for the entire incident. After a hard campaign, an exhausted RFK wanted nothing more than to rest at the Malibu home of a family friend, the film director John Frankenheimer. Kennedy had made plans to watch the final results on Frankenheimer's television set, but when television crews refused to lug their equipment to Malibu to watch the senator watching the results, Kennedy reluctantly agreed to make the trip into LA to the Ambassador (as reported in Moldea 1995:24, Clarke 2008:266 for a slightly different account).

Media accounts of the murder of RFK were filtered through the assassinations of his older brother in 1963 and of MLK just two months prior. For some like the *New York Times* (June 6, 1968) the sequence was evidence of a general moral decline: one of its headlines that day proclaimed a "World Morality Crisis" under which followed:

> The assassins of President Kennedy, the Rev. Dr. Martin Luther King Jr. and Lee Harvey Oswald and the attacker of Senator Kennedy may merely be deranged demons, tormented by frustrations and intoxicated by fear or revenge. But there is something more than that. This is not merely rejection of the view that life is essentially decent, rational and peaceful, nor is it even a decline into individual moral insanity. There is something in the air of the modern world: a defiance of authority, a contagious irresponsibility, a kin of moral delinquency, no longer restrained by religious or ethical faith.

While the *Times* saw moral decline, one "overseas American" reported in the *Washington Post* (June 6,1968) that he found himself numbed and hardened by events in "our faraway homeland...the murder of John Kennedy evoked a stunned disbelief, followed by profound grief. The assassination of Dr. Martin Luther King Jr. created melancholy and despair. Now, nearly 12 hours after first hearing of the shooting of Robert Kennedy, I am still waiting to be stunned." The themes of moral decline and shocked disbelief were several of the general themes that can be reconstructed from media accounts in the days following the murder of RFK. A related theme was that of the United States as a "sick society." This conception was evoked by President Lyndon Johnson himself in response to claims from home and abroad. The Cold War and America's image were important aspects of this. The *Washington Post* of June 6 carried the headline "Communists see sickness in U.S.," and two days later reported, "President Johnson said: 'It would be wrong to conclude from this act [the murder of RFK] that our country is sick.'" To which the paper's editors responded, "Now is the time to prove it. I mourn for a president who says that our country is not sick, who appoints yet another commission—to study the cause of violence...our society is sick. I mourn the death of two leaders who might have healed us, Martin Luther King and Robert F. Kennedy. Our humanity dies, and I mourn" (*Washington Post* June 8, 1968).

Some blamed the media itself for contributing to both this moral decline and to the state of the nation's health: "We hear tear-jerking comments of TV newsmen who try to outdo each other in an effort to dramatize the sickness of all Americans. As they so emotionally indicate, every man and every woman of America must take credit for the sickness and crime we have today. I am an American-born citizen, and I consider this a grave insult" (*Washington Post* June 11, 1968). A central dividing line in this public discourse lay between those who found in these murders an underlying societal problem, a collective sickness, and those who saw these acts as perpetrated by sick individuals. As one reader put it, "The argument between those who ascribe Sen. Robert F. Kennedy's murder to a 'national sickness' and those who insist it was simply the act of a single man seems to me to miss the point," which for this individual was that it was too soon to tell and that answering such questions must be left to future historians. Yet on June 13, the *Washington Post* headlined "2 of 3 Americans Now Believe Something Deeply Wrong in U.S.," and President Johnson looked to yet another commission to investigate the underlying causes of violence in America, the one cited in the first chapter.

America's apparent fascination with violence was another of the themes that structured this discourse. The *New York Times* (June 6, 1968:3) carried a statement from historian Arthur Schlesinger Jr., an adviser to RFK and a close friend of the Kennedy family: "The United States [is] a land of violent people with a violent history, and the instinct of violence has seeped into the bloodstream of our national life." "What sort of people are we, we Americans?...The answer, Mr. Schlesinger said, "is that we are today the most frightening people on this planet." The sources of violence, which the Presidential Commission set out to investigate, were a major source of contention. Two main culprits were identified: a national fascination with guns, and the crime and violence as represented on television and in the movies. The same author who wrote in the *Post* (June 8, 1968:5) mourning for a president "who says our country is not sick," was certain that the "roots" of the country's problems lay in "the effect of TV violence,"which included nightly news broadcasts from the war in Vietnam. The fascination with violence was connected to that of a national culture in free fall. America was described as a society out of control, driven by internal contradictions that could be traced back to its origins:

> Robert F. Kennedy is only the latest victim of a modern world that has turned loose greater forces than it can control...In America itself, the combination of poverty, in the midst of great luxury, plus the old American frontier tradition of violence as part of life and even as an achievement, impress thoughtful students of psychiatry as contributing to the decline of public order. (*New York Times* June 6, 1968:4)

And in the *Washington Post*, "Violence is the most primitive means of solving problems; and yet this Nation to which so many others look for a leader it is erupting like a social leprosy. What occurred this week was not a tragedy: it was the symptom of a tragedy, which is the slow derangement of our society and the members of that society" (June 11, 1968:1). In its cover story, *Newsweek* (June 24, 1968) asked, "Has Violence Become An American Way of Life?" while the *Philadelphia Enquirer* proclaimed, "The country does not work anymore" (both quoted in Perlstein 2008:274).

"AMERICA THE VIOLENT": FROM DRAMA TO TRAUMA

In mapping the public discourse following the assassinations of Martin Luther King and Robert Kennedy, one can also map the evolving cultural trauma as it unfolded in the aftermath of these shocking occurrences. The themes gleaned from these mass media accounts reflect a struggle to define the situation, to establish its meaning, its root causes, and to identify perpetrators and victims. Through this trauma drama, it was made clear that both victim and perpetrator were larger and greater than those murdered individuals. The victim was the nation itself and the perpetrator not merely those individuals who pulled the trigger, but some deep-seated values and underlying tensions

at the base of the social order that drove them to it. The root causes were identified as cultural and institutional, and their repair, it was proclaimed, would
require fundamental changes not only in social organization but in how the
collectivity understood itself. The murderous acts were seen as representative,
in the same way as those murdered and those responsible were representative
of larger social forces. These killings were assassinations, not murders, in
that they were surface acts that reflected deep-seated currents and cleavages.
They were construed and constructed as engaging the entire community: it
was this that made them *political* assassinations. It is not merely a question
of whether or not those murdered were public officials, more important was
that they were *representative* figures. These deaths were narrated as symp-
tomatic at the same time as they were tragic and horrific, serving to bring to
light hidden faults and underlying tensions in the social order.

Cultural trauma can be a double-edged process, where tragedy and possibility converge; this was recognized in the mass media discourse: "As all
these slain leaders have tried to tell us, this is an era when the survival of
the Republic requires the most sweeping reform of our institutions... But
let us now have the will and the purpose to forge our sorrow into a constructive force for public order and progress, justice and compassion. This
is the spirit that has sustained the nation in all the years of our history"
(*Washington Post* June 11, 1968:2). While fundamental faults may lie at the
root of the tragedy, so too lay the will to repair, proclaimed the *Post*. This
was a performative statement, a set of words, which, it was hoped, would
lead to action.

There were, of course, equally powerful forces who understood the situation differently, as the acts of lone madmen, not at all reflective of any basic
systemic fault. From this perspective, nothing fundamental, beyond mourning the dead and tracking down the killers, needed to be done. The only issue
was who and how many. Truman Capote, the author of the widely acclaimed
true-crime novel *In Cold Blood,* appeared on the popular television program
the *Tonight Show* and described the killers of King and Kennedy as "patsies
brainwashed by plotters determined to bring America to its knees" (quoted in
Perlstein 2008: 274). At least one American congressman blamed the Soviet
Union: "Rep. Mahan Links Reds to Slayings" proclaimed a *Washington Post*
(June 15, 1968:2) headline.

For those who believed in "sweeping reform," there were also major dis-
agreements about what exactly this would imply. Liberal commentators, such
as those that dominated the *Times* and the *Post,* called for gun control, while
conservatives were prone to call for less violence in popular culture, stricter
punishment for criminality, and more control over the content of education.
"Several months ago in this column I advocated that no law should be passed
regulating guns. One reason was because I believed that man is basically

good in human nature. After recoiling in horror at recent events, I wish to repudiate that naïve stand. Man is basically evil, and guns should be taken away from him" (*Washington Post* June 11, 1968:1). "The shooting of Senator Robert F. Kennedy following so closely after the murder of Dr. Martin Luther King Jr. and preceded five years by the murder of President John F. Kennedy must force the realization upon the United States Congress that individual citizens must not be allowed to bear arms indiscriminately" (*New York Times* June 9, 1968). Television and Hollywood came under attack for contributing to a "culture of violence": "The fantasy of American literature, television and the movies provide a contemporary gallery of dark and ghastly crime, which undoubtedly adds to the atmosphere in which weak and deranged minds flourish" (*New York Times* June 6, 1968:4). "No, there is no sure way of protecting Presidents and would-be Presidents no matter how many Secret Service men we deploy. The long-range solution is a change in the American people's passion for televised crime and violence" (*Post* June 10, 1968:2). "The networks, after a decent period of mourning, have now resumed the full schedule of violence. And they have already lined up two dozen shows for the next season featuring gunplay, brutality, sadism, and terror" (*Post* June 21, 1968:1). "It requires no study to understand that so long as television continues to drill into the immature and the disturbed members of our society that pulling out a gun is the way to solve every problem—and the manly, the heroic and the laudable way—that long will we suffer from shootings and assassinations" (*Times* June 30, 1968). Both papers carried "positive" reportage as well: a *Times* headline revealed, "Hollywood Writers and Actors Lead Fight on Movie Violence" (*New York Times* June 17, 1968), and two days earlier the same paper reported, "1000 pupils in Queens scrap toys of violence" June 15, 1968). For liberals, American foreign policy, particularly the war in Vietnam, was also a culprit.

On the opposite side of the political spectrum, blame found another source: the lack of law and order and the permissive "consumer" culture of postwar United States. The perpetrator here was also representative and indicative: the root cause of the current wave of violence, which included urban riots and antiwar protests as well as political assassination, were rooted not only in a popular culture apparently fascinated by violence, but were also debased by permissive upbringing and a lack of respect for authority. The conservative editor and syndicated columnist William F. Buckley wrote:

> In a civilized nation it is not expected that public figures should be considered proper targets for casual gunmen. But in civilized nations of the past it has not been customary for parents to allow their children to do what they feel like; for students to seize their schools and smash their equipment; for police

to be ordered to stand by while looters empty stores and arsonists burn down buildings." (quoted in Perlstein 2008:274)

Ronald Reagan was making similar charges in his run for the presidency in 1968 and his fellow California Republican, Max Rafferty, campaigned for Congress by indicting the "sick sixties" and "the cowardice of young men who refused to fight in Vietnam—tying it all to progressive education, the 'fraud of the century'" (Perlstein 2008:277). These were themes that would help make Richard Nixon president when he beat Hubert Humphrey by the slightest of margins in November 1968. From this perspective it was the American people, or the "silent majority," the middle Americans, who were the real victims, while the perpetrators were those liberal leaders, "gurus," Richard Nixon called them, those "teachers, preachers and politicians" who were "leading our children astray" (quoted in Perlstein 2008: 280). These "gurus" included Dr. Benjamin Spock, a pediatrician and antiwar activist, whose handbook on child rearing was identified as one of the main sources of "permissiveness." The cover of *Newsweek* (September 23, 1968) asked, "Is Dr. Spock to Blame?"

In the summer and fall of 1968, the battle to name victims and perpetrators was carried out in the press, the political campaigns, the houses of government, and religious institutions, reaching into the private homes of all Americans from all these sources and being reflected back out again in the form of public opinion surveys. Senator Strom Thurmond, among many others, used the floor of the Senate to name the "liberal media" and popular culture as prime suspects in this meaning struggle. Thurmond railed against Broadway shows like *Hair* and *New York Times* film critics who lampooned patriotic films like John Wayne's *The Green Berets*. The "nation's pastor," Billy Graham, led "crusades" against sex-education in schools, family-planning agencies, and other sources of "permissiveness" diluting America's foundational Christian values. He was joined at the pulpit by thousands of other religious leaders in their weekly sermons. The American people, it was claimed, were being victimized by a small, yet powerful group of "Communists, Socialists and liberals" who sought to undermine American values through the education system and mass media. One pamphlet distributed in a California campaign against sex-education in schools proclaimed: "Socialists Use Sex Wedge in Public Schools to Separate Children from Parental Authority" (quoted in Perlstein 2008:408), and California Congressman James Utt linked "the Beatles and their mimicking rock and rollers" and Communists using "Pavlovian techniques to produce artificial neuroses in our young people" in speeches on the House floor (Perlstein 2008: 409). When the Federal Bureau of Investigation (FBI) head J. Edgar Hoover linked Martin Luther King to "Communists," the "tragedy" of his death could be interpreted in a different light, than if he were identified as a "Negro leader" or "civil-rights advocate." Similarly, if Robert Kennedy was identified as a "liberal," his death meant something different than if it were placed in relation to his other brother or his family. King and Kennedy were clearly murder victims, but the meaning of their deaths depended on how they were narrated. In the midst of this trauma drama process, America was at war with itself, and the designations "victim" and "perpetrator" were fluid and shifting. Much depended on where one stood at any particular time and what interpretive frame one applied.

REMEMBERING ROBERT KENNEDY

In death as in life, Robert Kennedy lives in the shadow of his older brother. One eyewitness heard him murmur, "Jack...Jack," as he lay mortally wounded on the pantry floor (Clarke 2008:275). A famous photograph, which appeared on the cover of *Life Magazine* in 1966, shows Robert Kennedy standing in front of a larger-than-life photograph of his brother, which captures not only how he is generally remembered, but also how he viewed himself. Robert Kennedy entered public life as the "younger Kennedy" and honed his political skills as his brother's campaign manager, first in JFK's senate race in 1952 and then in the presidential campaign in 1960. Robert Kennedy had his own career, of course; he worked as an aide to the infamous Senator Joseph McCarthy, gaining a reputation as a tough, crime-fighting and union-busting lawyer. But it was in association with John Kennedy that he really gained prominence, as political manager and adviser and then as attorney general in his brother's cabinet. It has also been said that Robert Kennedy became another person, more liberal, more compassionate, after John Kennedy's death (Schlesinger 1978). The murder of Robert Kennedy was immediately associated with that of his brother and with the Kennedy family at large. "We've Lost Another Kennedy," was a common mass media theme in the aftermath of his assassination. Even his funeral procession was modeled after JFK's, though greatly modified with respect for the differences in political status. This is not to take anything away from the emotion unleashed by RFK's death that,to some extent, exceeded the emotion displayed after the death of JFK, in part because these emotions built upon each other, but also because of the hope many placed in RFK's political future. But the fate of the two brothers was intimately linked in the contemporary public mind and in American collective memory.

Media coverage of Robert Kennedy's death constantly made the association to JFK and also to their younger brother Ted, and this association has permanently affected how Robert Kennedy is remembered, as a member of a great and tragic family. The *New York Times* (June 6, 1968) obituary covered a full page under the headline, "Robert Francis Kennedy: Attorney General, Senator and Heir to the New Frontier," the last being the name given to JFK's program during his presidency. The obituary was framed by large family photographs. This focus on family can be contrasted to how Martin Luther King is remembered, as described above. King's *New York Times* (April 5, 1968:25) obituary was headlined "Martin Luther King Jr.: Leader of Millions…" While there are many public buildings and highways that bear his name, Robert Kennedy is commemorated more as family member than as a representative figure in his own right. Even the ceremonious awards named in his honor, the annual Robert Kennedy book award, for example, and the Robert F. Kennedy Center for Justice and Human Rights are the results of the efforts of family members and personal friendships. RFK is buried in a simple grave just a few steps from his brother's more substantial tomb in Arlington National Cemetery. The mass-media discussion following RFK's death swiftly declined, especially when contrasted to that following King's death. There have been commemorative programs on the anniversary of RFK's assassination on the mass media, but these have been sporadic. On June 5, 2008, the 40th anniversary, ABC News broadcast a memorial featuring former *Life* photographer Bill Eppridge's photographs and aligned with their publication in book form. In November 2001, on what would have been his 76th birthday, President George Bush renamed Washington's Justice Building in honor of Robert Kennedy, and on what would have been his 80th birthday in November 2005, a memorial ceremony featured Senators Obama and Clinton. The prime carrier of the memory of RFK, however, remains the Kennedy family. It should be said, however, that this family is not an ordinary one, in that the Kennedy name is very firmly connected to a particular set of values and the liberal political tradition. This focus on family is in stark contrast to MLK where though important, King's family, perhaps despite attempts by the mass media, has been overshadowed and challenged by the claims made on his memory by a social movement and a racial/ethnic identification. Kennedy was identified with the Catholic faith and with his Irish heritage, but these associations were not activated and continually renewed by any organization or movement.

That RFK was connected with the Kennedy family in the public mind is not difficult to understand. The Kennedys were given special symbolic place as America's first family with the ascendancy of JFK. John Kennedy was an attractive, photogenic figure, and his charismatic good looks were enhanced by his equally attractive and photogenic wife, Jacqueline, and their two young children. A family (young parents and small children) in the White House was a celebrated rarity, and the media devoted much attention to them. Photojournalism was at its height in the 1960s, with popular weekly magazines like *Life* and *Look* offering easy access to millions of

American homes. The "first family" was a major attraction. The Kennedys were represented as a closely knit, extended family, and through the presidency, America and the rest of the world was made well aware of this. Not only were the younger Kennedy brothers, Robert and Ted, household names, so too were the names of their mother and father, commonly identified as the Kennedy matriarch and patriarch. Robert Kennedy was himself the father of 11 children, and along with his wife Ethel, they were constant companions in media reportage. The public knew that Ethel Kennedy was pregnant when she accompanied her husband during the 1968 California primary, and she was at his side as he lay dying on the pantry floor in the Ambassador Hotel, an unforgettable image caught on camera and broadcast around the world.

American collective memory informs and is itself reproduced through state funerals. When officials were planning the funeral ceremony after the assassination of JFK, they were careful to check the protocol of the funeral of Abraham Lincoln, the first assassinated American president (Steers 2001). The president's widow also consulted references on Lincoln's funeral in preparation for her husband's (Mossman and Stark 1991). The body of President John Kennedy was placed in state in the East Room of the White House, where Lincoln's body had lain almost exactly 100 years earlier; his remains rested on the catafalque(a bier or platform used to support a casket) used during the other state funerals. The public response to the funeral train, which carried RFK's body after the ceremony in New York's St. Patrick's Cathedral to Washington, D.C., was similar to the one that carried Lincoln's body from Washington to Springfield, IL. In both cases, the tracks were lined with mourners paying their collective respects. The official funerals of John and Robert Kennedy were, for the most part, the responsibility of the American government, as both were public officials when they died. The family did exert some degree of control over the proceedings, however, though much was determined by established protocol and tradition. This was especially the case for John Kennedy, whose position as president carried more determinant symbolic weight. Though both funerals were organized through the military, the physical presence of the latter was much more constrained at Robert Kennedy's funeral. This came at the personal request of his widow. Most of the plans for RFK's funeral were prepared by family members, most particularly by his brother Ted and brother-in-law Stephen Smith, with Ethel Kennedy giving final approval (Mossman and Stark 1991:324). When informed of the family's plans, President Lyndon Johnson ordered military transportation to carry the senator's body and the Kennedy family from Los Angeles to New York and set the formal ceremonial preparations in motion: flags on government buildings were ordered to fly at half-mast, and a day of national mourning was proclaimed for Sunday, June 9. At the widow's request, military presence was kept at a minimum for most of the ceremonies, except for those inside Arlington National Cemetery. Crowds along the trackside were so great that the funeral train arrived five hours late at Washington's Union Station. It was past 9:00 P.M. and already dark when the train arrived and the ceremonies began, marking Robert Kenney's burial as the first to take place at night. The thousands who had gathered at Arlington included "residents of Resurrection City, the symbolic shanty town that had been erected on the nearby mall under the sponsorship of the Southern Christian Leadership Conference," the organization formerly headed by Martin Luther King (Mossman and Stark 1991:336). The transportation of Kennedy's body from Union Station to the gates of Arlington was carried live on television and viewed by millions.

CONCLUSION

The assassination of President John F. Kennedy in November 1963 is forever imprinted in American collective memory. Those old enough remember exactly where they were when they heard the news, and many are still moved to tears at the recollection. When his younger brother was assassinated less than five years later in June 1968, it reopened a festering sore. The assassination was the catalyst that brought an ongoing cultural trauma fully into the open. The assassination of Martin Luther King, just two months earlier, itself coming after the assassination of two other African American leaders, Medgar Evers in 1963 and Malcolm X in 1965, were other significant occurrences in this cumulative process. The deaths of these black leaders were, in themselves, tragic and shocking, but because of the racial as well as political polarization in the United States at the time, they could be restricted to the traumatic, collective memory of a particular group, a social trauma rather than a cultural trauma in Neil Smelser's sense. However, the death of Robert Kennedy fused these two trauma drama processes. Robert Kennedy had been viewed by many as the one person capable of bridging the ever-widening and ever more brutal gap between whites and blacks (if not the gap between left and right), and his assassination was the final blow in a process that began in 1963. As a period of great hope and polarization, the 1960s began with an election and ended with an assassination.

Why did these assassinations lead to cultural trauma? The assassination of John F. Kennedy was a tragic and shocking event. It left a lasting impression on American collective memory, but was not in itself a cultural trauma. The murder of JFK raised many questions and much public debate, but in a society where war and violence were relatively common, where political leaders were often the target of violent attack, it did not, by itself, give rise to a public debate where the foundations of American society, its collective identity, were called into question. This was in part the result of past experience and tradition: the American Constitution provides clear rules for political succession, and as Theodore White (1965) suggests, this was greatly aided by the power of television to visualize both the national mourning and the political continuity, the respect for law and protocol amongst the country's leaders. With the whole world as well as the nation watching, the United States revealed itself as a law-abiding and secure nation, this despite the lack of civil repair a trial of the accused assassin, who was himself assassinated, would have provided. Coming after the murder of the world-renowned civil rights leader Martin Luther King, the assassination of Robert Kennedy reopened the old wound with much greater force and consequence.

Robert Kennedy's death extinguished what was perceived by many as the last hope of reconciliation between blacks and whites, a polarization that had become increasingly violent. At the same time, it reopened the issue of violence and its place in American culture, more generally. What kind of society is it, many asked, where young and vibrant leaders could, with such regularity, be gunned down? Who were the victims and perpetrators? Who was responsible? How would this be resolved? The carrier groups in this move from social crisis to cultural trauma were the mass media, the houses of government, and two significant social movements, the African American and black movement for recognition and the antiwar movement. The mass media acted as more than a medium in this cultural trauma; it was a major actor, taking positions and offering substantial commentary as well as providing voice and visibility to others. The houses of government provided space for opposing sides to speak with great visibility and emotion. The movements brought the conflict to the streets and, through the mass media, into private homes across the nation. While much of this dramatic dialogue was clearly political in the narrow sense of interest-related gain, there was much more at stake than instrumental acts or strategic positioning. This public discourse was an emotional outpouring, which went far beyond the politics of self-interest. It raised substantial existential issues: Who are we? What is our purpose? How will we go on? This discourse fused past, present, and future, recalling both collective memory and collective identity as resource and stake.

CHAPTER 4

THE END OF INNOCENCE: THE MURDERS OF OLOF PALME AND ANNA LINDH

THE MURDER OF OLOF PALME

As discussed in the opening chapter, Sweden was one of the last countries in the world where one expected the murder of a national leader. Though extreme political violence had occurred in the recent past, these incidences affected the representatives of foreign governments. The last assassination of a Swedish political leader in the country had occurred centuries earlier. Then, on February 28, 1986, Swedish prime minister Olof Palme, who was accompanied by his wife, was shot shortly after leaving a cinema hall in central Stockholm. He died before his body hit the pavement. A second bullet grazed his wife, Lisbet Palme, but the wound was slight and she was later given only first aid. Seventeen years later, on September 10, 2003, Foreign Minister Anna Lindh was stabbed while out shopping with a friend in a central Stockholm mall. She died the next day. Both occurrences shocked the Swedish nation, but the second seemed worse than the first. Two days after the attack on Anna Lindh, one journalist wrote,

> This feels worse than the Palme murder. The shooting of Palme was unique in our Sweden. Such a thing couldn't happen here and when it did it was totally exceptional. In a short while we were back to the old rule—such things don't happen here. The murder of Anna Lindh means it did happen again. The murder of Palme was not unique...this time it feels worse: Lindh was young and cheerful. She had most of her life in front of her. She was killed before she became prime minister." (Jan Lindström *Kvällsposten*, September 12, 2003: 20)

Though nearly two decades separated the occurrences, it was impossible not to think of them together. Every newspaper made the connection, and every

Swede old enough to remember put them together. Despite the sentiments expressed at the moment, when measured in terms of social and political impact, the murder of Palme was perhaps most meaningful in its consequences. This chapter will attempt to explain why. If the murder of Anna Lindh marked the end of Swedish innocence, the murder of Palme marked the closing of an era, the end of the Swedish middle way.

THE CONTEXT

Olof Palme was 59 years old when he was killed. He had been the Social Democratic Party (SAP) leader for nearly two decades and prime minister for more than one. When he took over in 1969, becoming only the fourth leader in the party's long history, Olof Palme represented a voice of renewal for a party that had been in power nearly continuously since the early 1930s. Swedish social democracy gained international prominence through what was popularly known abroad as the "Swedish model," a middle path between American free market capitalism and Soviet communism. Known internally as a "people's home" signifying the image of a large family, with the prime minister as paterfamilias, the social democratic model society called for strong state regulation of the economy, but not state ownership; it steered through a centralized state apparatus, with a large public sector and formal ties with powerful, centralized trade unions. Redistribution of resources and regulation, rather than state ownership, was its byword; its argument was that big capital and big labor could coexist under its guiding hand. While continuing this tradition, Palme promised to make the influence of employees over their working conditions, what was termed economic democracy, even stronger. His real interest, however, lay in international politics—in the relations between rich and poor nations, and in the countering of the superpower politics of the United States and the Soviet Union. Palme became an international figure through his energetic articulation of these policies. He was the focus of global media attention, especially when he appeared at the head of mass demonstrations, those against the war in Vietnam, for example, where at least on one occasion (in 1968) he marched together with the North Vietnamese ambassador to the Soviet Union. This was all the more dramatic as Sweden's national defense was largely dependent on the United States and on the North Atlantic Treaty Organization (NATO) though it was not a member. Palme's international ambitions, and especially his symbolic politics, put him at odds with many members of the national political and military elite.

The 1960s–1970s marked a high point in Palme's long political career, when he found his voice as a Western spokesman for third-world radicalism (Östberg 2010). The head of a small nation with a population of under 8 million and no military power to speak of, Palme articulated an alternative vision with great forcefulness. These were also very good years for the Swedish economy; unemployment rates were among the lowest in the world, and the standard of living of the population was among the highest. Upon receiving the 2008 Nobel Prize in economics, American economist Paul Krugman said that Sweden in the 1980s represented his ideal model of the relation between government and economy.[1] Internationally, European social democracy was also at a high point: when, after six years in the opposition, Olof Palme returned as prime minister in 1982, Francois Mitterrand had been elected as the first socialist president in French history, and the Spanish socialist party had assumed control of the government. The following year, the Portuguese socialist party leader Mario Soares would be returned to power as prime minister. Yet in Sweden, a leading member of the Socialist International, cracks were appearing. During 1970, SAP received 45.3 percent of the vote in the national elections; in 1985, it was still close to that, winning 44.7 percent of the vote. However, the Conservative Party had risen from 11.5 percent to 21.3 percent, nearly doubling its mandate. Discord on the labor market re-emerged as the system of centralized collective bargaining, so important to the economic prosperity of the 1960s, broke down. There were waves of strikes in 1985, including a national lockout of centrally organized government workers, university teachers among them. In October 1983, right-wing opponents of a new socialist imitative to allow workers more influence over their workplace through the creation of *löntagarefond* (a system of employee funds) marched through the streets of Stockholm. It was the first time in modern memory that conservatives took to the streets, and the symbolic effect was electric. Though the Social Democrats won the election in the fall of 1985 and managed to pass a greatly modified version of the employee fund program through parliament (later repealed when conservatives seized power in 1991) signs of internal dissention within the party were apparent. A splitting of the ranks that would be called the War of Roses (the red rose being the party symbol) would eventually lead to the severing of formal ties between the party and the labor movement. More personally, there was the hint of a scandal surrounding payments for a lecture that Palme had given at an American university. At the same time, an emotionally intensive campaign against his person and his politics was being waged by political opponents on the left and the right. The so-called *Palmehatet* (literally, Palme-hate), stemming primarily from right-wing opponents who saw Palme as a Soviet lackey, had almost reached the level of frenzy in the Cold War 1980s (Åsard 2006:165). There were rumors of organized opposition within the police and the military, who viewed him as a traitor and a threat to national security. The middle path was never an easy one to steer, and it now began to take its toll on its chief representative. Friends and colleagues report a tired and irritable prime minister in the weeks before his death, and rumors circulated that he might resign (Wall 1996:23–29).

THE MURDER

Friday, February 28, 1986, was a normal workday for Olof Palme.[2] After returning home in the early evening and releasing his bodyguards for the day, Palme and his wife arranged to see a film with their son and his fiancé. This was all done rather spontaneously over the telephone, as they agreed on the film and the time to meet almost at the last moment. The couple left their apartment in Stockholm's old town just after 8:30 P.M., walking the few blocks to the nearest subway station to take the train into the central city. Olof and Lisbet Palme left the movie theater on foot at approximately 11:15 P.M., slowly walking in the direction of another nearby subway station, looking in store windows as they went. Three short blocks from the theater, a man suddenly appeared behind them, firing two shots in quick succession at close range. The first shot hit Olof Palme in the back, around his shoulder blade; the path of the bullet crushed his spinal cord, slicing major arteries and the windpipe before exiting through the chest cavity. The second shot, apparently aimed at Lisbet, entered through the back of her suede coat at around shoulder height, but only grazed her back, leaving a long scratch, before exiting through the right side of her coat. The time of the murder was approximated at 11:21 P.M. Bullet fragments later found at the scene revealed that they were of a special metal-piercing variety meant for use on targets who were wearing protective body armor. During the police investigation, this and other indications raised the issue that the killer might have been a professional. After firing his shots, the killer hesitated for a few seconds before fleeing on foot through a darkened cross street.

Overall, there were 25 witnesses (some accounts say 22) to the shooting, 2 of whom observed the incident in its entirety. Of the ten who saw the killer clearly, no one could give a description of his face, though the lighting around the scene was judged to be good. The most important witness—Lisbet Palme—was interviewed in her apartment the day following the murder. She reported seeing the back of the murderer as he escaped after the shooting, and recalled that he hesitated a second or two to look back at the scene before turning again and continuing on his way. She described him as a man in his forties, about 180 cm in height, with a compact body and a short neck. "He was dark, but not in a directly southern European way, his hair was more brown than that" (SOU 1999:88, 719). Lisbet Palme could give no clear description of his face beyond that. The fact that no one clearly saw or remembered the facial features of the killer is not unusual. In cases of violent assault such as this, witnesses are more focused on what is happening than on the details of the actors. What is unusual, according to many commentators, is that the police waited so long to interview the chief witness and that her testimony was not recorded. This has been explained by the witness's relation to the victim, her social standing, and the unprecedented nature of the occurrence. As we will see, not only were the police well aware of such mistakes when investigating the murder of Anna Lindh, but several of the eyewitnesses to that attack reported that they had made an extra effort to observe and remember details because of what they had learned about the unsolved Palme murder.

MEDIA REPORTAGE

The first mass-media reportage of the murder of Olof Palme went out over the radio. At ten minutes past one on the morning of March 1, Swedish radio broke into their regular light music to announce that the prime minister had been shot in central Stockholm.[3] It gave the time and location of the attack and reported, mistakenly, that Palme had died in hospital. This was followed by the statement that an emergency meeting of the government had been called and was being chaired by Vice Prime Minister Ingvar Carlsson (Wall 1996:15). At 4:00 A.M., Swedish television, which was usually off the air at this time of day, broadcast a special news program on the murder. It began with a picture of Palme and the facts as they were then known, mistakenly reporting that he had died in hospital. There were pictures from the scene and on-the-spot interviews with the police, including one supervisor who reported that this was the largest police engagement of the year. Beyond the facts of the murder and the police pursuit, two issues dominated the broadcast; the first was that of security and the fact that Sweden had now experienced a form of political violence more common in other parts of the world. This issue was directly connected to what changes in security might mean for Swedish democracy. The word *demokrati* (democracy) was used by almost every commentator in public discussions of the murder. The second issue, political succession and stability, followed from this. Pictures of a tired Ingvar Carlsson entering the main government building and heading for an emergency meeting were broadcast, giving the impression that order would be maintained. The early Saturday morning children's television program was interrupted by a special news bulletin; for many families with small children, this was their first encounter with what had occurred. At this time, television in Sweden consisted of two noncommercial stations. Normally, the first broadcast of the day was a children's program, which began at 5:00 P.M., except on Saturdays. The stations went off the air before midnight. Both a broadcast in the middle of night and an interruption of children's programs was extremely unusual.

The morning newspapers were already being printed when the story broke, and many editions of March 1, 1986, carried only first-page headlines over a photograph of Palme and essentially the same bare facts that had been reported in the radio broadcast. *Arbetet* (Labor), a social democratic daily published in Malmö, promised a large memorial edition for the next day. During the following days, *Arbetet* and all the other major dailies were filled with accounts of the murder, the search for the killer, and most prominently, visual and textual representation of a shocked and grieving nation. The main focus was on Olof Palme the man, who he was, and what had now been lost. *Arbetet's* memorial edition of March 2, 1986, carried the front-page headline, "The Whole World Mourns," along with a photograph of Palme and the massive pile of flowers spontaneously placed at the scene of the murder. Inside were stories of "shock and grief" from around the nation and the world, with statements from the pope, European political leaders, and the American president Ronald Reagan. The lead editorial on the following page called the murder "a horrible act that will seriously affect Swedish society." It was, it wrote, "a great tragedy not only for social democracy, but also for Swedish society and for the international politics Palme represented." As to what the consequences would be, the editorial predicted that "the conditions of doing politics is going to get tougher. The relative great openness we experience and the social calm we have will not remain. New security measures are bound to follow, the fear of terrorist attack will rise and democracy will be threatened" (*Arbetet,* March 2, 1986:2 my translation). Further on in the paper a headline announced, "The Swedish Ideal Has Disappeared." This was followed by pages of photographs from Palme's life and political career. The following day's headline said simply, "Thanks." The reportage in Stockholm's liberal *Dagens Nyheter,* Sweden's largest morning newspaper, was similar. The March 2 edition carried the headline, "Sweden Mourns," along with a large photograph of a massive candlelit expression of grief in a main city square. The left side of the front page carried a photograph of Ingvar Carlsson and the text "Carlsson New Prime Minister," while the right side reported "Shock, Grief, Confusion" among the population. The editors apparently felt that it was important not only to represent feelings, but also to represent political continuity: there are formal procedures to ensure stability, even in the face of tragedy. The focus on succession and formal political continuity was highlighted on the inside pages, with a photograph of Carlsson and Palme together, along with the text "Carlsson takes over" and an editorial entitled "Politics after Palme," which discussed the transition and what could be expected from the new party leader.

There were also many pages devoted to the spontaneous demonstrations of collective grief from around the country. A headline announced, "60,000 Honor Palme" in Göteborg, and a storyline from Ådalen, an honored historical site for the SAP, where five demonstrators were killed by Swedish military forces in 1931, was headlined, "As the World Mourns So Does Ådalen." Interspersed with the photographs was the usual array of advertisements that offered the viewer a sense of normality and comfort to accompany the tragic news. The more populist afternoon papers offered similar yet more personalized accounts to accompany their many photographs. The headline of Malmö's *Kvällsposten* on March 1 read simply, "Palme Murdered," and its lead editorial under the banner "Sorrow and Anger," began with the sentence, "We share the grief—we have often criticized [Palme] but we share the grief" (2). Their March 2 headline, "Lisbet Palme Reveals 'the Killer Disappeared Like a Shadow,'" was placed over her photograph. Along with the photographs and comments from many mourners were statements from the chief investigating police officer regarding his suspicions about the attacker, and a photograph of the Swedish king, together with the new prime minister, with the hopeful prediction, "He's going to unite the country." After these first days of focus on the shocking character of the murder, the spontaneous public expressions of grief, and the political repercussions, news accounts shifted their main attention to the murder investigation, and especially to Hans Holmer, the man heading it. Holmer became a national figure through this event, the virtual representative of Swedish justice, a role he shouldered with great enthusiasm. Like a figure from an American police drama, dressed in a black leather jacket, surrounded by bodyguards, and bearing the expression of a man who knows the seriousness of his allotted task, Holmer gave the impression of the man in charge. This carefully rehearsed image led one Swedish paper to call him "Sweden's Clint Eastwood" (*Kvällsposten*, March 10, 1986:8).

SELF-PRESENTATION

Hans Holmer's first appearance before a national audience was on March 2, when he appeared on an extended 9:00 P.M. television news program. Dressed in a rumpled, open-necked shirt and looking tired and haggard, but in firm control of the situation, Holmer again stressed the extent of police engagement and answered questions about the status of the investigation.[4] He was convinced, he said, that the murder had been planned and that a group of conspirators was probably involved, even though only one man was seen fleeing the scene, and as yet no group had claimed responsibility. A leading member of the SAP was interviewed for this broadcast about any changes in government policy that might result from the death of Olof Palme. She replied that party policy did not depend upon one person, and that things would continue as they had been collectively agreed upon. It was also announced that there was no need to declare a national day of mourning (given the overflowing spontaneous demonstrations of grief), and that the funeral, planned for March 15, would be under SAP direction. A national weather forecast followed, functioning in much the same way as do newspaper advertisements, after which the discussion about the murder was resumed. What had been lost, proclaimed opposition leader Ulf Adelsson, was the scope for politicians to move freely. This introduced a series of newsclips concerning recent occurrences of political violence from around the world, the murder of John Kennedy, Martin Luther King, and Robert Kennedy in the United States, the attacks by the German Red Army Faction (RAF or Baader-Meinhoff) and the Italian Red Brigade. Also shown were pictures of the murdered Egyptian leader Anwar Sadat, India's Indira Gandhi, and an Irish Republican Army (IRA) bomb attempt on the life of Britain's Margaret Thatcher. The purpose, it appeared, was to show that Sweden had now joined the rest of the violent world, something that was unavoidable, according to an academic guest in the studio. Hans Holmer raised the issue of the role of the police in maintaining the freedom of mobility for politicians in an open society, which led to a comparison with the Soviet Union, where the powerful were kept under tight control. Sweden, the reportage seemed to suggest, must find a new middle way between its earlier complete openness and the rigid, Soviet-style control.

Hans Holmer became a common figure in the mass media and he used it for his own purposes—to promote his view of the crime and himself. During the course of his year-long tenure as head of the investigation, he held 25 press conferences, most of them during the early stages of the investigation, when his public meetings with the press occurred nearly every day (Wall 1996:55). Holmer used the media to push his particular version of what had motivated the murder of Olof Palme and who the perpetrators were. As we shall see later in connection with the murder of Anna Lindh, the police authorities often use press conferences to gather, rather than to give, information. They will often appeal to the public for help, using the occasion to disseminate a photograph or a description. The dynamic between police authorities and the mass media will be discussed in more detail later on in this chapter. Holmer was convinced that the murder was a political assassination carried out by organized groups of conspirators, and his press conferences had a different purpose from the one outlined earlier. At the beginning of the investigation, his team worked on several conspiratorial possibilities: the American CIA, the Soviet KGB, groups in South Africa, Chile, Iran, and Iraq. He eventually became convinced that the Partiya Karkeren Kurdistan (Kurdistan Worker's Party) or PKK, which had been responsible for several murders around Europe, including three in Sweden, were the killers. All this was dutifully reported in the media and was later recorded in the book he wrote after his resignation. Contrary to the more common approach, Holmer ordered his investigation around the possible motive, rather than from clues and evidence from the crime scene itself; there was nothing that linked the PKK to the crime scene (Åsard 2006:175). Not satisfied merely with press conferences to put forward his views on the murder of Olof Palme, Holmer made a secret agreement with the chief editor of *Dagens Nyheter* in the first week following the murder (Wall 1996:55). The agreement provided this newspaper exclusive rights to Holmer's story of the ongoing investigation, which would be published under the byline of one of the paper's journalists (Nilsson 2001:44). When this agreement was later discovered, several journalists resigned in protest. After Holmer's own resignation, these articles were later published in book form and, during his retirement, Holmer went on to a new career—that of writing crime novels.

On March 8, International Women's Day, a week after the murder, large demonstrations filled the squares in Stockholm, Malmö, and other cities. Lisbet Palme participated in the Stockholm demonstration, and *Arbetet,* (March 9, 1986) published photographs of these demonstrations under the headline, "Women and Immigrants Honor Palme." Television reportage showed that much of the Stockholm demonstration was dominated by Palme's murder. One broadcast contained an interview with Anna Lindh, then head of the SAP youth organization, who discussed how much Palme had meant to her and to other young socialists. When demonstrators attempted to march toward the murder site, they were hindered by the teeming multitudes already present. Two days later, a national moment of silence halted all transportation as trains and buses came to a halt and individuals stopped their automobiles to stand silently by the roadside. Workers stood beside their machines and desks with heads bowed, and the Swedish parliament recessed for a two-hour memorial ceremony, carried live on television.

MOVING FORWARD

After days of demonstrations of public mourning, Olof Palme was buried on March 15, 1986. The funeral service attracted great media coverage as well as the attention of the nation. It was also closely guarded, as some feared a terrorist attack on the world socialist leaders who were in attendance. More than 2,000 police guarded the ceremony (Bundeson 2005:66).[5] The televised funeral ceremony drew a large audience, international guests, and banner headlines. The march through the city followed a path choreographed by the SAP leading the marchers through some of the historic sites of the Swedish labor movement. All of Sweden's local labor organizations were included, and each carried its own red flag. The city was draped in red as much as in yellow and blue, the national colors. This too was followed by television cameras moderated with solemn descriptions of the significant places passed along the route—places heavy with symbolic meaning for Olof Palme and the Swedish labor movement.

To commemorate this, on March 16, *Arbetet* published another special memorial edition in its second section, while its front-page headline read,

"Farewell Olof Palme, You Live On In Our Hearts." The memorial section featured a full-page photograph of Palme and a second-page photograph of the widow and children under the headline, "A World United in Grief With Lisbet and Her Sons". It featured many photographs of visiting dignitaries, including one of German socialist leader Willy Brandt beside Palme's casket,another of the new prime minister, Carlsson, and the text of his funeral oration. A statement by the Swedish king about his personal feelings of loss accompanied his photograph. Here again, political continuity was represented in text and image. *Dagens Nyheter* followed this theme of stability and continuity, yet with a different slant. Its front page of March 15 featured a photograph of the ceremony with the headline, "Summit Meeting After the Funeral." The funeral, it suggested, provided a chance for world leaders to meet and discuss important issues. Their following day's editorial stated this more bluntly: "Everyone Wants to Move On," and featured a photo of Ingvar Carlsson beside Palme's casket.[6]

Moving on meant the assumption to power of the new social democratic government. Ingvar Carlsson, who had been Sweden's first environmental minister in addition to being vice prime minister and a close colleague of Olof Palme, was formally confirmed as prime minister by parliament on March 12. He announced his new cabinet the following day.[7] There were few changes. However, moving on did not mean an immediate resumption of political debate. There was, in fact, an unexpected and unspoken moratorium on open conflict, which lasted several months and involved internal and external opposition. The country became united around its fallen leader. Although stunned by the murder, the death of Palme—in a perverse way— helped the SAP to resolve its internal tensions as well as to quell the sometimes tense external opposition. Palme represented many of the long-standing socialist values that some in the party (and, of course, many more outside it) considered outmoded in the contemporary world. He was a strong proponent of worker participation in the running of the firms they were employed in; though a latecomer, he was in favor of collective employee funds as a means of combating unemployment as well as of increasing the power of employees over their working conditions. He was, in other words, a most powerful representative of the Swedish Model.

Although internal opposition was quieted in the immediate aftermath of this death, it soon re-emerged and was only strengthened by his absence. The internal criticism of Palme (and by implication the Swedish Model) came primarily from those who favored a closer alliance with liberal segments of the nonsocialist bloc, especially concerning economic matters. There was of course also opposition from the Left, both inside and outside the SAP, pushing for more radical reforms. Although a close confidant of Palme's, Ingvar Carlsson had an entirely different leadership style and eventually steered the party in another direction. Describing himself as a "team player," Carlsson was pushed by those in the social democratic leadership (his team) toward polices that brought the party closer to the political center and thus toward the nonsocialists. Gunnar Wall (1996: 34) lists the following as noticeable changes in SAP orientation after Palme's death: a softer tone in the criticism of American foreign policy; a push toward the European Community; an endorsement of an economic policy that brought them closer to the nonsocialist parties and that favored high-income earners; and dropping not only the employee funds but also the entire argument that employees must participate in those company decisions that affect them. These were major changes even though the effects would not become visible for some time.

THE POLICE INVESTIGATION

On February 28, 1996, the tenth anniversary of Olof Palme's death, *Aftonbladet's* front-page headline proclaimed, "This Fall We Will Know Who Killed Palme," quoting Sweden's chief prosecutor. This prediction, like so many others before it, proved to be false. One year after taking charge of the investigation, which involved a fruitless pursuit of several conspiracy leads and constant battles with the district attorney, Hans Holmer resigned. Responsibility for the investigation now shifted from the Stockholm police district, where Holmer had been administrative chief, to the federal police, and a new investigating officer was appointed. In the absence of real progress, rumors flourished and public skepticism grew. One of the most prominent rumors concerned right-wing members of the Swedish police complicity in the murder which some leading members of the SAP believed to be true (Borgnäs 2006). This view was circulated in the mass media and remains one of the continuing threads in the conspiracy theories concerning the murder (see Borgnäs 2006 for supporting evidence and Åsard 2006 for an opposing view). In 1988, the social democratic minister of justice was forced to resign after press reports that she had been actively involved in supporting an unofficial investigation into Palme's murder. Sponsored by the SAP, this investigation ran parallel to the official, police investigation, yet with the apparent knowledge of the heads of both the national and secret police. Its aim was to continue on the path laid out by Holmer's investigating team, which was now only one of several paths and leads being investigated by the police. The ensuing scandal ended with nationally televised hearings before a parliamentary commission, which included formal hearings with the former minister of justice. During the process, responsibility for the Palme investigation was again shifted, this time to the National Crime Bureau, and a new lead investigator was appointed (Borgnäs 2006:11–12).

In December 1988, newspaper headlines announced the arrest of a 41-year-old suspect in the killing. This later turned out to be Christer Pettersson, a petty criminal living on the fringes of the Stockholm underworld. Pettersson fit much of the profile of political assassin as outlined by the American commission, a fact orchestrated in the Swedish mass media. He was a loner, a former acting student, who after a serious head injury went spiraling down a path toward substance abuse and violent crime. Pettersson had been interviewed by the police in the early days of the investigation because of his record of violent offences, some of them committed in the vicinity of the crime scene (Åsard 2006:178). When the investigation turned its focus to foreign political conspiracy, Pettersson was dropped from serious consideration. He became interesting again with the new investigations, and when Lisbet Palme picked Pettersson out of a police lineup, he became the prime suspect. This was nearly three years after the murder.

Christer Pettersson was convicted of the murder of Olof Palme in July 1989 and sentenced to life imprisonment. In October 1989, this conviction was overturned on appeal. In reversing the conviction, the high court pointed to the lack of technical evidence: no murder weapon or fingerprints had been found, and no motive had been firmly established. Most dramatically, the court pointed to what it considered the questionable identification made by the chief witness, Lisbet Palme (Åsard 2006:182). Pettersson was freed and the case reopened. He died in 2004, after having achieved something of a cult status, being portrayed as a scapegoat and as a victim of established authority. A performer to the end, just before his death, Pettersson first "confessed" to the murder and then retracted his confession. Much more significant was the fact that Pettersson had been pointed out by Lisbet Palme as the killer of her husband. This made it difficult for any further investigation into the crime in that any new suspect would have to resemble him: anything else would appear to challenge her judgment. Given her status, especially after the murder, this was something few would attempt (Borgnäs 2006).

CULTURAL TRAUMA?

The murder of its prime minister clearly shocked the Swedish nation, and its representation and reconstruction through the mass media did raise issues about the fundamental grounds of Swedish collective identity. From the first moment, there were concerns raised about Swedish democracy and how a democratic nation would react in the face of such a tragedy. Although the Swedish monarchy was brought to bear as a symbol of national identity, it played a minor role. More important were the quick transition of power within the political system and the lack of any controversy concerning succession. The assumption of leadership by Ingvar Carlsson, pictured with

Palme in media reportage from the first day onward, went very swiftly and was significant in buffering the shock and quelling the emotions brought about by the murder. Sadness and grief, rather than explosive anger, were the most commonly represented emotions. This may have been a political murder, but the loss felt personal, like losing a family member—something clearly reflected in the survey results mentioned earlier. The nation that was revealed to itself and to the world in this process was inward-looking and dignified as well as democratic. The fact that political opposition was also quieted for this period of mourning only reinforced this. Just as he had while alive, in death Olof Palme brought international attention and respect to the nation, a fact that was pointed out often in the commentaries voiced in the immediate aftermath of his death. Through the performance of national mourning and the demonstrations of unity and political stability, the nation reaffirmed its sense of significance well beyond its size and military strength. Even without this representative figure, Sweden could continue its role as model nation, at least temporarily. As the young Anna Lindh so poignantly said during her funeral oration, the best way to honor Olof Palme would be to carry his ideals further. These words would be repeated at her own funeral.

There were no significant carrier groups that were interested in pushing this traumatic occurrence to another level. In this relatively homogeneous and law-abiding society, social conflict was highly institutionalized, with well-established and accepted rules and procedures. This was largely a result of the long tenure of social democratic rule, which had seen to it that one of the most fundamental conflicts in modern society, the one between capital and labor, was well formalized through centralized collective bargaining. In this sense, the "Swedish Model" itself played an important role through the manner in which the emotions aroused by the murder were managed. What could have pushed things in another direction were the rumors of right-wing conspiracy, the suspicions of police and military involvement in the murder, which surfaced for a while. Although rumors of foreign involvement were common, they were less threatening than the idea that Swedish citizens would conspire against one of their leaders (Borgnäs 2006).[8] The Soviet news agency TASS, (as reported in *Dagens Nyheter,* March 2, 1986:12) claimed that the CIA was behind the murder. Hans Holmer was convinced that the Kurdish PKK was the party responsible. Had these or other conspiracy theories been proven true and orchestrated, more dire consequences might have followed. No one really took seriously the Soviet claim, and after Holmer's pursuit failed, the focus of investigation turned to viewing the killer as a lone individual, most likely with psychic problems.

From the point of view of cultural trauma, the most potentially threatening of the rumors was the claim that an internal conspiracy existed, with

supporters within the Swedish police and military (Borgnäs 2006 maps this
in great detail). If it were true or even widely suspected, this could have
raised serious issues about the democratic foundations of Swedish society and
potentially called into question one of the nation's most sacred beliefs: the
faith in authority. Just after Palme's murder, the first thought of many close
to the investigation was that a politically motivated conspiracy was involved.
This was also the view of Ingvar Carlsson and others in the SAP leadership. In reflecting on this possibility, Borgnäs (2006:281) goes so far as to
suggest that there was a conscious effort among Swedish elites to "seek the
alternative that was least politically harmful" and which "would be easiest
for the country to take." In this case, he suggests, the PKK seemed to be
the most likely candidate. One need not accept the notion of a conspiracy
among Swedish elites to believe that the suspicion of active engagement of
Swedish citizens, especially those—such as the police—who were in positions of authority, would have to been the most "politically harmful." We
will probably never know if there was any substance to these rumors, but the
fact remains that the suspicions were never actively investigated, as least as
far as was officially stated. Several authors have called for a new investigation
that would seriously consider this as well as other leads in the case (Nilsson
2001 and Borgnäs 2006, for example). A very popular three-volume novel by
criminology professor Leif G.W. Persson follows this lead to its conclusion.
The murder of Olof Palme is portrayed here as a conspiracy organized by a
high-ranking member of the Security Police (SÄPO) with a background in
the extreme right. The novel's hero, who solves the crime, is also a member
of the security police. The pursuit of Palme's killer is portrayed as an internal
affair, and the public is never aware of either the investigation or the final
punishment. This raises issues regarding how much truth a democratic society can endure and when it is best to keep the pursuit of justice hidden from
the public.

Even if there had been such an investigation, any findings of complicity or
conspiracy among Swedish authorities would have had to be substantial, even
overwhelming, given the legitimacy awarded to those in positions of authority, especially the police. Public opinion surveys have consistently shown that
Sweden places high on the list of those countries where authority is legitimate
and consensual (see, for example, Holmberg and Weibull (eds.) 2004:71). This
is why the American study mentioned in the first chapter placed Sweden at
the bottom end of its scale of political violence. This is also why the murder of
Olof Palme was so shocking. Even if there had been a carrier group, the SAP
for example, to drive a claim of conspiracy, and media support to orchestrate
it, it is doubtful whether such a claim would have found a receptive audience
among the Swedish population. This is not to say that conspiracy theories do
not have their public. Besides the accounts by academics and journalists, in

the university town of Lund a lone individual stands a few hours each day, as he has done since 1986, bearing a placard declaring conspiracy and a cover-up in the murder of his beloved prime minister.

For the majority, after the period of national mourning, any traumatic effects of the murder of Olof Palme would lay deep under the surface in collective memory, and their long-term effect would become apparent only with the murder of Anna Lindh, seventeen years later. The possibility that the shock caused by the murder of a powerfully symbolic figure such as Olof Palme could be transformed into cultural trauma was effectively scuttled through firm management of the crisis and the apparent lack of agents who would be interested in seeing this happen. One can more easily mark the long-term traumatic effects in regard to two central institutions of Swedish society: the SAP and the agencies of law enforcement, most especially the police corps. For the police, the murder of Olof Palme shaped institutional memory and influenced the handling of the Lindh murder at every level, including the selection of the chief investigating officer. Through a stroke of bureaucratic irony, the room where the new team of investigators in the Lindh murder had gathered for the first time was, in fact, the Palme Room— the same room where that investigation had been quartered and had faltered. And the chief prosecutor at the trial of Lindh's killer was named Krister Pettersson. For the SAP, Palme became an iconic figure whose memory was invoked on many ritual occasions in party ceremonies. His shadow, as Ingvar Carlsson recounts in his memoirs, fell everywhere that party members gathered. During the initial meetings following Palme's death, his chair at the head of the table was left vacant. This shadow encompassed the entire nation when another party member, said to be his apprentice, was similarly murdered.

THE MURDER OF ANNA LINDH

THE CONTEXT

Although not directly evident when measured by the election results of 2002, the Swedish political landscape had altered radically in 2003, when Anna Lindh was murdered. The SAP had been in office continuously since 1994 and won re-election in 2002, receiving 39.8 percent of the vote, to the conservative party's 15.3 percent. The Social Democrats formed a coalition government with the Left and the Green Party. What had changed was not so much the numbers, but the general attitude of the party and the country at large and, most importantly, the global political situation. One of the most important changes since 1986 was that Sweden was now a member of the European Union (EU), having joined in 1995 with support from the Social Democrats, the liberals, and the conservatives. A national referendum on the issue was passed in 1994 and was formally confirmed in parliament in December of that year. As early as 1967, Sweden had begun negotiating with the European Economic Community (EEC), as this body was then called, to secure grounds for participating in the expanding economic cooperation within Europe. Olof Palme had opposed formal application, primarily for foreign-policy reasons, favoring European trade agreements but not formal political alignment. He was concerned with maintaining Swedish neutrality and was opposed to NATO, at least officially.[9] Palme was a fervent advocate of disarmament and placed that issue as high on his agenda as labor issues. The fall of the Berlin Wall in 1989 and the uprisings in Eastern Europe marked the end of the Cold War and the victory of capitalism over socialism, at least in most of the Western world with Sweden still being somewhat the exception.

To many, the idea of a middle way seemed as ideologically outdated as it was difficult to maintain economically. In the early 1990s, Sweden was mired in an economic crisis and the SAP in an ideological one. The two were related in that the SAP's ideological crisis stemmed in part from a major tax-reform that had been passed under its leadership in cooperation with the nonsocialist parties that were in the middle of the political spectrum. The tax reform was seen as a step toward resolving the economic crisis. This angered those on the political Left, both inside and outside the party. The SAP was slowly but surely drifting toward a more market-oriented economic policy and a more favorable stance toward the EU.[10] Joining the EU was represented by the party leadership as a way out of both crises, ideological as well as economic. As a whole, however, the party was split nearly down the middle regarding membership, as the national referendum had revealed. The main forces opposing membership, however, came from the outside: from the Left communist party; the Green Party, which had emerged as a vibrant force in Swedish politics just after Palme's death; and activists in the agriculturally based Center Party. After 1994, any attempt to reformulate a Swedish Model would now have to add Brussels to the list of contending forces.

Though she was often compared to Olof Palme and portrayed as his political apprentice, Anna Lindh operated in a political world that was radically different from that of Palme's. Lindh was a Europeanist in the way that Palme was an Internationalist. The SAP that spawned her was now committed to Europe, and its dealings with the wider world were necessarily filtered through that frame. Lindh was killed in the midst of a national referendum on the European Monetary Union (EMU, which would decide whether or not Sweden's monetary system would be more obviously and intimately tied to that of Europe. The SAP leadership was firmly on the "Yes" side with Anna Lindh as its most visible proponent. The shopping trip she took in the early afternoon of September 10, 2003, was in search of a new jacket to wear in a televised debate on this referendum, and pictures of her supporting the "Yes" side were plastered all over the city (Franchell 2009). Wherever Anna Lindh went, she was recognized and recognizable for who she was and what she stood for.

Around 3:45 P.M. on September 10, 2003, Anna Lindh and her longtime friend and former press secretary left the building of the Foreign Ministry on Gustav Adolfs Torg in central Stockholm to walk to the nearby shopping malls (my account builds on Jennekvist 2005, Unsgaard 2005, and Franchell 2009). They stopped to look at the shops in one of the malls before moving on to the next mall, about a half block away, in one of the busiest areas of the city. Entering the building, they took the escalator to the women's clothing section on the second floor. As they were standing by a clothes rack placed just inside the entrance of a fashionable boutique, a man rushed toward them. Pushing her friend aside, he leaped on Anna Lindh with such force that she fell backward as he began jabbing her with the quick, short motions of a boxer. Thinking that the man was punching her, the friend hit his arm and shoulder, shouting, "What the hell are you doing?" He turned and looked at her coldly before rushing down the escalator and out of the mall. It was only after Lindh said she had been stabbed that the friend noticed the blood on her clothes. Other shoppers rushed to help, and an ambulance was called. Before it arrived, one of mall's security guards leaned over the victim and asked if she thought the attack was "political." Anna Lindh looked up and replied, "Of course it's political" (Unsgaard 2005:112). The emergency call was intercepted by a police patrol in the vicinity, and two police officers arrived at the scene at approximately the same moment as did the ambulance. There was some confusion as to where the victim lay and whether the crime scene should be marked off and secured first, before the rescue workers could move in. One of the central criticisms of the police investigation into Palme's murder was precisely that they had failed to secure the scene of the crime, thus losing potentially valuable evidence. As it was, the rescue personnel had to force their way through the 75–100 onlookers surrounding the victim, but within minutes of the attack, Anna Lindh was on her way to hospital.

A few minutes later, at 16:41 P.M., a radio bulletin announced the attack to the world. Two journalists happened to be in the mall and called in the news. The bulletin stated that Foreign Minister Anna Lindh had been attacked and stabbed in a downtown department store. At that same moment, Prime Minister Göran Persson, a close colleague of Anna Lindh, received the news by phone on an airport walkway just as he arrived back in Stockholm from a referendum rally in another part of the country. The extent of the injuries was not reported until about an hour later and was represented as "serious, but not life threatening."[11] A press conference was hastily scheduled for 6:00 P.M.. In front of the assembled mass media, his voice cracking with emotion, Göran Persson gave the bare facts: "At twenty minutes after four this afternoon Anna Lindh was stabbed at a Stockholm department store. She is now being operated on and the situation is serious…Security has been increased around official buildings and the government and other authorities have been informed. For our part, we halt all activities concerning the coming referendum." He then called this an attack on "our open society…[a]bout which I feel great dismay and anger" (Jennekvist 2005:46). When asked how he felt when receiving the news, Persson replied, "It felt unreal" (Unsgaard 2005:128–29). There was enormous international media interest in the incident; Unsgaard (2005: 130) reports that in the first eight hours over 800 calls from journalists around the world were recorded. As it happened, there were many international journalists in Sweden at the time, some to cover the referendum and others to cover the European basketball championships. They were all soon forced to change their focus to politics and murder. Like the Swedish media, international journalists were quick to link the attack on Anna Lindh to the murder of Olof Palme. Among the first questions to be asked was, "How could this happen again?" Sweden was now a part of Europe, and Anna Lindh was a well-known and respected figure throughout the continent. Swedish newspapers would also ask, "Have We Learned Nothing?"

Doctors (there were nearly 30 closely involved in the proceedings) operated throughout the night, as the bleeding from the stab wounds continued unabated. At around 3:00 A.M.,they announced a halt, saying that the patient's condition was improving. Friends and relatives who had been waiting in the corridors were advised to go home and rest. Two and a half hours later, at 5:29 A.M. on September 11, 2003, Anna Lindh was dead. She died on the operating table, her body, in the end, unable to cope with all the bleeding and the 15 blood transfusions. Hospital representatives delayed making the formal announcement to the media so that family members could be informed first. The announcement was made at just after 9:00 A.M., and a radio bulletin followed directly after. Then came the official announcement from the prime minister. It was, writes Evard Unsgaard (2005:155), the most difficult moment in Göran Persson's political career: "Everyone knew what he was going to say. No one knew how he was going to say it." Göran Persson simply said, "It is with great sorrow that I received the message that Sweden's Foreign Minister Anna Lindh died this morning at 5:29 from the wounds of yesterday's attack."

MEDIA ACCOUNTS

"Anna Lindh Stabbed," proclaimed the headline of *Dagens Nyheter* on Thursday, September 11, 2003. This was followed by a quote from the prime minister: "This is an attack on our open society." Its editorial, headlined "The Attack Sends a Shock Wave Through Sweden," drew the connection to the

Palme murder seventeen years prior to this one, and noted that the murder took place just four days before an important referendum, which made it difficult not to think about possible political consequences. A signed "debate" article blamed the secret police for not providing proper protection.[12] "The attack shows that the police do not have control of the security of leading political figures," proclaimed the author (*Dagens Nyheter*, 2003:3). This was followed by a graphic diagram of the crime scene and the headline, "Attack Was Probably Planned." The next day's headline, "A People In Shock and Sorrow," was accompanied by photographs of weeping individuals. The unsigned editorial began with the words "Sweden has suffered a difficult loss. The shining political star of her generation has met the same fate as Olof Palme." A signed editorial on the same page (2) sought an explanation "for our innocent Swedish attitude":

> We want our elected officials to be ordinary people, so that they can move freely through town and talk to everyone...at the same time as we live in a cold, hard world both at home and abroad...we should have known better before this tragedy occurred. The tragic parallels to the Palme murder 17 years ago are many. No body guards in central Stockholm, a random attack, a lone perpetrator who escapes on foot. Since the police failed to arrest the assailant there is a growing uneasiness that there will be a repetition of the Palme investigation. Swedish democracy cannot afford another prolonged trauma, with conspiracy theories and all the political consequences which follow from that. (Niklas Ekdal, *Dagens Nyheter*, September 12, 2003:2)

It did not appear possible to discuss the murder of Anna Lindh without reference to the Palme murder and the use of words such as "shock" and "trauma." The murder and the failure of law enforcement to find the murderer weighed heavily on collective memory. For many, including one leading journalist, it was a national disgrace (Borgnäs 2006) Reportage in all the major newspapers made the immediate connection, and most papers carried photographs of the two, Palme and Lindh, together. The political editor of *Aftonbladet* wrote on September 11, 2003:2, "Sweden is in shock as it was after the murder of Olof Palme in 1986. On public transport on the way to work eyes meet, the atmosphere is depressed. How could it happen again? Is this the final end of the open, popular movement (folkrörelser) democracy?" The opening lines were typical for these first days after the attack. What marked this as a comment in a Left-leaning newspaper was the rooting of Swedish democracy in popular movements.[13] The conservative *Svenska Dagbladet* also found a nation in shock, but made no mention of a threat to democracy, much less to any claims about its origins. Their inside headlines cried, "No, Not Again" (September 11, 2003:9) and proclaimed "Yet Another Swedish Trauma" (September 12, 2003:20). The fact that Anna

Lindh had been one of the featured speakers at Palme's funeral was also widely reported, often accompanied by photographs of her on that occasion. In his emotion-filled funeral oration, Göran Persson quoted Anna Lindh's own speech at Palme's funeral. "This is what Anna said to Olof: 'With all our resources we will carry on your struggle. The struggle for freedom, for international solidarity, for a free and open Sweden, a Sweden without racism and the fear of Otherness.'" Earlier in the week, speaking at a large demonstration in Stockholm's Sergel's Square, Persson noted that Olof Palme had been Lindh's role model and inspiration.

Media representation after the murder of Anna Lindh followed the pattern established seventeen years before with the murder of Palme. This was also the case for the spontaneous as well as official demonstrations of grief. A mountain of flowers, notes, and other personal items appeared at the murder scene; crowds of grieving people gathered in displays of mourning, and the official funeral followed a similar pattern, with the exception of the dramatic and solemn march through the streets of Stockholm. Lindh, after all, was neither the prime minister nor the symbolic head of the labor movement. Just as it had been for Olof Palme, the funeral of Anna Lindh was the occasion for a gathering of political dignitaries from around the world, but this time, most especially from Europe. For one foreign dignitary, Lindh "died for Europe" (*Kvällsposten,* September 13, 2003:4). The media represented a nation in mourning and spoke of trauma and of the possible political consequences. On Friday, September 12, 2003, for example, the chief political editor of *Dagens Nyheter,* wrote, "The trauma the Swedish people are now experiencing after the murder of Anna Lindh can have great political consequences. The normal succession in the SAP is broken…The referendum's result can be questioned and Sweden's position in the EU can be weakened" (2). This suggested that the present crisis was not so much a national crisis as one for the SAP and its policies. Anna Lindh was a popular figure in Swedish politics, "one of the highlights of her generation," as a conservative newspaper put it, but she was first and foremost a member of the SAP and, within that party, a leader of those who supported the EU.

Several themes can be gleaned from the media accounts of the days following the attack: the threat to Sweden's open, democratic society; the threat to women; the need for better protection of political leaders and, related to that, Swedish naivete in the face of the world's evil. The likelihood of the murderer being a mentally disturbed individual was also strongly put forward as was advice from mental health professionals on how to deal with children exposed to such trauma. Comparing these with the media themes that emerged in the coverage of the Palme murder, one significant and obvious difference can be found: Anna Lindh was a woman. This difference can be marked in two rather opposite ways; the first was the clear reference to Lindh's role as mother and wife, as well as politician. In an editorial on the day of the attack, the conservative afternoon paper *Kvällsposten* began its reportage by identifying Lindh as a mother of two children. Under the headline, "The Attack," the editors wrote, this is "first of all an attack against her person. The mother of two, Anna Lindh is another victim of violence in today's Sweden. Too much violence, too many easily available weapons, then comes the politics, the referendum" (*Kvällsposten*, September 11, 2003:2).[14] The second angle was less traditional in its approach to gender. Writing in the liberal *Dagens Nyheter*'s debate column, Agneta Stark, identified as a gender-researcher and author, wrote beneath the headline "Freedom is Shrinking" that Anna Lindh "was in an obvious way a pragmatic feminist. For very good reasons many women are fearful of violence. But there exist free zones. A quick shopping trip with a friend felt secure. But does it now? Will it ever again? I feel the safe zones around me shrinking" (*Dagens Nyheter*, September 12, 2003:4). The same day, and also in *Dagens Nyheter*, a Danish author wrote, "There is a brutality in Scandinavia which we tend to forget. Anna Lindh was controversial because she was a woman... It's enough to be a woman and also have power—that by itself is provocation to some. A consequence of the murder is that women who want to become politicians, or are already, are fearful and that of course was one motivation for the attack" (Hanne-Vibeke Holst, *Dagens Nyheter*, September 12, 2003:7). Many agreed that Anna Lindh had been an important role model for young women who might now think twice about public service as a career choice.

As was the case after the murder of Olof Palme, the issues of national security and the protection of public figures were raised in the media. This time, however, the representation of and by the police was very different. Like Hans Holmer, Leif Jennekvist, the lead police investigator in the murder of Anna Lindh, became a frequent figure in television reportage. But the contrast was striking. From the beginning, Jennekvist appeared in uniform and was usually surrounded by other high-level authorities from law enforcement, several of whom were women. Jennekvist was clearly a team player with less need for personal aggrandizement. This difference is also revealed in the books both he and Holmer wrote about their experiences during their respective investigations. Whereas Holmer placed himself at the center of activity, Jennekvist made it clear that his own role was encased within a chain of command and stressed his need for support from colleagues and family. The failed Palme investigation weighed heavily on all those involved in the Lindh murder. Jennekvist writes of his own anxiety and that of others, especially when meeting the press, which in effect meant facing the nation. Their actions were filtered through the memory of that failure even if one had not actually been involved with that investigation (Jennekvist 2006:68–69). At press conferences it was always a team that appeared before the cameras and microphones, usually with Jennekvist in the middle, flanked by his immediate supervisor and lead prosecutor, both of whom were women, each with ample opportunity to speak.

From a police standpoint, these cases were also very different, despite their public significance. Anna Lindh was attacked in broad daylight in a very public place. Not only were there many eyewitnesses, but closed-circuit cameras were in use, offering investigators a much better chance of identifying a suspect. The knife used in the attack was found near the scene the same day, as was a cap worn by the attacker. This was in stark contrast to the Palme murder, where not one of the witnesses caught a clear view of the perpetrator's face, and the only technical evidence found at the badly protected crime scene was two bullet fragments. A significant proportion of television reportage was devoted to the new technologies available to police since the Palme murder, including closed-circuit television and, most importantly, the use of DNA. Within two days of the attack, the closed-circuit images of the suspect were leaked to the media and published in the afternoon papers. The image of a young man dressed in a Nike-hooded sweatshirt and a baseball cap with the logo "Just Do It" was now available to everyone. It contrasted sharply with eyewitness descriptions and the first police reports, which described an unkempt, "Swedish-looking" man, possibly a homeless person, dressed in camouflage clothing. With the aid of the violent criminal profile and the CCTV images, police arrested a suspect within a week of the attack. Whereas some television reportage wondered if this was the right man, *Aftonbladet* devoted more than 13 pages to the suspect, including his school performance and his "racist" attitudes; like much of the press, they seemed convinced of his guilt (Unsgaard 2006:239). This suspect was released one week later when the results of the analysis of the DNA abstracted from the knife and cap arrived at police headquarters. On the same day, September 24, the chief prosecutor made a dramatic announcement. After it was announced that the suspect, now in custody, was being released for lack of sufficient evidence, an audible tension could be felt among the assembled press corps. Without missing a beat or changing expression, but perhaps with a note of triumph in her voice, the prosecutor went on to say that a new suspect, a 24-year-old for whom stronger evidence was available, was in custody. The new suspect was formally charged two days later, pleading not guilty through his lawyer. In most cases, Swedish norms prohibit the public disclosure of a suspect's name until formal conviction; in this case, however, the court decided to release his name. On September 24, 2003, two weeks after the attack, Mijailo Mijailovic, who had identified himself to his police interrogators only as "Tom Cruise," was announced as arrested and charged with the murder of Anna Lindh.

In effect, there were three trials to legally settle the murder of Anna Lindh. The first lasted three days, during which time the court was satisfied of Mijailovic's guilt, but requested a complete psychiatric examination before imposing sentence.[15] When the medical experts found him to be free from serious mental illness at the time the crime was committed, Mijailovic was sentenced to life in prison. This sentence, not the murder itself, was appealed, and a higher court changed the ruling to closed psychiatric care instead of ordinary prison, where no such care is given. This sentence was in turn appealed, and finally the Swedish Supreme Court reversed the ruling and reaffirmed the lower court. Mijailo Mijailovic is now serving a life sentence in a Swedish prison, which in practice means about 20 years, as media discussions have confirmed. He has since asked to be allowed to serve this sentence in a Serbian prison and has renounced his Swedish citizenship. This request has been denied. During the negotiations, Swedish television presented pictures showing the conditions in Serbian jails and interviewed some other Swedish inmates with a Serbian background who had considered making the same request. One of them said that the images shown on Swedish television had caused him to change his mind. As the experts interviewed argued, this inmate concluded that it was better to remain in a Swedish prison. Mijailovic remains unconvinced.

WHO WAS THE PERPETRATOR, AND WHO THE VICTIM?

Mijailo Mijailovic's defense attorneys argued that he was not in full control of his actions when he stabbed Swedish foreign minister Anna Lindh on September 10, 2003. The sequence that led to her death, they argued, was the result of the unplanned, impulsive behavior of a mentally ill person directed by inner voices. The choice of victim, it was contended, was purely random and thus, for all intents and purposes, could have been anyone. In other words, this was not a political murder, much less an assassination. The perpetrator, they argued, was himself a victim—a victim of a malfunctioning mental health care system. It had come forward during police investigations that Mijailovic had been suffering from mental illness for some time and that in the days before the stabbing he had sought emergency hospital care and had, in fact, been driven there by two police officers, only to be released with a prescription. When the police searched his room they found a pile of prescriptions, the last written two days before the attack. Mijailovic was taking antidepressants and other medication related to mental illness and to insomnia. His mother and sister also had a history of mental illness and his father, sick-pensioned for many years, suffered from alcoholism.

The prosecutors did not seek to deny this medical history, nor that Mijailovic might have acted impulsively when he killed Anna Lindh. However, they were convinced and managed to convince the court that he had targeted just her. CCTV images revealed the perpetrator walking through the balconies of the shopping mall looking not for items, but seemingly for someone. They show him exiting the escalator on the mall's third level, turn suddenly around, and head back down. Although there were no images of him actually seeing the victim, prosecutors were able to show that he had both the time and the opportunity to do so. This established opportunity and challenged the claim to unplanned behavior. As for the murder weapon, there was no need to question the perpetrator's claim that he carried the knife because he felt pursued by enemies. Whatever the reason or wherever this Mora hunting knife came from, DNA evidence revealed that it had been in contact with Anna Lindh and that he had held it. Although in the absence of an admission, it could not be proven that Mijailovic's actions were politically motivated, many, including the victim, believed this to be so. What would "political" mean in this case? Would it refer to the victim's or the perpetrator's views? Was Anna Lindh attacked because of what she stood for or what she had done? Was she targeted as a politician, as a female politician, or as someone representing a policy or a party? Just who was Mijailo Mijailovic, and why did he attack Anna Lindh?

The depressing picture of Mijailo Mijailovic's life, which emerged in the courtroom and after, referred primarily to the recent past; as Edvard Unsgaard (2006) describes it, his early childhood appears to have been much happier. Mijailovic was born in Stockholm in December 1978. Six years earlier, his father, then 21 years old, had followed his own father in emigrating from what was then Yugoslavia. His mother arrived a year later, in 1973. Like the majority of immigrants to Sweden from Yugoslavia, the Mijailovic family were Serbs. In the 1960s, Sweden, like other European countries, activity sought to import workers, primarily from western and southern Europe. Yugoslavia was the only Eastern European country that permitted some of its citizens to emigrate. Sweden differed from other countries, such as Germany and the Netherlands, in that it did not categorize these laborers as "guests" who would soon return home, but rather, was more liberal in allowing families to immigrate together. As we will see in the case of the killer of Theo van Gogh, the Netherlands would later change its immigration laws to permit some family members to join those already in the country.

Mijailovic's extended family lived and worked in Lidingö, an exclusive suburb on the outskirts of Stockholm, where a margarine factory permitted the presence of a small immigrant population. When he reached school age, Mijailo Mijailovic, together with his mother and sister, was sent back to Yugoslavia and remained there until war broke out between the various territories of the country. This was not an uncommon practice. They returned to Sweden in 1991, when Mijailo was 12, as the war moved nearer. After a year in a special school class that was organized to make the transition into the Swedish school system easier for the children of immigrant parents,

Mijailo entered a class of 30 students, most of whom had been together since grade school. He was one of the few with an immigrant background. From this point on, a good student turned into one with problems. Problems at school were multiplied by those at home, where an already troubled relationship between his parents was further strained by unemployment. The years of tension within the family culminated late in 1996 when, intervening in a confrontation between his parents, Mijailo attacked his father with a kitchen knife. Arrested and charged with deadly assault, he was sentenced to supervised probation, with the added proviso that he be examined and treated for any mental illness. Mijailo Mijailovic had just turned 18. It was then that his involvement with mental health and law enforcement authority began.

The killer of Anna Lindh was a second-generation Swede with a Serbian background. Like Sirhan Sirhan and Mohammed B., Mijailo Mijailovic well fit the American-based profile of a potential political assassin: he was young; was a single male child of immigrant parents; had a troubled family life; had a bad relationship with an often-absent and distant father and with women outside his family. He was bright and relatively well educated, yet unemployed, with little future prospect. Although a motive for his actions in attacking the Swedish foreign minister has not been firmly established, the violent criminal profile used by the Swedish police in tracking him down offers a possibility: the expressive killer. In attempting to reconstruct the assailant's path toward murder, the Swedish police made use of a sophisticated profile of the extreme violent offender that had been developed in the United States (Unsgaard 2006:198ff). There were four basic variants in this model: (1) those need driven, the career criminal in search of money, either a professional or a substance abuser; (2) the severely mentally ill, who commit violent crimes for no apparent reason; (3) stalkers, who develop a fixation for a particular person, often someone well-known; (4) the expressive criminal, one who wishes to communicate something through a violent act. Through a process of elimination, using anonymous tips, the witness testimony, and the technical evidence they had on hand, the Swedish special task force was able to concentrate on the last of these categories. The expressive criminal falls into two types, inner and outer directed: those who act out their own fantasies through violent acts and those who want to express or represent something to others. Looking at the killers of Martin Luther King and Robert Kennedy through this model, one could say that they were persons who sought to overcome their social marginality through the killing of a public figure, an act that would bring them immediate attention and higher social status. The petty criminal James Earl Ray may well have been a racist for whom Martin Luther King Jr. was anathema, but he was also someone on the lower ranks of the criminal status hierarchy, someone whom a "big killing" would have catapulted to the top (Ayton 2005). The killing of MLK could be seen as his attempt to make it big, to show that he was not who everyone in his circle of acquaintances thought he was. In a similar way, Sirhan may well have had Arab nationalist sympathies and appears to have stalked his victim, but he was also someone on the lower ranks of the social order for whom a big crime would offer instant recognition. Mijailo Mijailovic may well have been a mentally unstable, socially marginal person for whom Anna Lindh represented all that made him feel that way. She was attractive, successful and, in this context, a political celebrity. In her person and in the politics she represented, she was Swedish society. As lead police investigator Leif Jennekvist put it, when reflecting on the killer's possible motivation, "she became the object of his disappointment." All the hurt and misunderstanding that he felt was being inflicted on him by Swedish society was reflected in this representative figure (Jennekvist 2006:196). His murderous act would communicate this to the world.[16]

Regardless of what could be shown in court, the murder of Anna Lindh was political in the broad meaning of the term. From the point of view of the killer and at the most abstract level, attacking Anna Lindh might well have been meant as an attack on Swedish society, as Jennekvist and others believe. Beneath this, Anna Lindh was also a representative of the governing party, of its policies in the Balkans, and those with regard to the EU. As a representative figure of what Swedish society might have meant to Mijailo Mijailovic, the targeted victim could in fact have been anyone, as the defense attorneys claimed—any Swedish citizen, that is. This was also the way the crime was first handled by the Swedish police, as we will see later. But the victim was not any citizen; she was Anna Lindh, the Swedish foreign minister, representing the government in power. In the television reportage from the crime scene one can clearly see a large poster just outside the entrance to the mall where Lindh was attacked. The larger-than-life poster shows her broadly smiling face accompanied by a text about the EMU referendum. In addition to this very public campaign, Lindh had been actively involved in formulating and implementing Sweden's and the EU's policies in the Balkans. In March 1999, Lindh was among those EU leaders who issued the final warning to former Yugoslavian president Slobodan Milosevic before the NATO bombing of Serbian targets. These targets eventually included Mijailo Mijailovic's hometown. Each day during the eleven-week bombing campaign, there were protest demonstrations led by Swedish Serbians in Stockholm's Sergels Torg, with increasing anger shown toward both the prime minister and Anna Lindh (Rönnegård 2008:118–19). Subsequent newspaper reports would claim that Mijailovic had made threatening remarks against both Göran Persson and Lindh during this period. Later, in March 2003, Swedish media reporters from Belgrade covering the assassination of Serbia's prime minister interviewed Anna Lindh, who had been only a few hundred meters away when he was killed. All this could not have escaped the killer's attention, especially given his keen interest in political affairs (Unsgaard 2006, Rönnegård 2008). This was, at the very least, a politically motivated murder, if not a political assassination.

MASS MEDIA AND THE POLICE

Especially since the murder of Olof Palme, the Swedish police have become increasingly aware of public relations and the role of the media in shaping public opinion, not least in relation to their own image. This new awareness was, of course, not merely a result of this unsolved crime; the exponential increase in the media's significance in contemporary society has been generally recognized, and though the media is highly regulated, Sweden is no exception. But Hans Holmer's attempt to use the media to amplify his own role in the first stages of the Palme investigation has become something of a reference point for police authorities. The police in charge of the Anna Lindh investigation were very aware of Holmer and his media-amplified shortcomings. This affected their concern with public perception and also their own handling of the crime. Not only were there new professionals, such as public relations officers and press secretaries whose job it was to mediate relations between the police authorities and the media, but those in charge of the investigation took the media into account nearly every step of the way. As stated earlier, the police were very skillful in their use of the now almost-obligatory daily press briefings. As an evidence-gathering agency, they were able to make use of these meeting with the media for their own purposes, appealing for help from the public, for example, as well as using the press as a vehicle for maintaining public sympathy for their ongoing efforts. A conscious effort was made to balance the need to keep the press corps satisfied and to satisfy their own need for information and goodwill from the public. The entire situation had to be delicately balanced and treated tactically and with care. It could not be left to chance.

The mass media served as a conduit to reach the public while, at the same time, being a collective actor that needed to be taken into account. Those leading the police investigation were forced to devise a media strategy and to even develop diversionary tactics with regard to the mass of journalists covering the story. For example, as recounted by Leif Jennerkvist (2006), police investigators sent a group of officers to decoy reporters so that they themselves could attend to their real goals without media disturbance. This was the case during the arrest of Mijailo Mijailovic. Police officials knew that a sudden deployment of officers would arouse the curiosity of the press corps assembled outside the police headquarters. To avoid having their tactics exposed, they deployed a party of police in another direction, hoping that the press corps would take up pursuit. The plan worked, and the subject was arrested without added drama. When later queried as to why they had not arrested Mijailovic earlier when there was enough evidence to do so, the officer in charge said that it was to avoid putting him through the media barrage of attention that would certainly have followed. They waited until they had gathered more certain evidence of his guilt, such as his DNA.

FRAMING THE PERPETRATOR

The Palme investigation offered several perpetrators, first the generalized and faceless conspirators, the PKK and other "terrorist" organizations; then the so-called phantom man, an artist-generated and media-circulated composite image of the "33-year-old"; and finally, Christer Pettersson, who gave not only a real face but a personality to the perpetrator. Pettersson's life story became the subject of thousands of pages and hours of media representation. From this the Swedish public learned a great deal about criminal life on the social margins.

The first image of a perpetrator was an artist composite based on witness testimony, which Hans Holmer released in a televised press conference on March 6, 1986, six days after the murder. This image was reproduced in the print media, and there were lines of people awaiting the afternoon papers, which carried it in large format on their front pages. Interviews by television reporters found that people desperately wanted to see "what the murderer looked like" (*Svt nyheter*, March 6, 1986). Holmer said Swedish police had all to gain and nothing to lose by sending these pictures through the media. The lack of technical support for this distribution among Swedish police was duly noted, as most police stations around the country lacked the machinery necessary to receive an electronic image, so they had to be sent by ordinary mail. This image of the perpetrator could have been of almost anyone, but at least it was someone; a believable face of the killer, as one of those anonymous Swedes said in response to a reporter's question. On March 24, the police released another image, which they said represented an accomplice of the killer. This image was popularly known as "the shadow," while the first one was called "the phantom." The second image was also based on witness testimony, which differed from the testimony that had been responsible for the phantom image. It later came to light that this witness, a man with an immigrant background, came forward to produce a counter image to the first image, as the former looked "too much like an immigrant" (Nilsson 2001:58). Both images (each of which turned out to be based on mistaken identity) were widely circulated in the media. The police received hundreds of telephone calls about them, including one mentioning that Christer Pettersson looked very much like "the shadow," and another claiming that he looked like the "phantom." (Nilsson 2001:112). Several leads were pursued in the following weeks, all of which turned out to be false. The most damaging, the rounding up of 22 members of the PKK in January 1987 and their almost immediate release, brought to a head an ongoing conflict between those members of the police force leading the investigation and the district attorney. This eventually led to Holmer's resignation in February 1987. After this, the investigation ground to a halt as the federal police, now in charge, were forced to retrace the steps of the old investigation. One of their first actions was to plough through all the tips that had been amassed, and it was in this pile that the name Christer Pettersson appeared again and again.

As previously mentioned, the police had already interviewed Pettersson in connection with the murder two days after its occurrence. He came to their attention because his name appeared on a list of those who had committed violent crimes in the vicinity of the crime scene. After his testimony was taken, Pettersson was released. Although the police never lost interest in him, it was not until Lisbet Palme pointed him out in a videotaped lineup in December 1988, nearly three years after the murder that he became a prime suspect. Pettersson was in that lineup because investigators could place him near the scene of the crime at the time of the murder and knew that he had once been observed with a weapon similar to the one that had killed Palme. Pettersson was tried and convicted for the murder of Olof Palme in the summer of 1989. He was freed by a higher court in the fall. All this was followed closely in the mass media.

ANNA LINDH

From the point of view of the police, the murder of Anna Lindh was resolved within two weeks. CCTV cameras provided images of a suspected perpetrator within days of the attack. The Nike-clad suspect was given the name "the NK-man," from the name of the shopping mall where the images had been taken and the murder had occurred. After one false arrest, which led to the media barrage described, Mijailo Mijailovic was arrested and tried. Because Swedish norms protect the suspect, the only images that were broadcast were artist renditions that showed a hunched-over human figure covered with a blanket. At the first hearing, there was as much focus on the defense attorney, who was also a member of parliament, as on the suspect himself. As it was in the defense's interest to focus on its client's mental health, it was not long before this became the central theme of media reportage. This followed the police framing of the suspect, a young, mentally unstable individual. The fact of his immigrant background was of course a subject, but never a major one. This in part followed from the general norms of media reportage, where mentioning the social background of suspects has been the subject of great debate and much criticism. *Dagens Nyheter* printed its own reflections and readers' responses to the pros and cons of using constructions such as "the 33-year-old," rather than the name and photograph of a suspect. From the day of his arrest, media coverage of Mijailo Mijailovic referred to the "24-year-old," while reportage focused on the technical evidence and on his history of mental illness. The first background description in *Dagens Nyheter* on September 26, two days after his arrest, identified the suspect as someone born in Sweden, but whose parents came from a village outside of Belgrade. The report went on to give an account of his youth and informed readers that he had spent his earlier school years in Yugoslavia before returning to Sweden at the age of 13. An account was also given of his arrest in relation to the stabbing of his father. This was immediately followed by what would become the main story line, the history of mental illness surrounding the family, and Mijailovic himself. An editorial in the same paper carried the headline, "Many Do Not Get Sufficient Care" (6), which was followed by a criticism of the state of mental health care in the nation. This would become one of the dominant themes in all discussions of the perpetrator. The unsigned lead editorial in the following day's paper noted that the perpetrator's "tattered background once again points a spotlight on Swedish psychiatry and the criminal justice system" (*Dagens Nyheter,* September 27, 2003:2), while an inside headline on September 28 carried the story that the police had dropped off the perpetrator at the mental health emergency room on the evening before the attack.

The more sensationalist afternoon papers were a little less self-reflective. *Kvällsposten,* September 25, 2003, carried the huge headline, "He Shaved His Hair and Eyebrows, the Day After the Murder," over a blurred image of the perpetrator. This was followed by stories and photos of his friends, neighbors and, most significantly, his "role model," a man with a Serbian name, identified as a *torped* (hired gun) . The main theme here was the perpetrator's alleged hatred for Anna Lindh.

As an alternative, media reportage could have focused on the perpetrator's immigrant background and the possible implications this might have for his political views or, from another angle, for the political views of some of its readers and viewers. *Dagens Nyheter* carried accounts and photographs from the Serbian press the day after the arrest, revealing the latter's keen interest in the perpetrator. Playing up the immigrant background might have attracted some and alienated others, but it clearly was a possible narrative frame that could have been pursued. The first media reports from the scene, based on interviews with those in the mall at the time, describe a man with a "Swedish" appearance as the attacker. The Nike designer sweatshirt and "Just Do it" cap did not signal "immigrant" to these witnesses, though some of them apparently saw camouflage pants and an army jacket instead of the sweatshirt and cargo pants actually worn by Mijailovic, which might have done so. He was also reported as *ovårdad* (unkempt) and, possibly, a homeless person. One of the key witnesses interviewed by the police was a barber in a nearby mall, who reported a very stressed and tense young man demanding to have his hair cut just minutes after the murder. This turned out to be Mijailovic, who thus seemed to be keenly aware of his appearance. The notion that a homeless person would be the perpetrator was quickly ruled out by the police as unlikely, given the upscale character of the mall, where any such person would have clearly stood out and been observed by the many private security guards in the building. This was a perpetrator who was very conscious of his appearance and sensitive to the eyes of others. Given his background as one of the very few "immigrants" in an upper-middle-class neighborhood, this does not seem at all strange. This was a perpetrator who not only was used to being seen, but who wanted to be seen—but not as an outsider. Mijailo Mijailovic wanted to fit in, but for a multitude of reasons, could not. His murderous act was his way of closing that possibility. He was now a Serb and, in his own eyes, a political exile. In January 2004, Swedish television broadcast an interview with Mijailo Mijailovic's grandfather in his Serbian village, in which the latter apologized to the Swedish people for his grandson's actions.

PALME AND LINDH

In comparing the murders of Olof Palme and Anna Lindh, one is struck by the differences as much as by the similarities. Both took place in a public space, marking them as an attack on the basic democratic principle of free movement, but they differed dramatically in their mise-en-scène. We still do not know who killed Olof Palme or why, but the attack took place late on a Friday night on a relatively uncrowded city street. While this might be a time to be out on the town, this was the end of February, which meant that many would be away during the traditional winter-sport vacation that closed Stockholm schools for the week. This also affected the police corps, as many heads of department were away, including Hans Holmer. Even if it had been an impulsive act, the killer had chosen a time and place with relatively few people, with a clear escape route, and where the chances of being observed were minimized. This appears to be a cold-blooded assassination by a cold-blooded assassin. In contrast, Anna Lindh was attacked in broad daylight in a crowded shopping mall, where there would be little chance of remaining unobserved and a slim likelihood of escape, even if one could probably count on getting lost in the crowd, as the killer did. The attacker wanted witnesses; he needed an audience because he had something to express. Mijailo Mijailovic may have acted impulsively out of personal frustration, but he chose both a target and a location that would bring attention to himself, well beyond the confines of that shopping mall. His audience was not merely the anonymous crowd that would gather around the victim, but the larger national and international audience that could only come through attacking an iconic figure. The fact that he chose a political celebrity rather than some other official implies that he sought to send a rather specific political message, drawing attention not merely to himself, but also to what the person he attacked represented. This was a communicative act, but in any such action what it might mean to an audience must be taken into account. Anna Lindh may have represented his particular vision of Swedish society, but she represented something different to others. Although Mijailovic could not know exactly who that audience was or how they would react, he knew that killing Anna Lindh would send a meaningful message, one that would grab their attention and demand interpretation.

One could ask why the current Swedish prime minister was not the target. One will never know, of course, but it is possible that Anna Lindh was the victim of an opportunistic attack. Since the murder of Olof Palme, the protection of Swedish political leaders has significantly increased, although, as the murder of Lindh suggests, not sufficiently.[17] Göran Persson was under constant protection and was not one for close contact with the public. His public performances were always stylized and distant, taking the form of ritualized press conferences and public speeches (Franchell 2009). On such occasions he was always well protected. Shopping in a Stockholm mall was not one of his habits. In this sense, Lindh made herself available in the same way that Olof Palme did when he attended the cinema without bodyguards. But there was more to it than opportunity: Göran Persson may have been the prime minister, but beyond that, it would be hard to call him a representative figure. A skillful politician, Persson was not a public figure in the same sense as Olof Palme or Anna Lindh were.

The choice of weapon also marks a difference between the two murders. Olof Palme was killed with a handgun, which, like its user, was anonymous and impersonal. A handgun creates distance and requires discipline to use, but requires no personal contact between perpetrator and victim. Using a handgun necessitates a certain technical competence and self-control. Using a knife, on the other hand, demands closeness, contact with the victim. It also requires physical strength and involves the risk of coming face-to-face with one's victim. The knife is an emotional weapon in a way that the handgun need not be. Moreover, the choice of either of these weapons affects not only the relation between perpetrator and victim, but also the way others interpret the act. Palme was shot—executed—one could say. Lindh was attacked—brutally beaten—in front of an audience of onlookers. Palme's killer carried out a task in a more or less rational and instrumental way. Lindh's attacker performed his action: he engaged an audience in a meaningful act of communication. He had something to say and the choice of weapon helped him say it. This choice was not simply a practical matter, as Mijailovic owned a handgun, but rather a meaningful choice, a communicative act. The knife helped him communicate his message.

The choice of weapon also affected the search for the perpetrator. The use of a handgun requires a particular set of skills and a social network, especially in a social context where they are strictly regulated. It implies a conspiracy and professional skills. The fact that Palme was shot helped lead the police investigation in a particular direction—toward politically motivated conspiracy. One of the most infamous images from the early stages of the failed Palme investigation is one of Hans Holmer holding up two handguns of the type used in the murder. A knife, on the other hand, is easier to come by; anyone can buy one, but not everyone can use one to attack another human being. This led the police investigation and the mass-media reportage in quite another direction—in search of a lone, mentally unstable individual with a history of violence. The knife helped move the narrative away from political conspiracy and away from serious consideration of the more politically sensitive possible motives of the killer. The fact that Anna Lindh was stabbed and the attack labeled *grov misshandel* (felonious assault), immediately turned police attention away from political conspiracy and to a lookout for a mentally disturbed individual (Rönnegård 2008:21). This had immediate consequences; because it was not classified as an extraordinary occurrence but as a regular criminal act, the number of police involved in the search for the attacker was severely limited, and a national alarm was not issued. It was not until later that the status of the crime was raised and police tactics were dramatically altered. The attack weapon thus affected the original police framing, their definition of the situation. As we shall see, the SÄPO defined the situation differently and went into another mode of operation. When they received the report of a knife attack against the foreign minister, the Stockholm police chief in charge made the decision to classify it as an ordinary, rather than an extraordinary, crime, which would formally have brought special rules (implemented since the murder of Olof Palme) into play (Rönnegård 2008). For the police, the status of the victim did not change the characterization of the crime. The police chief later justified this by saying, "Everyone should be treated equally" (Rönnegård 2008:13–14). The victim, in other words, could have been anyone.

The above offers an example of how a particular element, in this case a knife, can more or less shape a narrative. Something to also consider is how narrative shapes actions. The knife attack on Anna Lindh was labeled as a serious, but not overly dangerous, attack on a private person. This had major consequences for how the investigation was organized and carried out, at least in the first hours. Since it was not labeled as "extraordinary," no extra resources were made available and no strategic command center was set up (Rönnegård 2006).[18] On the other hand, the security police, those in charge of protecting political figures, focused not on the level of the assault or the means, but on who was attacked. For them, an attack against the foreign minister, regardless of the degree of its severity, was a threat to national security—something that set in motion a wide range of response. In the first case, the knife closed a narrative; in the latter, it had no meaning.

CONCLUSION

How do we explain the fact of these two political assassinations, in relative close proximity, in a country with no recent history of political violence? The American study mentioned in the opening chapter placed Sweden on the very lower end of a scale and would not have predicted their occurrence. In fact, its special appendix on Sweden seemed to suggest that this was the exceptional case in a world full of political violence. This confirms very nicely Sweden's view of itself. The idea of being different, exceptional, that things like political assassinations don't happen here, is one of the founding myths of modern Sweden. This myth was first formulated with the idea of the *folkhem* (the nation as a large family with a place for all, including the rich and the unruly). This grounding idea of modern social democracy, which also underwrote the great compromise between capital and labor, was first formulated by Per Albin Hansson in 1932. It was central to the idea of the middle way and to the Swedish model, Olof Palme being its last representative figure. One can say that the two died together. One function of a founding myth is to provide a grand narrative through which a collective understands itself, providing a point of reference for collective identification. The folkhem was, for many Swedes, what made their nation unique. Part of this uniqueness was that violence was an exception and, in its extreme forms, happened elsewhere. Swedes knew how to compromise, how to mediate conflict, and how to control themselves; they took care of themselves and of each other. The benevolent state and its noncorrupt and caring representatives were the prime vehicle for ensuring this collective good. Forms of behavior that did not conform to—or confirm—this myth were considered aberrations. This came out clearly in the reactions to the murder of Olof Palme. For those who chose to see it, there were plenty of indications that Palme could be the object of an assassination. There were a number of threats made to his life, from inside as well as outside the country. There were also a number of incidents of political violence, including the occupation of the Yugoslavian embassy in Stockholm in 1971 and the hostage-taking at the German embassy in Stockholm in 1976, both of which occurred within the recent past. There were members of the Swedish police corps and the military who made no secret of their extreme dislike for Palme and what he represented. All this was known, yet not seen. When it did become the object of media orchestration, in the so-called *polis-spår* (police-lead or trail) it remained merely that—a matter of media-fueled exaggeration, the stuff of crime novels and films.

Palme was himself a victim of this myth of Swedish exceptionalism. In choosing to release his body guards—the fact that he had some is revealing—in the middle of the day based on the reasoning that he would be working in his office and would then be at home over the weekend, he was acting on this belief and on the principle that was connected to it. Beyond the formality of selecting its leaders through regular elections, one cornerstone of an open, democratic society is that all citizens, including elected officials, have the right to assemble and to move freely through public space. Palme was applying this principle and was shot as a result. In this sense, he could have been anyone, and the principle would still have been breached. But Palme was not anyone. He was the charismatic Swedish prime minister. And it was in this capacity that he was shot: as a representative figure of the nation, more than just any citizen exercising a basic right. Why did this happen in a nation where it should not happen? Answering this question does not depend on who the actual killer was: there was motive enough to go around. But political murder had not occurred in such a long time. Why now? And with Anna Lindh, why again? The simple answer to both questions is "because it was possible." Both Palme and Lindh made themselves available, in part because "such things don't happen here." But there must be more to it than mere opportunity, means, and motive. Palme and Lindh were killed precisely because they were representative figures of a nation that thought itself to be exceptional, to be above and outside of the violence that permeates the rest of the world. We know who the killer of Anna Lindh was, and we have discussed his possible motives in this chapter. We don't know who Palme's killer is, but the motivation does not really matter. Both are cases of political assassinations in the sense that they were directed against representatives of the collective, the body public, in a country that considered itself exceptional. This is no longer the case. In this sense, one can speak of a cultural crisis if not a cultural trauma: although the assassination of Palme and Lindh did not lead to prolonged public discourse on the foundations of Swedish society, their cumulative result was to explode one of its myths.

CHAPTER 5

THE END OF TOLERANCE: THE MURDERS OF PIM FORTUYN AND THEO VAN GOGH

"Pim Fortuyn is a victim of the Sixties,"
Sander van Walsum (*De Volkskrant* editor) May 8, 2002
(According to Van Walsum, his murder marked the definitive end to the 1960s!)

THEO AND PIM

In a television interview recorded in 1997, Theo van Gogh spoke with Pim Fortuyn on the latter's views on the European Union (EU). It was a serious and factual conversation, with Fortuyn presenting in very clear terms his position against the idea of a united Europe with its own parliament and governing elite, as he put it. Fortuyn spoke eloquently for a federation of European nation states.[1] At that point (1997), Van Gogh, who appeared in jeans, a white T-shirt, and suspenders, was a fledgling filmmaker and media commentator, and Fortuyn, impeccably dressed in suit and tie, was a professor at Erasmus University, specializing in employment conditions within the public sector. Both took their respective roles very seriously. Fortuyn would soon leave his academic career behind and set out as a freelance author and lecturer, whereas Van Gogh would continue his career as a filmmaker and producer, finally achieving a career breakthrough in 2003 with the film entitled *Interview*. Although he began to make a name for himself as a columnist and commentator with his critical views on Islam and Dutch multicultural policy, Fortuyn's real breakthrough would come with the republication of his book, *The Islamization of our Culture*, in the wake of the 9/11 attacks on New

York's World Trade Center. The new edition of the book carried the same message as the one originally published in 1997, but now it had a new cover and a new audience. The cover featured a photograph of Fortuyn, seated face-to-face with an Islamic cleric. Both were dressed in their finest "uniforms." Fortuyn, with his characteristic shaved head and perfectly tailored suit and tie, appeared in stark contrast to the fully bearded Imam, dressed in flowing robes and a turban. The message was clear—Fortuyn, representing Western culture, dared to confront the "Islamic threat," but through conversation, not violence. The subtitle shown on the cover proclaimed, "My words are my weapons."

Fortuyn's words became increasingly sharper and his style more confrontational as he warmed to his new theme, Muslim integration and the ostensible Islamic threat to European culture. As he moved from the academic culture of critical discourse—as Alvin Gouldner, one of Fortuyn's sociological referents called it—to the more simplified, black-and-white rhetoric of media-based political discourse, Fortuyn's already-beaming self-confidence became more pronounced, appearing to some as arrogance. He was a formidable opponent for those who chose to confront him in his native realm, on a sofa or around a table in front of a microphone and television camera. This can be clearly seen in his confrontations with political rival Ad Melkert, especially in the last interview, broadcast the Sunday before his death. Fortuyn was ruthless with the staid Melkert. His voice changed timbre with his manner and his message, and went from harshly confrontational to sarcastic. He laughed in his opponent's face at the implied suggestion that he, Fortuyn, was aligning himself with Hitler and Mussolini with his repeated calls for a "strong man" who would stand up for European values. This occurred after the Dutch Labor Party (PvdA) leader's reference to the Dutch "history of occupation and the Holocaust," and that residue of collective memory, which the phrase "strong man" calls to mind. From this harsh style, Fortuyn moved easily to a serious and knowledgeable tone when Melkert confronted him with the issue of unemployment. Here, Fortuyn was again on familiar ground, given his academic research credentials and his neoliberal solutions: reduce the bureaucracy and create an efficient public sector, he proclaimed. In this confrontation, one can observe something more than a conflict between political points of view; there is also a generational struggle going on in which a generation shaped by the Second World War is confronted by a postwar generation seeking both to confront that past and to move beyond it. Fortuyn's sarcastic laughter at references to the Dutch experience during the Second World War signaled both an acknowledgement of this past as well as a dismissal. Yes, you and your voters were shaped by that experience and interpret the contemporary world through its frame, but for me and my generation things look different, he seemed to be saying.

There is something more than rhetoric and performance to consider in all this. Fortuyn was an adept media performer, and at the same time, a vote-seeking populist (see also Pels 2003). He clearly wanted to be prime minister, or at the very least, an influential politician, and he appeared ready to do what was necessary in order to achieve that goal. But he did undergo something of a conversion with regard to his political beliefs, something that moved beyond opportunism. In the amateur YouTube video *De Nacht van Pim Fortuyn* (Fortuyn's Night) depicting his last meeting with representatives of Leefbaar Nederland (LN) an antiestablishment, locally based political movement , during which he attempts to convince party officials to keep him on as their leader, Fortuyn revealed another side of his personality and of his politics. When the crucial issue of a newspaper (*Volkskrant,* see below) interview and his statements about Muslims and Islam came up for discussion, Fortuyn became extremely angry. He started gesturing wildly and forcefully, much in the manner of a demagogue, claiming that he was the lone individual standing up for "our civilization," defending it against those who would destroy it, those Turks and Moroccans who "steal from our old people." "This is what our supporters want," he shouted, injecting an element of opportunism. Yet, from the force of his statement, it seems clear that he was also speaking out of conviction.

THE MURDER OF PIM FORTUYN

When Volkert van der Graaf shot and killed the maverick politician Pim Fortuyn on May 6, 2002, there had not been a political murder in the Netherlands since the 1600s.[2] It was a week before an election that promised to place Fortuyn in a leading role in the precarious coalition-building that marks Dutch politics, with some polls indicating he could very well become prime minister. A former sociology professor, Fortuyn had seemingly come from nowhere to a central role in party politics with the aid of a skillfully orchestrated campaign. For the political establishment he was, as one party leader put it, "a very dangerous man" (G. Zalm, cited in Faber 2008:228). For others, he was a new Jorg Haider, a contemporary representative of National Socialism and the extreme right. For his killer, he was "a populist with a huge ego," who endangered not only vulnerable social groups such as pensioners, immigrants, women, and Jews, but also animals and the environment (Faber 2008:229). Whereas his political opponents thought he must be defeated, Volkert van der Graaf thought he must be stopped.

The murder of Pim Fortuyn distinguishes itself from the other murders discussed in this book, in that this was clearly a political assassination. Although not yet elected to political office, the victim had become a major figure in public debates, representing a newly formed constituency around issues to which he helped give voice. The head of a new party, Fortuyn would, at the very least, have become an outspoken member of parliament after the coming election. His death aroused the emotions not only of a community of supporters, but also of the nation. The perpetrator was also clear in his motivations; he viewed Pim Fortuyn as a danger to social life: "*Hij werd in mijn ogen een gevaar voor de samenleving*" (In my eyes he was a danger to society; cited in Faber 2008:227) and set about to kill him in the name of humanity. At his trial, defense attorneys did nothing to deny this, though the question of his exact motives became an issue at the sentencing hearing: Did he kill in the name of animal rights or human rights? Was he following a political or a moral agenda? There was never a claim made to mental instability. Van der Graff was a married man with a young daughter. He was college-educated, and had no history of mental illness, though he had once attempted suicide. He was solidly Dutch, with blue eyes and thinning blond hair, and was born in 1969 in the Zeeland city of Middelburg. His father was a schoolteacher and his mother a homemaker, and he was raised in the conservative Protestant atmosphere of the western provinces. Always an avid bird-watcher and naturalist (interests shared with his father), Van der Graaf became interested in environmental politics in his first year of college and a full-time activist during his second. This too distinguishes him from the other assassins we have discussed. Volkert van der Graff clearly set out to kill Pim Fortuyn and took full responsibility for his actions at his trial. The murder and the escape were carefully planned; this was not an impulsive action and the perpetrator was not an impulsive man. The killer viewed his act as one of duty, a duty to society and to humanity. In his eyes, Fortuyn was a danger to the Dutch way of life, to the democratic, law-bound state, as well as to those human beings most in need of its protection. Yet it was he who broke the law when he set out to murder Fortuyn. Why this was the case warrants further investigation.

In a television interview two months prior to his assassination, Fortuyn had himself proclaimed the possibility of an attack on his person. Already the victim of two pie-in-the-face assaults, Fortuyn accused the Dutch government and the mass media of creating an atmosphere in which another more serious attack appeared imminent. To great applause from the live studio audience, he said, "If something were to happen to me, they are in part responsible..."[3] Fortuyn was referring to the way he was being portrayed in some parts of the mass media and, most directly, to the way his political opponents, primarily on the Left, were reacting to his popularity. He claimed that party leaders and the press were "demonizing" him, by which he meant that they were associating him with right-wing Europeans like Le Pen in France and Haider in Austria. According to Margry (2003:109), "Despite what his own supporters considered 'demonization' and thanks to his cultivating his status as a political underdog, his popularity only increased. Fortuyn was able to strategically use demonization, the so-called 'underdog effect,' his role as a victim, and his openness about his shortcomings and peculiarities." It was thus possible at the time to view these remarks as strategic, as part of a plan to paint himself as an outsider who was feared by the political establishment and was thus a viable and powerful alternative to "politics as usual." When Fortuyn was murdered, his words looked more prophetic than strategic. This was neither the first nor the only time Fortuyn had expressed such fears. There was thus a story line already in place before the attack on May 6, and it would be drawn upon by the mass media in their construction of the murder as a significant event. It was a theme also drawn upon by Fortuyn's supporters, who were quick to blame the Left—from the PvdA to anarchists—for instigating his death. As part of its first reportage, on May 7, 2002, the conservative *De Telegraaf* offered the headline "Fortuyn's Great Fear Becomes Reality" ("*Fortuyn's grote angst werd waarheid*") quoting from an earlier interview in which Fortuyn expressed the fear that something would happen to him before the election. Although Van der Graaf was the obvious perpetrator and Fortuyn his victim, the struggle to define the meaning of the murder began the moment the shots were fired. The mass media would play a central role in this process—they helped set the tone and provide the themes for how this occurrence would be narrated.

Pim Fortuyn was a formidable personality. He was born Wilhelmus Simon Petrus Fortijn (he changed the spelling later because it added more flair) in 1948 to a Catholic family in a small village northwest of Amsterdam and grew up in what he once described as "a Catholic school, Catholic hospital, Catholic work organizations, Catholic pillar" (quoted in Chorus and Galan 2002:127). Fortuyn studied sociology in Amsterdam, receiving an advanced degree in social science from the University of Groningen, where he later taught and conducted research. His academic interests centered around the quality of working life and organizational effectiveness. These interests were reflected in his politics—his interest in work relations brought him close to the PvdA, and the interest in organizational effectiveness re-emerged as Fortuyn moved politically rightward after quitting the PvdA in 1989. In the mid-1990s, he joined the Volkspartij voor Vrijheid en Democratie VVD (a center-right party), and in this sense, his political trajectory bears some similarity to that of Hirsi Ali, as will be discussed below. The interest in organizations and public administration was put into practice when Fortuyn outlined his political program as prospective leader of LN. He highlighted two central issues: reducing the bureaucracy in local government and limiting the number of political refugees. In one graphic interview, Fortuyn made his views clear when he stated that "the Netherlands is full," there is no room for more immigrants, especially from Muslim countries. "I say: everyone who is in, will stay in. They are our Moroccan boys, we cannot burden [Moroccan]

King Hassan with them…But I do say it should be over now. We have enough" (cited in Uitermark 2010:78). Fortuyn was also in favor of national military service and nuclear power, both contentious issues at the time. When he assumed leadership in 2001, LN was a fledging organization, an attempt at creating a national party out of a string of surprisingly successful locally based citizen's groups, all bearing the name "Leefbar." The term translates as "livable," and was used in front of the name of the city or town, for example, Leefbar Utrecht or Leefbar Hilversum. The "Leefbar" movement began as a series of urban grassroots citizens' initiatives that focused on issues such as better schools and care for the aged and that achieved surprising success in local elections. The possibility of having Fortuyn as a national leader marked a major step and required a program with a broader appeal. Fortuyn's fame as a media personality—he was a constant figure on radio and television and was well known as a commentator, lecturer, and author—was something that could make this possible. With the charismatic Fortuyn as its representative, popular support for the party soared.[4] Until the previously mentioned infamous interview in the *Volkskrant* (February 9, 2002), in which he raised the possibility of changing Article 1 of the Dutch Constitution, which contained an anti-discrimination provision, the main themes mobilizing his supporters were the more typical antiestablishment populist ones. Before the interview, Theo van Gogh, whom he consulted on occasion, advised him to condemn racism and said that the following day's headline ought to read, "Pim Fortuyn: I Find Racism Reprehensible" (Chorus and Galan 2002:138). However, things didn't turn out that way. The headline of the *Volkskrant* on Saturday, February 9, 2002, read "Fortuyn: Close the Borders to Islam." The content of this interview, particularly his labeling of Islam as a "backward culture," offended many in the leadership of the "Leefbar" movement, and Fortuyn was forced to resign. He reacted by forming his own party, the Lijst Pim Fortuyn (LPF), and it was in this capacity that he appeared on the verge of a sweeping victory in the elections of May 15, 2002.

THE MURDER

Pim Fortuyn was shot a few minutes past 6:00 P.M. on Monday, May 6, 2002, in a Hilversum Mediapark parking lot just after recording an interview. His killer waited for over an hour, hidden behind a parked car.[5] As Fortuyn walked toward his own automobile in the company of his chauffer, he stopped momentarily to converse with the moderator who had interviewed him; the killer rushed to meet them, but stopped about five feet away, apparently because he did not want to come face-to-face with his victim. With his weapon wrapped in a plastic bag to avoid leaving fingerprints, Van der Graaf raised both hands and fired off five shots. The first bullets struck Fortuyn in the chest and throat. The killer then fled the scene, with Fortuyn's chauffeur in pursuit. He was captured by police officers within six minutes. In his car, police found maps of the area and a schedule of Fortuyn's appointments, all taken from the Internet. In fact, the killer's image of his victim was gleaned from mass media. Van der Graaf learned about his victim through magazine and newspaper articles and through the television interviews he viewed online. As he recounted at his trial, he had never met the man or seen Fortuyn before that day, but recognized him immediately through his voice and his movements. Fortuyn was a media figure and a public performer, and according to Van der Graaf, one was never sure if he was serious or was merely playing. It was a pair of interviews, however, one televised and one printed, that apparently convinced Van der Graaf that Pim Fortuyn was a serious threat that must be stopped. A televised interview on the weekly newsmagazine *Business Class,* where he was a regular commentator, in which Fortuyn spoke out in defense of animal breeders and against animal-rights activists and called them "fundamentalists," was the first to capture his killer's attention. The second was the *Volkskrant* interview mentioned above.

The perpetrator was very careful in his choice of clothing and was mindful of his appearance before the act. He chose a bomber jacket, baseball cap (much would be made in media reports about the baseball cap), and a hooded sweater, with sunglasses to cover his eyes and latex gloves his hands. While driving to Hilversum, he stopped to buy an electric shaver because he felt he needed a shave (Faber 2008). When he tested it in the car and found that it didn't work, he thought about returning to the store, but realized that he lacked the time, being well aware of his victim's schedule. This bad purchase upset him as much as his grizzled chin. He later claimed to have acted alone and out of duty, telling no one, neither his wife nor his activist friends, what he planned to do. Killing Fortuyn had been something that animal-rights activists had talked about, as a police wiretap made before the murder revealed. After a series of fire bombings and other incidents involving animal-rights activists, police had begun tapping the phones of some offices and leaders; Volkert van der Graaf was not among them, however. But the possibility of attacking Pim Fortuyn was in the air, discussed in activist circles and in the mass media by no less than Fortuyn himself.

Why Van der Graaf attacked Fortuyn then and there is easier to answer than why he decided to kill him. The timing concerned the upcoming election. It is true, as some have speculated, that he could have waited to see how well Fortuyn actually did in the election before killing him. But recent newspaper accounts reported Fortuyn to be far ahead in the polls, something that actually turned out to be false, but which must have pushed Van der Graaf into action (Pels reports that the polling results were wrongly declared). Better to kill him before he and his party achieved a great victory, which would have ensured them parliamentary representation, even in the absence of Pim Fortuyn. The place itself appears to have been chosen primarily for pragmatic reasons; there were likely to be few witnesses in a media park with restricted access. Van der Graaf was able to avoid the attendants and sneak into the parking lot undetected. The attack and the escape were well planned, at least on paper.

Like the perpetrator, the victim was also very mindful of his appearance. Always impeccably dressed, Fortuyn wore a business suit and a characteristic brightly colored necktie at the time of his death. He was once voted the best-dressed man in the Netherlands, and flamboyancy was part of his public persona. He claimed to model his political image after JFK, who he said was "open, stylish and energetic," but Fortuyn went far beyond the former U.S. president in his pursuit of these ideals.[6] He was openly gay, dandyish, and decadent in his lifestyle, and the political energy he manifested was aimed at issues that were in direct opposition to his supposed role model. Fortuyn's openly professed homosexuality would provide a thread in the narratives around his death that differs substantially from that of the others whom we have studied. The day after his assassination, the *NRC* (May 7, 2002:3) reported that a Dutch organization, aimed at protecting and promoting the rights of homosexuals, called the murder a threat to Dutch democracy.[7] The homosexuality that Fortuyn professed was always cloaked in traditional masculine mannerisms, however, and his confrontational argumentative style, especially when he performed for the media, was as tough as that of any of his opponents. He also joked about his erotic conquest of Moroccan youth, something that must have made supporting him easier for those to whom homosexuality was anathema.

MEDIA ACCOUNTS: MANAGING THE PUBLIC MOOD

Given the time and place of the murder and the personality of the victim, the first media coverage occurred simultaneously with the real-time occurrence. As with the other assassinations analyzed in this book, the role of live coverage, not only in spreading information but also in prompting emotional response, must be recognized. Not only was there a large national audience, but coverage of the circumstances surrounding Fortuyn's death spread quickly around the globe. According to Margry (2003:111, see also Pantti and Wieten 2005), "A large portion of Dutch adults only turned off the TV in the early hours of the morning. In the following days, from most of the television and newspaper commentators, and many of those interviewed, it appeared that there was a general consensus that The Netherlands would never be the same again." The normal six o'clock radio and television news broadcasts were interrupted by bulletins and on-the-scene reportage. The first reports were heard almost immediately, over the radio, which is not surprising as Hilversum is a center of

Dutch mass communications. The on-the-scene reporter, clearly emotionally upset and out of breath, gave a factual account of the attack (as it was then known), while the police, and he himself, were pursing the killer. A few minutes later, the regular television news broadcast was similarly interrupted, and one could observe the emotional changes occurring as the newsreader shifted from his prepared text to the live message coming into his earphones. He first reported that Pim Fortuyn had been stabbed, only to change that a few seconds later to report that he had been shot. The identity of the attacker and the extent of the injuries to the victim were still not known, he continued. These accounts were followed by a broadcast from a news magazine that regularly reports from The Hague, the center of Dutch politics. The Hague reporter was asked to recount the spontaneous reactions of political leaders to the news that had just been announced. They were shocked, he said and then went on to make the prophetic remark that this attack would shape Dutch politics for the coming decade. Subsequent reports that evening would confirm Fortuyn's death and provide the identity and background of the suspect, who was now in custody.

Newspaper accounts on the morning of May 7 reflected (as well as reinforced) a shocked, angry, and confused nation and a dazed political elite. The dailies were filled with comments and commentary from all sections of society and from political leaders in the Netherlands and around Europe. The *Telegraaf* offered on-site reactions from those who had gathered in the Hilversum Mediapark, where an instant memorial of flowers and notes was being erected from the first hour of the attack onward. A 25-year-old-man compared the situation to the violence in the United States, and his comment was made into a headline: "It is like America"; another, an angry well-dressed 49-year-old, screamed out, "Melkert is the murderer," referring to the head of the PvdA, and a fierce opponent of Fortuyn. The two, Melkert and Fortuyn, had been the subject of several bitter confrontations, including the previously mentioned televised debate, the night before the murder. Like the victim himself, this man blamed what he described as the country's political polarization for the murder, assigning culpability to the context and not to the actual killer. In the *Volkskrant's* Forum (May 7, 2002) Albert Verheij seemed to agree, writing under the headline: "Political Murder in the Netherlands. After the past months' continuous media frenzy a madman has been created amongst us. Dutch politics has now been terribly defiled." He then called for a sympathy demonstration for Fortuyn, and for the media and the political parties to seriously reflect on their role and responsibility. Supporters made the comparison to the murder of JFK: "Fortuyn was a symbol of change, now everything is crushed. This is as bad as the Kennedy murder" (*Trouw*, May 7, 2002:16) and many blamed the Left for Fortuyn's death. "You all have a price on your heads. Murderers. You are all guilty of his death," shouted one

Fortuyn supporter, as leaders of the PvdA arrived in The Hague (*Trouw,* May 7, 2002:17).

The theme of the nation's "lost innocence" was headlined in *Trouw,* a daily with a denominational orientation (Johan Ten Hove byline:, p 16) on May 7)—"The Netherlands has lost its innocence." The Netherlands, it was claimed, has been a fortunate country, where political violence happened "elsewhere," a country in which discussion, compromise, and tolerance reigned, and now, all this was lost. The same paper's political editors wrote, "The Netherlands is no longer the Netherlands" (*Trouw,* May 7, 2002:3). In a related manner, the Associated Press (AP) reported on the hundreds of supporters waiting in line at the Rotterdam city hall to sign a condolence log and the tens of thousands who marched through the city's streets. It also reported, "Many Dutchmen said the killing, the first political assassination in modern Dutch history, was a jolt to the self-image of a nation of 16 million that saw itself as more sensible, better organized, and less violent than others. Dutch political leaders typically do not have body guards and many ride public transportation." It quoted a Leiden University political scientist to the effect that "Holland has entered the 21st Century. This has gotten rid of Dutch smugness" (Anthony Deutsch, AP, May 7, 2002, LexisNexis.nl). As we have seen, similar claims were made about Sweden after the murders of Palme and Lindh, as if modernity was characterized by assassination. Many cries were heard after the murder of Fortuyn, claiming that this could not happen here, that political violence was "unDutch" and happened elsewhere. This was also the case in Sweden, where the two assassinations were seen by some as the end of Swedish exceptionalism. The victim here, then, was not so much Fortuyn, but the nation itself. It is interesting to note, in this regard, that not long before the murder of Fortuyn, the reigning Dutch government felt it necessary to resign in light of an official report in which the Dutch military was held, in part, responsible for the murder of thousands of civilians in Srebrenica. Why this was not considered a "loss of innocence" can only be speculated upon. One can, perhaps, speculate that this was not considered as a loss of innocence because of the past colonial history of the Dutch military, which was far from innocent, or because it involved an institution of declining importance to the face of the nation. Whatever the reason, the elections of May 15 were, in part, the result of this resignation and Fortuyn's own rise to power.

One could also take a longer historical view, back to the 1960s and a new generation's confrontation with their elders' behavior during the German occupation in the Second World War, when the dominant narrative, taught in school and represented through mass media and the arts, that the Dutch were a nation of heroes, was challenged. As I have argued in a previous book (Eyerman 2008), this myth of the "good Dutchman," resistant to the occupiers and protector of Jews, was shattered. This too could be considered as "loss of innocence," as could the revelations about the treatment afforded to local populations in former Dutch colonies. With all of this shadowing the recent past, why would one speak of a "loss of innocence" only after the murder of Pim Fortuyn? Political violence was not exactly absent in Dutch politics; environmental activists had contemplated and carried out violent actions since the 1980s. What would the phrase mean, and who or what would be served in the use of such a phrase? What were the Dutch innocent of, and what exactly was lost? One thing that was lost (a loss felt also in Sweden, after the assassination of Olof Palme) was the myth that public figures could move about freely in society, without the need for protection. Fortuyn was hardly a man of the people; in fact, he made a point of being extraordinary. For instance, he would never dream of riding on public transportation or taking a bicycle to work. He also had a bodyguard, though this appeared more a matter of style than of substance. However, just as in Sweden, it was part of Dutch mythology and of national self-identification that elected officials were just ordinary citizens. Fortuyn himself punctured that myth through his lifestyle, and then, in his death; perhaps this was a "loss of innocence." There was also the notion that political violence happened elsewhere and, as the studies cited in earlier chapters confirm, this was more than myth, but the idea that something was lost assumes an idealized, as well as a shared past (Pantti and Wieten 2005:306). With the murder of Pim Fortuyn, political assassination was a fact, and indeed, there was something lost because of it. Whether one called what was lost "innocence" or "smugness" was a matter of political and social perspective.

Another theme in media narration was the murder as an attack on the democratic process, as much as on a person. Both domestic and European political leaders reported being shocked by the murder and, like EU chair Prodi, viewed it as a threat to the democratic process. "This is an attack against democracy," the *Volkskrant*, (May 7, 2002:3) headlined, quoting a member of parliament. The country's prime minister, PvdA leader Willem Kok, called for calm while telling the *Volkskrant* (May 7, 2002:1), "I am crushed. I am totally crushed by what happened, in this country, today. A murderous attack. This is deeply tragic for our country, for our country and our democracy, the democratic rule of law" (my translation). Other Dutch politicians agreed. Muslim leaders, quoted in the *NRC* (May 7, 2002:3) and *Trouw* (May 7, 2002:4) condemned the murder, also seeing it as a threat to the democratic process. Such statements by political and community leaders can be seen as attempts to manage emotions (here with the aid of mass media) as much as they may reflect strongly held views or values. In a statement made by Kok in a television interview we can see the attempt to present the former, managing emotions, but appealing to the latter, the views and values. Speaking of Fortuyn's murder right after it occurred, Kok said,

> "This is deeply tragic for his next of kin. Deeply tragic for our country and our democracy…In The Netherlands! In a tolerant country with respect for each other's opinions…These are my personal feelings. I feel shattered. I felt an urgent need to tell you this. Let's in God's name keep calm! At the same time when one is inclined to be quite furious, quite angry. Calm is perhaps the best service now that we can render, in dignity, to the rule of law and democracy and to the memory of Pim Fortuyn."

In a performance of authority aimed at calming an aroused populace, the prime minister appealed to his own emotions (Cited by Pannti and Wieten (2005:304).

Much attention was paid in the center-left press to the reaction from immigrant groups. This was the case for at least two reasons; first, Fortuyn was an outspoken opponent of current immigration policy and thus seen by many as an enemy of immigrants and immigrant groups. Second, it was widely suspected when the murder occurred that the obvious assassin would be an immigrant, and more specifically, a Muslim. Even though the killer was caught within minutes of the act and was identified the next day as "a white, Dutch man" (*NRC*, May 7, 2002:1), these suspicions remained. The fact that the perpetrator was indeed a white male was given much attention in the media because it was the cause of a collective sigh of relief. As one television news editor recounted,

> "I remember that we, at that moment at 8 o'clock, as editor of the day, did something that we had not done before; told the presenter that he should say that the man who had been apprehended, that it concerned a white Dutch male. I found it important to say that, because everyone first expected no doubt that the man concerned would be an immigrant. If it had been an immigrant the situation would have been even more chaotic and aggressive…" (quoted in Pantti and Wieten 2005:309)

It seems clear that even journalists had expectations about who the murderer of Pim Fortuyn would be. Pantti and Wieten argue that both this expectation and the sense of relief when it was not fulfilled are indicative of the Dutch media's interest in containing and minimizing ethnic conflict and in promoting national unity in a highly inflammable situation. Their analysis of Dutch television coverage is supported by my own examination of the print media. This raises the question of what would have happened if there had been a media source with the opposite aim, a sensationalist tabloid, for example. Although not represented in the mainstream media, those interested in exploiting the situation for more divisive ends were plentiful on the Internet.

Political assassination, as such, was also a theme. Whereas many drew comparisons to the United States and specifically to the murder of JFK, and some to RFK and MLK, *De Telegraaf* (May 8, 2002, Rolien Creton byline) drew the link to Sweden and the murder of Olof Palme. Beneath the headline "Politics Wildly Opened After the Murder of Palme," the article quoted Swedish prime minister Göran Persson as saying, "The murder of Fortuyn shows how vulnerable our democracy is." This is a theme he would return to a year-and-a-half later when Anna Lindh was murdered. Danish Social Democratic leader Poul Nyrup Rasmussen is also quoted as saying, "After the murder of Palme we in Scandinavia were all in agreement that our political culture [of open democratic dialogue] must be cherished and fostered." In its second publication after the murder, *Elsevier* (May 18, 2002), the conservative newsweekly in which Fortuyn published a regular column until his turn to active politics, also made the link with Sweden and to Palme. Beneath the headline "A Shattering Of the Soul," reporter Oene van der Wal wrote, "Like the ice-cold wind that swept over Sweden after the murder of Palme in 1986, so the murder of Fortuyn has brought dread and shock to the Netherlands... Sweden was a model country, then with one blow this ended when Palme was shot down after a visit to the cinema in central Stockholm." The comparison might appear a bit forced. Palme was prime minister at the time and the representative of the Swedish model; he stood for Sweden, or at least part of it, both in the formal and the symbolic sense. Can one say the same about Fortuyn? What did he represent for Dutch society? What did he represent for *Elsevier*? This raises the issue of who and what was attacked in Hilversum on May 6, 2002; for *Elsevier*, the answer appears to be a new force for change in the Netherlands, someone who could get the country back on the proper track, that is, what, for them, Fortuyn represented politically. This would again make the country as much a victim as the man himself, a country that had now "lost its innocence," a model country no more.

The previous week, *Elsevier* (May 11, 2002, n.19, 10–14, LexisNexis.nl) had run Fortuyn's obituary as its lead story. Following themes that were already in place within the broader media discourse, one headline called the murder an attack on democracy, whereas another reminded readers of "Political Murders in America," describing the murders of John and Robert Kennedy and Martin Luther King. This article began, "Every European above 50 knows exactly what he was doing at the moment... that John F. Kennedy was murdered..." (12), continuing with the implication that the same might well happen now, with the murder of Pim Fortuyn. *Elsevier* reports focused on Fortuyn's popularity, the fact that he was irreplaceable, and the role of freedom of speech and expression in Dutch society. Reporting on the spontaneous gatherings on the evening of his murder, they wrote, "People gathered on Monday evening near the Hague Binnenhof, as one said 'to raise my voice for Pim Fortuyn.' One woman said, 'My mouth is now sewn shut.' Near [Fortuyn's Rotterdam] home crowds mixed rage with sorrow and resignation. This public was strikingly mixed: men in jogging outfits, men in business suits, an old woman with a rollator, white as well as black: 'At last, someone who speaks his mind, and for that he his shot down'" (*Elsevier*, n. 19 2002:12, my translation). The theme of free speech was one that would become central to the commentary on Fortuyn's death and would reemerge as a mobilizing force with the murder of Theo van Gogh.

The crowds outside The Hague Parliament building may have been mixed, but they were also rowdy and violent, something not mentioned in the *Elsevier* articles, perhaps because it was more interested in creating an impression of unity in grief, rather than showing anger and discontent.[8] Television reportage showed groups of young men, many with shaved heads, boots, and Lonsdale shirts—the uniform of the neo-Nazis—who loudly vented their anger and frustration.[9] Fires from burning cars and the smashed windows of government buildings could be seen in the background. Support for Fortuyn among extreme right-wing groups was apparent and well known and this is a paradox that must be explained. Fortuyn's openly gay lifestyle would not easily lend itself to the support of such groups. Quite the contrary; in another time and place, what Fortuyn symbolized would have been the target for verbal attack, even violence. Somehow Fortuyn became "Our Pim" for this group and also for others who would normally hold negative views about homosexuals, such as conservative religious groups. What made Fortuyn "acceptable" in their eyes? Although it might seem obvious that it was his outspoken views on Muslims and Islamic religion that was the key factor, this was not necessarily the case with regard to religious conservatives, for despite the obvious differences in theology, they shared some fundamental cultural values with conservative Muslims. Fortuyn's radical views on immigration and his catch phrases about Muslims were probably what attracted extreme right youth to his cause, but not necessarily those more moderate conservative groups. In this sense, the *Elsevier* reportage was correct; those present at the demonstrations immediately following the news of Fortuyn's death were a mixed group. One of the powers of a representative figure, especially in death, is the ability to symbolically represent a wide range of often contradictory messages and thus to bring together individuals and groups that would not normally have much in common. "Our Pim" was precisely such an individual.

THE FUNERAL

The funeral of Pim Fortuyn on May 10, 2002, received widespread media attention, including a photo essay in *Time*, the global newsmagazine. It was carried live on two Dutch television stations and had "'the scale and style' of a national funeral" (Pantti and Wieten 2005:308, quoting a Dutch television commentator). With support from those actively involved in media coverage, they argue that this was part of a conscious effort to "design and manage the public mood," to create consensus out of a contentious and potentially dangerous incident:

> The cabinet's reaction was: we must make this a national event, just to be able to keep it in hand more or less. And to some extent this is how we felt…The funeral got the character of a national event, while it was not of course. For it was the mourning of one group, of people opposed to the other people who walked along with them and who were opposed to us who filmed it." (Dutch television news editor Hans Laroes cited in Pantti and Wieten 2005:304–5)

Turning a partisan issue into a national event was thus a conscious and creative strategy in which visual imagery provided through television would play a central role.

In the print media, there were two prime interests; the first was the event itself, as a social and cultural phenomenon, and the second was the impact of Fortuyn's death on the coming elections of May 15. On the day of the election, the editors of the *Washington Post* (May 15, 2002 :A18) remarked on the "tens of thousands who showed up" at the funeral, while pointing out, "For a brief moment, Pim Fortuyn flickered on the stage of European politics, forcing the Dutch to face their fear and fascination with the 'problem' of Muslim immigration . … The Netherlands has lost a charismatic personality. More tragic yet would be if in concentrating on that loss, it ignores the opportunity to address the fears Fortuyn brought to the fore." London's *Daily Telegraph* (May 11, 2002:16) compared the funeral to that of Princess Diana, pointing to the broad range of people among the thousands present, including a representative of the Dutch queen. It cited an oration by Fortuyn's brother, who adamantly denied that Fortuyn was an extremist, quoting him as saying his brother was "most of all humane and a committed democrat," and that the crowd outside the cathedral was spontaneously singing the British football anthem, "You'll Never Walk Alone."[10] There was much iteration here, from the "spontaneous" memorial and the laying of flowers and written notes—the creation of a scene, one could say—to the way the funeral procession was choreographed, with Fortuyn's body carried in a white Cadillac driven slowly along Rotterdam's streets to the applause of thousands of onlookers, and his two lap dogs in a central role. Fortuyn was sent away(his remains eventually being buried in Italy) in a style meant to project his self-image, but which also closely resembled not only that of other media-generated celebrities such as Princess Diana, but also the more stately funerals of John and Robert Kennedy.

In its stately grandeur, Fortuyn's commemoration created something of a dilemma for Dutch authorities, as reflected in the presence of a representative of the queen, rather than she herself. This was no ordinary funeral. The manner and timing of Fortuyn's death, as well as his enormous popularity, made it seem necessary that the royal family be represented at the funeral ceremony. Fortuyn's supporters seemed to expect the queen's presence. However, since Fortuyn had no formal standing or representative function, this was not possible. This was the source of some disappointment for his supporters. The royal family would adopt a different position when Theo van Gogh was assassinated a year-and-a-half later. The queen would then take a more active role in an attempt to unify the nation and to blunt the violence that followed that incident and was present at Van Gogh's funeral.

Perpetrator/Victim

The news that the killer was a Dutchman and an environmental activist went out in the media later in the evening on the day of the murder. The Dutch news agency Algemeen Nederlands Persbureau (ANP) released this information four hours after the murder at 10:20 P.M., and it was immediately picked up by the international media. The English edition of the Agence French Presse reported, "The man named Tuesday [May 7] as the suspect in the killing of Dutch far-right leader Pim Fortuyn is reportedly a militant animal right activist. The man, 32-year-old Volkert van der Graaf is being held over the shooting of anti-immigrant Fortuyn..." (http://academic.lexisnexis. nl.uva). Here we can find the key aspects of the narrative that will become the dominant one regarding the perpetrator and the victim. The victim is characterized as a far right, anti-immigrant politician and the victim as a far-left political activist. These frames were readily available and easily understood. Immediately following its news release, the ANP reported that what it identified as a Dutch extreme right-wing party, the Nederlandse Volk Unie (NVU), linked the murder to the extreme Left, calling for a demonstration on the following Saturday. The killer's identification was expanded somewhat in London's *Daily Telegraph* (May 8, 2002:7), where he was identified as a "vegan animal rights activist," while the British Broadcasting Corporation (BBC) called him an employee of the organization *Milieu-Offensief* (Environmental-Offensive). The *Times* (May 9, 2002) headlined "Accused Vegan was 'a Fanatic Who Cared Only For Animals.'" The Dutch press was a little more cautious. The *Volkskrant* (May 8, 2002:7) identified the killer as "a 32-year-old from Harderwijk, active in the organization Milieu-Offensief," noting that his motive for killing Fortuyn was not yet known. The *Telegraaf* (May 10, 2002) still insisted on calling the suspected killer Van der G., though other news sources had already released his full name and cautiously remarked that the link between him and radical activists was now confirmed, after dispute and discussion with movement activists.

A central issue in the following weeks concerned whether it was a madman, an enraged activist, or the environmental movement as a whole that had killed Fortuyn. *Elsevier's* lead article for May 18, 2002 (Simon Rozendaal byline, academic.lexisnexis.nl/uva/) began, "The jester was killed by a madman, not by the environmental movement perhaps... But even madmen have supporters. In the cluster of environmental researchers, environmental civil servants and the environmental movement it was well known that with the arrival of Pim Fortuyn environmental issues were taken off the table..." Environmental organizations, most especially Milieu-Offensief, were forced to clarify their position and to take a stand with regard to the action of Volkert van der Graaf. As the suspect chose to remain silent about his motives, a great deal of attention was paid to his past and present life, to understand what he had done. Was he a madman, a highly motivated activist, or an ordinary young father driven to the brink? Did he act alone or in concert with others? The *Volkskrant* (May 25, 2002:3) headlined that there was no proof of help for Volkert van der G. and had reported on May 18, 2002 (2) that "he lived in his head, what thoughts inspired him, no one knows." One week earlier, the same newspaper had attempted to get inside the world in which they thought de Graaf lived. Under the headline "Volkert's World," reporter Jeroen Trommelen linked Van der Graaf with an extremist wing of the animal rights movement, which he termed the Dutch branch of a "fundamentalism" (*De Volkskrant* [May 16, 2002:V1]). Since Van der Graaf had chosen to remain silent, Trommelen interviewed activists in the movement to get an idea about how they viewed the world. What he discovered was a group of individuals who attempted to order their lives in a way that was least harmful to animals, not only in terms of diet, but also in avoiding such things as musical instruments, which made use of animal products. Van der Graaf, Trommelen then claimed, belonged to this group, moving from vegetarianism to the much more radical veganism. Others, identified as vegans, were quick to deny any link between their beliefs and the murder of Fortuyn. One said, "I don't know Volkert and do not think that his motivation for murder came from veganism. There must be something else. Like everyone else, we hope he was psychotic. That would be a relief." The article ended, however, with a list of violent acts carried out in the Netherlands in the name of animal rights, most of them arson attacks—and the list was rather long. On May 7, *De Telegraaf* summed up its position: "Fortuyn murdered. The Netherlands deeply shocked by Pim's death. The killer extreme left" (Dominique Weesie, byline). The same day it also reported (Rob Sebes byline) under the headline "LPF: The Left is Guilty of Murder," (the LPF being Fortuyn's party) and quoted a party member as to the cause: "The hate campaign was set in motion by the left, with the Labor Party at the head."

THE TRIAL

The trial of Volkert van der Graaf was closely watched around the world, most especially by those who shared Fortuyn's fears of Muslim migration.[11] Fortuyn supporters filled the courtroom, and the atmosphere was tense during the weeks of formal hearings and the actual trial itself. These events were widely covered in the national and international media. Was he a madman or an activist? Did he act out of psychosis, jealousy, or cold-blooded reason? Was he alone, or acting with others? Was this a political assassination or an ordinary murder? These were some of the central questions that arose during the trial and sentencing of Volkert van der Graaf. Prior to the trial, Van der Graaf had maintained strict silence about his motives, and this opened the door to profuse speculation about a possible conspiracy. This possibility was raised primarily by those connected to Fortuyn's supporters, including leaders of LPF and LN, who suggested possible links to al Qaida. Such charges were later dismissed by the court for lack of evidence. During the early stages of the hearings, Van der Graaf's wife was arrested and then released, this too for lack of evidence. The Dutch criminal system calls for a complex process of hearings and trial for crimes of this seriousness, with final judgment and sentencing made by a judicial panel. There is no jury, though the public may be present, and in this particular case, demonstrations took place both inside and outside the courtroom. In the first "pro forma" sitting, both sides presented their arguments without the accused being present. The accused watched these proceedings on CCTV from his prison cell. It was decided here that Van der Graaf should undergo psychiatric evaluation to determine his mental state. Before this was to occur, however, the Public Ministry announced that Van der Graaf had confessed to the murder, but the content of this confession was not released to the public. After seven weeks of evaluation at a mental health evaluation center, it was found that Van der Graaf suffered from relatively minor forms of mental illness—a neurotic, compulsive personality—but that this was not serious enough to affect his behavior during his murderous act. There was, the report concluded, no "diminished capacity" during the actual murder. A second sitting then took place, with the accused present. Here, the issue of motivation was central, and Van der Graff was asked to explain why he killed Fortuyn. He acknowledged that murder was wrong and that violence was not proper to the democratic political process, but claimed that in some cases, extreme cases, violence was necessary in the face of even greater violence. Van der Graaf also acknowledged that he had done wrong, but justified his actions through an appeal to higher principles and a higher good. He did this in a seemingly thoughtful, polite, and reflective manner. Prosecutors would later claim they had never met such a perpetrator before; always polite, never losing his temper or raising his voice, always ready to acknowledge another's point of view, and to reflect on what he had done and accept responsibility for it. The third sitting set the dates for the actual trial and sentencing, where the final arguments of the attorneys were presented to a panel of three judges and the formal sentencing pronounced. As guilt was assumed by this point, the proceedings were concerned primarily with the manner and length of punishment. Van der Graaf was formally charged with premeditated murder, the illegal possession of weapons, and threatening the life of Fortuyn's chauffer by pointing a gun at him during the chase. At this point, Van der Graaf was again asked to describe his motivations and whether or not there were others involved. Van der Graaf denied the involvement of anyone else, claiming that he had never even spoken to anyone of his plans, and that the final plans had not been formulated until the actual day of the murder. He ended by saying that though he recognized that murder was wrong, he had acted in good conscience to stop what he claimed was a grave danger to society. Not to act would have been similar to being silent in the face of a threat like Adolph Hitler. He was found guilty and sentenced to 18 years of imprisonment. Following Dutch law, which requires that he serve at least two-thirds of this sentence, Van der Graaf could be released in 2014.

MEMORIALS AND COMMEMORATION

A spontaneous memorial of flowers, notes, and pictures was created at the site of Fortuyn's murder within moments of his death. This was the beginning of a wave of memorial celebrations and shrines, including the funeral itself, meant to commemorate Fortuyn through public outpourings of collective emotion. Margry (2003:111) lists six "major" shrines, including personal ones like Fortuyn's home and the site of his death, general ones like the Homo Monument in Amsterdam, and also national monuments like the monument to William of Orange and the National War Monument. These commemorative acts were the first such expansive display of public grief in modern Dutch history, bringing to mind the more joyful public celebrations at the end of the Second World War or a royal wedding. Here also, television had a constitutive role to play:

> Because there had never before in The Netherlands been such a massive, spontaneous and public display of mourning for an "ordinary" citizen, these places received constant media attention, and thus through the television screen they appeared in every living room as virtual sites of remembrance, to fulfill a memorial or mourning function there. As a result of the media attention, new visitors were in turn mobilized to go to the shrines." (Margry 2003:112)

As one of those ironies of history, Fortuyn was killed on May 6, a day that follows two days of traditional and ritualized public commemoration. May 4 is National Remembrance Day, when those who died during the Second World War are commemorated, and May 5 celebrates the liberation from German occupation. Followers of Pim Fortuyn have since suggested that May 6 become an official day of remembrance for Pim Fortuyn, whereas others have appropriated some of the previous days' celebrations to commemorate their fallen leader.

On the first anniversary of the murder, May 6, 2003, media commentary was extensive. *De Volkskrant* asked politicians to recall how they had reacted to the news. *De Telegraaf* asked supporters and opponents to comment on Fortuyn's significance and listed all the commemorative events scheduled for the day, most of them broadcast over mass media, including a documentary entitled *The Murder of Pim Fortuyn, One Year Later*, with studio commentary by his associates and supporters. Two themes dominated the discussion: the motivation of the murderer and Pim Fortuyn's legacy—his politics and his party. The killer's motives were still unclear and the issue of whether he was a lone, angry young man, either mentally unstable or out for notoriety, or whether he had acted out of conviction as a member of a movement, still went unanswered. The fate of Fortuyn's legacy was easier to answer. His party had won a major victory in the May 15, 2002 elections, but would later lose most of these votes. The LPF came in second, in terms of the total number of votes. The center right Christian Democratic Appeal CDA was the big winner, winning 28 percent of the vote and 43 out of 150 seats in the second chamber of Parliament. This was an increase of 34 seats from 1998. The LPF received 17 percent of the total votes and won 26 seats in parliament, the largest single gain by a political party in Dutch history. The election's largest losers were the VVD, which won 23 seats (down from 38), and the PvdA, which went from 45 to 23 seats. LN received 1.6 percent of the votes and only 2 seats.

In the next parliamentary election, held on January 22, 2003, these results were sharply modified. The CDA won only a narrow victory over a resurgent PvdA, the CDA gaining only one seat, bringing the total to 44, and the PvdA gaining 19 seats to 42 total. The VVD gained 4 seats to 28 and LPF was the biggest loser, down 18 seats to just 8 total. LN won no seats. On May 27, 2003, a coalition government was formed, led by the CDA; other partners in the governing coalition were the VVD and Democrats 66 (D66), with the PvdA as the main opposition. By the elections of 2006, the LPF had no seats in parliament. However, these elections results can be deceptive. It might appear that support for the politics that Fortuyn had advocated had diminished, even disappeared, in the years following his death. To believe that could be a serious mistake. The lack of seats for the LPF and the loss of seats for the LN could as well mean dissatisfaction (among those who voted for Fortuyn) with the representatives of those parties, rather than a change in attitude or belief. It is also the case that many of those who voted for LPF voted for Fortuyn and no other, recording the extraordinary fact that over 1.5 million people voted for the already dead politician. In fact, many of his supporters had come from groups that do not normally vote at all and are mistrustful of politicians and politics in the traditional sense. They may have been motivated to participate in the electoral process on just that single occasion. Chorus and Meno (2002) describe the typical Fortuyn voter but then say : "But one should here distinguish between a voter, who would fit this profile and a supporter, who may not under other circumstances be a voter at all. The June 7th 2010 election proved a surprise..."

Speaking about election returns and the rapid decline of political organizations is one way to gauge the long-term significance of the assassination of Pim Fortuyn.[12] But it is not a particularly good way to get at its *meaning*. For this, one would better look at the various narratives constructed in the aftermath and ask how they *could* have unfolded, if, for example, the murderer had been a dark-skinned immigrant. Where, for instance, do the various competing narratives begin, and where do they end? Fortuyn supporters, for instance, his adviser Oscar Hammerstein, begin their account of the murder with the "demonization" by the Left and specifically with the "pie-in-the-face" attack on his person, seen as symbolic violence that represented a step to even greater violence. The pie-in-the-face attack occurred a few months before the murder and was seen at the time as a form of nonviolent protest. Another such attack occurred a few weeks before the assassination. Since his death, supporters have linked the two incidents in a narrative, which blames the Left generally for creating an atmosphere in which the violent attack on political opponents was tolerated, if not condoned.[13] As noted, the killer is identified in this narrative with the political Left through his beliefs and affiliations, as an animal-rights activist, which is then located on the extreme Left. From this perspective, the 'Left' covers a broad spectrum, from the PvdA to anarchist squatters and the extremists of the environmental movement.

Fortuyn supporters seemed at first to have a hard time with Volkert van der Graaf; he was not their image of his killer. The same was true for the prosecutor and the rest of Dutch society. After interviewing Volkert, the lawyers and the police commented that they had never met a perpetrator such as him before—modest, totally conscious of what he had done, and ready to take full responsibility. At issue in the sentencing was the question of whether or not this was a political assassination or an ordinary murder. Did Volkert act out of personal, or political motivations? He claimed to be doing his "duty" and acting on the basis of a higher law, that of humanity. The problem he created for Fortuyn supporters was that he was so ordinary and so Dutch. They would have preferred the profile of a "typical" assassin or the dark-skinned immigrant, but if the perpetrator had to be white and Dutch, it would have been better if he were an obvious radical, a male with dreadlocks spouting radical rhetoric. No one knew what to do with a plain-looking, timid, and soft-spoken young father, especially one speaking in the dialect of the western provinces and with a solid conservative religious background. Painting him as a radical leftist, an environmental fanatic—a fundamentalist in Pim Fortuyn's words—was essential. "The Left killed Pim Fortuyn," screamed his supporters.

What would their ideal murderer look like? Clearly, not like the actual killer—perhaps more like Mohammed B.—the killer of Theo van Gogh. What would have happened had the killer of Fortuyn been an immigrant? A Muslim? A Muslim radical? The reactions would surely have been even more violent and divisive. And regarding the actual killer, why did Van der Graaf kill Fortuyn when he did, before the election? Why not wait until afterwards to see if he would actually win? Could this have been mere pragmatism, a question of opportunity, that it would be easier before rather than after, when his victim might be better protected? Or was there something else?

From a different perspective, it is likely that the story began much further back, with the rise of fascism, prior to the Second World War, linking Fortuyn with charismatic leaders like Hitler and Mussolini and then with what is identified as its more recent emergence in Jorg Heider in Austria and Le Pen in France. This played on a very alive segment of Dutch collective memory, which mixed fear with guilt. It recalled the ambivalent relationship with German occupiers, as well as the treatment of minorities, most especially Jews. Amsterdam mayor Job Cohen recalled the latter in his appeals for calm and solidarity after the murder of Van Gogh, whereas the latter called Cohen a "collaborator" for just such an appeal. The Left drew caricatures of Fortuyn, dressed in a Nazi uniform and sporting a Hitler moustache. The Right, including Van Gogh, spoke of "Islamic-fascism." All played on deep-seated fears, which especially after 9/11 and the assassination of Pim Fortuyn, had been brought increasingly to the surface in the ongoing debate about the foundations of collective identity.

THE MURDER OF VAN GOGH

It did not seem possible that it could happen again, and when it did, it was not possible to speak or to write about the murder of the filmmaker Theo van Gogh without referring to Pim Fortuyn. The two will forever be linked in Dutch collective memory. It was not simply that they were friends or that they shared many political points of view, or that they were members of a generation shaped by the 1960s; all this is true, but what linked them was the timing and and the manner of their deaths.

On November 2, 2004, the 47-year-old Theo van Gogh was shot and stabbed in broad daylight on a busy Amsterdam street, while cycling to work. He was on his way to prepare for a day of work on a film about the murder of his friend Pim Fortuyn. Van Gogh, the great-grandson of another Theo van Gogh, brother of the famous artist, was in the middle of a successful career as a filmmaker and journalist. He was attacked because of things he had written, and most directly, for a film he had directed and produced. That film, *Submission,* an 11-minute-long indictment of brutality against Muslim women, was written and narrated by Ayaan Hirsi Ali, a Somali-born member of the Dutch Parliament. The film alleged a direct connection between the Koran, the holy text of Islamic religion, and the mistreatment of women. It had just been shown on Dutch public television. The killer, Mohammad Boyeri, a 26-year-old Dutch citizen of Moroccan descent and a self-proclaimed Islamic fundamentalist, had been so provoked by the film that he set out to murder its producers. Because his main target, Hirsi Ali, was under constant police protection and because Van Gogh had refused such protection, the latter became a target for his wrath. Even after two trials, it remains uncertain whether he acted alone.[14]

MEDIA REPORTAGE

The first news went out over the radio minutes after the early morning attack on November 2, 2004.[15] By lunchtime, there was a press conference, and the regular news programs were filled with accounts of the murder. Morning newspapers carried special bulletins on their websites. The following day, *De Telegraaf* (November 3, 2004:1) featured the front-page headline, "Slaughtered," in large type with a black background over a photograph of the body of Van Gogh lying in the street. Superimposed on the photo was the text, "Exactly 911 days later, Theo van Gogh has been murdered 911 days after Pim Fortuyn, who was killed on 6 May 2002." In the paper, another headline announced, "Disgust and Anger Following the Murder of Van Gogh." From neighboring Belgium, *De Tijd* (November 3, 2004) also made the connection: "New Fortuyn—Trauma For the Netherlands: The Attack on Van Gogh Hardens Opposition." Dutch newspapers carried similar headlines: *De Volkskrant* proclaimed, "Hatred and Anxiety in Amsterdam" (November 4, 2004). Then came the news that the perpetrator was a Muslim, followed by headlines such as, "Searching the Link With Al Qaeda—Suspect of Murder Van Gogh is Mohammed B" (*Algemeen Dagblad,* November 4, 2004). There were even proclamations of war: "Holy War in Holland" (*Algemeen Dagblad,* November 4, 2004) and "We Are At

War," announced by Vice Prime Minister (and also Finance Minister) Zalm (VVD) in *Algemeen Dagblad* (November 6, 2004).[16] Later, commenting on the situation in the country at the time, historian Geert Mak called it tense and stated that the mass media were an important agent in spreading this tension. According to Mak, "...The media opened the gates and hatred against foreigners that was hidden for so long...suddenly splashed outside" (quoted in Bloomgaarden and de Vreese 2007:8). How hidden this hatred was at this time can be questioned, especially since the rise and murder of Fortuyn. What made the difference now was that the perpetrator was a self-described Islamic radical, a description that was fully orchestrated by mass media. In contrast to the murder of Fortuyn, a series of violent actions followed the murder of Van Gogh. Mosques and Islamic schools were bombed and burned, and in seeming retaliation, several Christian churches and Jewish sites were vandalized and burned. By November 3, just one day after the murder, media were linking not only the murders of Van Gogh and Fortuyn but also religious fundamentalism and the "War on Terror." *De Telegraaf* had already made that link implicitly, through using the highly symbolic 9/11 in its first-day reportage. By November 4, and the arrest of Mohammed B, they were making this link explicitly: "The perpetrator was the spearhead of a terror cell" (www.lexisnexis.com). The murder was now clearly an assassination and one that was of interest to political leaders around the world.

In the Netherlands, newspaper editorials called the murder of Van Gogh an attack on democracy, further raising the stakes from an attack against an individual to one directed at a collective and its foundational principles. Under the headlines, "A Black Day," and "Murder An Attack on Democracy," *Het Financieele Dagblad* (The Financial Daily) called the murder "another anxiety-producing blow to the foundation of Dutch society," while, at the same time, drawing the link to Fortuyn (www.lexisnexis. com). On its opinion page, the editors of *Volkskrant* (November 3, 2004) began a commentary with the headline "An Attack on Democracy," ending with the demand that Muslims accept the principle that religious beliefs be open to criticism—for Islam as well as for Christianity. The notion of an attack on democracy was specified even further, as the murder was soon framed as an attack on free speech, coupled with the right to criticize. Beneath the headline, "This is Worse Than the Murder of Fortuyn," the paper reported the words of a PvdA leader: "This is a struggle between free speech and religious fanaticism" (*Volkskrant,* November 3, 2004 www. volkskrant.nl/binnenland/article 188263.ece). The issue was now a matter of drawing the boundaries between free speech and blasphemy and secular and religious worldviews. It was not only the media that shifted the narrative in relation to the murder of Van Gogh, however. On the evening of the murder, there was a mass demonstration (reportedly attended by over

10,000 people, according to New York's *Daily News* [November 3, 2004])
held in Amsterdam's Dam Square, itself a symbolic site, where the right
to free speech was a major theme. This was followed a few days later by a
"silent demonstration" announced in the name of free speech, which was
held after the funeral ceremony.

Interpreting the murder of Theo van Gogh as an attack on a grounding
principle of Dutch society significantly widened the number of people who
could identify with the victim. Many media commentators prefaced their
remarks with the statement, "I was not a friend of Van Gogh, but…" This
most likely applied to many of those who laid flowers on the spot where Van
Gogh died and who gathered in the mass public demonstrations. What they
all had in common, if not any special attachment to Van Gogh the person
or his social and political views, was the sense that his murder was directed
at a foundational societal principle with which they could identify. Mass
media representation, which transmitted the voice of political authority,
including that of the royal family, was a significant force in formulating and
disseminating this interpretation of the murder. From this perspective, van
Gogh was killed because of what he represented, and the murder was, as one
Volkskrant columnist (also a former editor of the conservative weekly *Elsevier*
and a colleague of Pim Fortuyn) called it, "a *meningenmoord*," (a murder
of conviction). This commentator drew a connection between the killers of
both Fortuyn and Van Gogh on this basis: what Mohammed B. and Volkert
van der Graaf shared, he wrote, was "an intolerance for the freedom of
speech" (H. J. Schoo, *De Volkskrant*, November 3, 2004:4 [www.volkskrant.
nlbinnenland/article475272.ece]). And thus, by implication, an intolerance
for Dutch society, which was, in fact, grounded not only on the notion of free
speech, but also on tolerance for the views of others.

THE PERPETRATOR AND HIS AUDIENCE

The interpretation that this was "a murder of conviction," if not an attack
on freedom of speech, was enhanced by the perpetrator himself, by the way
the murder was carried out, as well as by the message he left pinned to the
body of his victim. Mohammed Bouyeri or Mohammed B., as he was first
known to the public, carried out his murderous act in a way that was clearly
intended to convey a broader meaning than a mere criminal act. Although he
was not dressed in the traditional clothing or sporting the long beard attributed to him by various eyewitnesses, Bouyeri did choose his apparel and the
mode and place of the murder with an eye to a multilayered audience. He
wanted his act to carry its own interpretation, by giving it a "preferred reading." This was a scripted performance, with a well-conceived mise-en-scène.
Mohammed B. stalked his victim as Sirhan Sirhan and James Earl Ray had

stalked theirs. With or without the help of others, he carefully selected the time and place where Van Gogh would be attacked—a busy street in the middle of the morning rush hour—where his act would be seen and reflected upon. His first audience was thus the anonymous Dutch citizens going about their daily routines, whose lives he sought to disrupt in the most dramatic way possible. The intention was to create a sense of general unease, with the message, "You are unsafe where you feel most at home." As he replied to a bystander during the murder, "...now you know what to expect" (Eyerman 2008:6). This might appear similar to the intentions of a suicide bomber, but Mohammed B. was not out to create terror in the same way. He did not murder innocent people indiscriminately. Rather, he saw himself as an assassin in the traditional sense, a religiously motivated actor carrying out an act of retribution against a known and impure enemy.[17] His act was thus more personal, which is why he used a knife as well as a pistol. As if this were not clear enough, Bouyeri carried a note in his pocket clarifying his aims and another, a five-page document, which he pinned to the upper body of his victim with a kitchen knife substituting for the traditional dagger. Mohammed B. had practiced all this in private, before actually doing it in public.[18] These actions, as well as the choice of dress (he wore a short, unkempt beard, a skullcap, and a jacket and baggy pants, the typical garb of the unassimilated, young male immigrant) were meant for several audiences. First of all, there were those everyday Dutch citizens who witnessed the murder (there were 53 witnesses interviewed by the police). Then, there was the wider Dutch public, as well as the Muslim community in the Netherlands and around the world, who might be inspired by this act and identify with the perpetrator and his cause, or at the very least, reflect upon its own position and situation. Understanding this, Muslim community leaders in the Netherlands were quick to disassociate not only themselves, but also Islamic religion, from Mohammed B. and to condemn his actions and call for calm.

The note in the perpetrator's pocket and the text pinned to the body of the victim confirmed the perpetrator's intent to murder with conviction and to die a martyr to a cause (for the text and analysis see, Eyerman 2008:6–7). That he failed in his attempt at the latter must have been a disappointment. Under the heading "Baptized in Blood," the note found on Mohammed B's person at the time of his arrest began with this statement "So these are my last words...Riddled with bullets...Baptized in blood...As I had hoped." At his trial, Mohammed B. was forced to create the role of living martyr; perhaps this is why he chose to remain for the most part silent, staring blankly as the evidence was laid out against him. He did, however, admit to the murder. Dressed in a black robe and with the Koran in his hand, he told the judges, "I did what I did purely out of my beliefs...I want you to know that I acted out of conviction and not that I took his life because he was Dutch or because

I was Moroccan and felt insulted" (As reported on www.msnbc.msn.com/
id/8551653). The trial ended in another type of conviction; on July 26, 2005,
Mohammed Bouyeri was found guilty of murdering Van Gogh, of attempting to murder several police officers and civilians, and of illegally possessing
firearms. In addition, he was found guilty of threatening the life of Ayaan
Hirsi Ali, then still a member of the Dutch parliament. During the sentencing, one of the three presiding judges called his actions "a terrorist act,"
which meant that he could be more severely punished, following a recent
change in Dutch law. In March 2006, Mohammed Bouyeri was included
in the indictment of the so-called Hofstad Group, a terrorist cell of which
he was allegedly a member. At this trial, he reversed the tactical silence and
made a long courtroom speech in which he expounded the virtues of Islamic
radicalism. He is currently in prison serving out his sentence.

Besides Van Gogh and Bouyeri, the third actor in this social drama is
Ayaan Hirsi Ali, who according to the notes left by the murderer, was the
prime target. Unlike Bouyeri, Ali was a recent immigrant to the Netherlands
from Somalia and a smashing success. Fleeing an arranged marriage, she
arrived at Amsterdam's Central Station in 1992 and applied for political asylum three days later.[19] Ali was 22 years old. In the refugee camp, Ali quickly
accommodated, learning the language and embracing the role of go-between
for other asylum seekers. She received an advanced degree from a prominent
Dutch university, worked as a researcher for the PvdA , and was elected to
parliament as a member of a center-right party (in 2003)—all in the space
of 11 years. As a young black woman from a decimated African country,
Ali's success was nothing less than extraordinary. This might well have been
a factor in why she became the target of such wrath from a less successful,
second-generation immigrant with a Moroccan background like Mohammed
Boyeri. The film *Submission,* which she made with Van Gogh, could have
been the last of a long line of factors that angered this aspiring Islamic radical. Ali was an outspoken defender of the rights of immigrant women, as
well as a critic of Islam and what she saw as Muslim culture. The film was
only one, if the most graphic, representation of her views. Ali was a media
celebrity in the same way as Fortuyn was, and for similar reasons. She was
an equally colorful figure in an otherwise drab political landscape. Unlike
Fortuyn, however, her celebrity status stretched far beyond national borders,
something that was only enhanced after the murder of Van Gogh. Her face
appeared on magazine covers and on television programs throughout Europe
and the United States, and she has received a number of international prizes
and other forms of attention. In addition, Ali claimed to be a former Islamic
radical herself, which in the eyes of true believers made her even more the
infidel. All of this kept her in the public eye, making her an exemplar of successful assimilation from one perspective and a legitimate target for a *jihadi*

warrior from another. Like Mohammed Bouyeri, Ali was a militant in the "clash of civilizations" and, until the assassination, a much more visible one. In the tense atmosphere following in the wake of Fortuyn's assassination, Ali was the subject of many death threats and was under 24-hour police protection, living for a time in exile and then in a designated safe house. Killing her would not be easy, and this made Van Gogh, who had also received death threats but refused police protection, the more available victim.

If this was to be a religious assassination, the murder of Van Gogh created problems of its own. In a strict religious interpretation, one would need the blessing of a religious leader, and though there would be no need to name the potential victim, it would be presumed that it was a fallen Muslim, rather than a non-believer. Special dispensation would be necessary in such a case, unless one accepted the proclamations of Osama bin Laden, who in a broadcast from 1998 had said, "To kill Americans and their allies—civilians and military—is the individual duty incumbent upon every Muslim in all countries... This is in accordance with the words of God Almighty: 'Fight the idolaters at any time, if they first fight you'" (cited in Eyerman 2008:72). Though they did not come from a legitimate religious leader, these words would have provided important justification for the murder of a non-Muslim like Theo van Gogh. At his trial, Bouyeri had said, "The law compels me to chop off the head of anyone who insults Allah and the prophet" (reported on French news www.france24.com/en). Taking this literally would explain why he tried, unsuccessfully, to slit his victim's throat on that Amsterdam street. The spectacular attack on New York's World Trade Center on September 11, 2001, of which bin Laden was the alleged organizer, was a most significant turning point in the evolution and growth of Islamic radicalism. It was also a major stimulus to debates about immigration and multiculturalism in the Netherlands. It was 9/11, as it came to be known, which turned U.S. president George Bush into the commander-in-chief of the newly declared "War on Terror," and Pim Fortuyn from a public intellectual into a front-running political candidate. It also revealed to alienated Muslims living marginal lives in Western countries that another path to self-fulfillment and confidence was possible.

This raises the general issue of the potential for radicalization among Muslims living in Europe and elsewhere and the particular issue of why this happened for Mohammed Bouyeri. After the murder of Van Gogh, an Amsterdam-based study of the potential for conflict and radicalization among its Muslim residents was commissioned by Mayor Cohen and other civic leaders. It divided the city's population into ten different categories, five categories each for Muslims and non-Muslims alike. The fifth category for Muslims was "the jihadis who recruit and train, maintain breeding places, spread hatred of the West and want to commit extremist acts" (Uitermark 2010:182). About 150 people fit into this category, according to the findings.

Another study found that about "two percent of the capital city's Muslim population, some 1,000 to 1,500 people, were orthodox and politically active" and "sensitive to radicalization" (reported on www.france24.com/en). As the sociologist Jean Tillie explained, "It concerns mostly the 16- 18-year-olds, who feel discriminated against and have a distrust of politics" (Uitermark 2010:182). This was an audience with whom the actions of Mohammed Bouyeri would have resonated. Bouyeri himself did not begin his life as an orthodox Muslim, much less an Islamic radical. On the contrary, his identification with the religion he was born into was thin, rather than thick. Like many urban youths in predominantly immigrant neighborhoods, Bouyeri lived in two worlds, the modern world of the street and the more traditional world of the home. In his own account of his conversion to radical Islam and a thick Muslim identity, Bouyeri cited the death of his mother from cancer and his father's disabilities after many years of hard labor at low-paying jobs in the Netherlands and France (Eyerman 2008:56ff).[20] But there were many other factors as well, such as his frustrations in school and with the Dutch authorities, including social workers and the police. Whatever frustration he might have felt at not being fully integrated into Dutch society (however one might interpret that) came after having absorbed some of the fundamental values of modern urban life. He played football, smoked and drank, and enjoyed the clubs and nightlife, while at the same time defending the honor of his sister in the traditional manner of the eldest son. He was a serious student in a secular school, with dreams of social mobility for himself and the community with which he identified. These are modern ideals, and if there were frustrations in his life beyond those connected directly with his family, they arose, perhaps, out of the attempt to combine traditional and modern ideals, not from any religious orthodoxy. That orthodoxy would come later, more as justification for his actions rather than the cause of them.

If not the prime target, Van Gogh was a legitimate target in Mohammed Bouyeri's eyes, but this was the case not only for his participation in the making of an insulting and blasphemous film. Van Gogh was the quintessential Dutchmen, at least as a representative figure of what, in Mohammed B.'s opinion, was a decadent postwar generation. In this, he resembled Pim Fortuyn. For the newly converted religious militant, Van Gogh was evil personified: a fat, foul-mouthed, blond-haired and blue-eyed devil, who called Muslims "goat-fuckers" and had dressed up as an imam in a public performance (together with the then deputy prime minister Gerrit Zalm and other politicians) where he defended Hirsi Ali and ridiculed Amsterdam mayor Job Cohen,[21] appearing to say and do as he pleased. Just as the perpetrator dressed for the occasion when he set out to murder Van Gogh, the victim was also dressed for his part. As he cycled to work that November morning, Van Gogh wore red, white, and blue suspenders to hold up the jeans over his substantial belly. He did this in preparation for an evening meeting to follow the U.S. election results. Red, white, and blue are also the colors of the Dutch flag and those suspenders gaily glorified this connection. In one column, he had written, "Since September 11...the knives have been sharpened and the fifth columnist goat-fuckers have been marching relatively unhindered forwards. I can't put it otherwise. We live in a nightmare of good intentions and wrongly understood idealism. I am too old to emigrate to America, that beacon of hope in a steadily darkening world" (cited on www.militantislam-monitor.org). The name he bore was itself expressive of a social attachment; thus, when Mohammed Bouyeri shot and stabbed Theo van Gogh, he also attacked a vision of Western society. With this act, he announced his own rejection of that society and all it stood for. In this sense, the murder of Theo van Gogh was both personal and representative. Although Mohammed B. could, in principle, have chosen any Dutch citizen, he chose this particular one for ritualistic assassination. This death could not be anonymous and indiscriminant; what was attacked through the body of this individual was an entire way of life.

ALTERNATIVE SCENARIOS

One could ask, "What if it had been Hirsi Ali and not Theo van Gogh who had been killed; would the effect have been the same?" The two were, after all, on the same side in the Dutch cultural wars. Would this have equally fueled the accelerating public discourse on the meaning of Dutchness and the foundations upon which it was based? The murder of Theo van Gogh not only evoked collective expressions of grief and violence, but also intensified an already fiery debate about immigration policy. It was one that touched the very foundations of national identity because it involved two opposing views of society: should the Netherlands be a multicultural ménage of various groups, or an integrated community based on shared norms and values? Who and what was Dutch was a question now being discussed in many forums—in the parliament, on the street and in the private home. These issues and this heated debate had come to the fore already in the 1980s, but they were restricted, for the most part, to the political realm and to a small number of politicians, which, of course, is not to say that others did not feel the same way. The attack on the World Trade Center and the voices of Pim Fortuyn and Van Gogh, among others, increased the volume and widened the audience. Immigration policy, who should be included in the collective of the nation and on what grounds, was now one of the most contentious and central issues on the public agenda. The most visible and vulnerable group in this debate were the Muslims, whose role and place within Dutch society was at issue. Fortuyn had helped to make this so, though he was far from alone. What Fortuyn had achieved in his short political career was to secure for this debate a more permanent place in the political arena and to open that arena itself to a much broader segment of the Dutch citizenry. His assassination further expanded those borders and the affected groups. The death of Theo van Gogh at the hands of a self-identified Islamic radical moved this ongoing debate to another level of intensity at the same time as it shifted the numbers and allegiances of the participants—those who felt themselves affected. All the taboos about political and social correctness, at least in public behavior, seemed to vanish. One could now, it was felt, say exactly what one meant. This is what both Fortuyn and Van Gogh preached, and their deaths, in such close proximity to one another, made their message that much stronger.

What if Hirsi Ali had been murdered by Mohammed Bouyeri instead? I believe the outcome would have been different. Although she was linked to Van Gogh through the provocative film they made together, Ali spoke to a different, more restricted public. Her audience, and thus, her sphere of influence, was largely political and intellectual, even though she spoke of cultural matters. Though a popular author and public speaker, she was most attractive to liberal and conservative intellectuals in Europe and the United States, which also made her more cosmopolitan. Ali was not a representative figure of Dutchness, or even of Western culture and society, in the same way as Van Gogh was. Or, if she was, it was at a different, perhaps more elite, level—a more restricted form of representation. Ali spoke out in the name of the Enlightenment and of liberal values. The *New York Times* dubbed her a "daughter of the Enlightenment," and although she may have represented those values to an already convinced Dutch public, her death would most likely not have unleashed the same kind of collective emotion and identification as the death of Van Gogh did. In addition, Ali was someone newly arrived and thus, in some eyes, not "one of us," something she herself expressed when asked to speak at a ceremony commemorating the end of the Second World War. For others, like Mohammed Bouyeri, she was not an authentic "immigrant," a member of that diverse group in whose name she often chose to speak; after a short period in the refugee camp, she had moved quickly up the ladder into Dutch society. From this perspective, Ali was (and remains) a woman without a nation, a free-floating intellectual claiming to speak for, rather than being rooted in, any particular group. To be sure, her assassination would have caused a political crisis. She was, after all, a formal representative of the government, and there would have been a variety of official ceremonies, but most likely not the same kind of spontaneous mass reaction as there was with the death of Van Gogh. An eventual assassination of Hirsi Ali could have been equally exploited by political entrepreneurs like Geert Wilders, but I do not believe this would have added as much force to the debates about the foundations of Dutch identity as the assassination of Theo van Gogh did. Though much less elegant and eloquent, Van Gogh, probably much to everyone's surprise, had a wide and broad representational effect. In a way that would have been difficult to foresee and predict, the

death of Theo van Gogh in the manner that it occurred—with this particular perpetrator and with the obvious links to Pim Fortuyn—catalyzed,
intensified, and focused a wide range of feelings that the murder of Ayaan
Hirsi Ali would not have, tragic and horrendous as it would have been.

As a true counterfactual exercise, one could also ask what would have
happened had Van Gogh not been killed, had instead been wounded, or
if nothing at all had happened to him on November 2, 2004. The debate
surrounding immigration into the Netherlands and the place of Muslims in
Dutch society would have continued, because it was well in motion, especially after the assassination of Pim Fortuyn. The debate surrounding the
film *Submission* would most likely have subsided, and Hirsi Ali would have
found other means to keep the issue of Islam and the rights of women on
the agenda. Others in her party would have exercised the means and policies to retain assimilation as an important item on the political agenda and
Geert Wilders would have done the same. Outside of formal politics, Van
Gogh would have played his part. After a while, this would all have become
politics as usual, part of the process of routinization in the wake of the charismatic Pim Fortuyn. A contentious issue would then have shifted from the
most divisive and dangerous sphere of civil society, that of mobilization and
social movements, to the more formalized and ritualized realm of professional politics. The Netherlands would have become even more like other
European nations, which is not to say that this could not be reversed with a
new catalyzing incident, another assassination, or a provocative act of terror.

CONCLUSION: THE ROLE OF CARRIER
GROUPS IN TRAUMATIC OCCURRENCES

Casting counterfactuals is a useful endeavor because it helps to parse the many
different aspects of a political assassination and to locate the nuances in their
meanings. However, it is crucial to also underscore the role of carrier groups.
In short, they are the central agents in the meaning struggle in the aftermath
of a traumatic occurrence. As Alexander (2004) points out, the struggle to
define the situation focuses on what happened, who the perpetrators and
the victims are, and most of all, what it all means in the broader sense. The
first carrier groups in the attempt to define the situation in the case of the
Van Gogh murder are the mass media; it is they who construct the facts and
give them coherence by creating a story. They produce the first narratives
that are diffused to the public. If we unpack the concept "mass media," we
find reporters and editors who select and adjust the frames through which
they define the situation, prioritizing what is important and the story lines
with which to organize and make sense out of what happened. Reporters and
editors also rely on experts, those who claim some sort of special knowledge
regarding either the specific type of incident, such as an assassination, or of

the persons involved. In this case, once it was established that it was a "radical Islamic militant," a "terrorist," or an "animal-rights activist" who was the likely perpetrator, experts on these topics were called upon by the media to express their opinions about the meaning of what had occurred. This was significant in the framing of the incident and its understanding by the wider public. These labels helped to simplify and to personalize a potentially very complex and confusing occurrence. There is nothing inherently sinister about this process of typification; it is something we do every day, but it does lend itself not only to simplification but also to stereotyping. At the same time, once a label is applied and diffused, it is difficult to change and adjust.

Inevitably, the process of meaning making involves contestation; so it is with political assassinations. There are other carrier groups that may dispute, counter, or enhance the narrative constructed in the mass media and the experts it invokes. One such example were the so-called Friends of Theo van Gogh a group of well-placed and media-savvy journalists and authors, who came together in an effort to influence the way the assassination of Van Gogh was understood. Since they were not politicians themselves, they could act as a countervailing force against attempts at political exploitation. In his own way, Van Gogh had been doing the same thing with his film about the death of Fortuyn. One of these "friends" is the journalist Max Palm, who is currently writing a book about Theo van Gogh (http://www.youtube.com/watch?v=p7F9kcf-3NU). Palm and others in the group were influential in the construction and placement of a memorial to Van Gogh in the park near where he was killed.[22] The theme of this memorial is "freedom of speech," and it carries the message that Van Gogh was a martyr to that principle. This is one example of the attempt by an individual or group to influence the meaning and also the memory of Van Gogh's death, as part of the meaning struggle surrounding a traumatic occurrence. Other carrier groups (or members of groups) in political assassinations are those who would exploit the traumatic occurrence for their own political ends. The individual who best exemplifies this is Geert Wilders, who had been a member of the VVD and an ally of Hirsi Ali in championing the issue of cultural assimilation of immigrants to the Netherlands. He took on the issue even more assiduously after the death of Fortuyn and is considered by many to be his heir. In 2004, Wilders formed his own party, the PVV (Freedom Party), which was a major winner in the last election. After the death of Van Gogh, he made a very provocative 17-minute political documentary *Fitna* (Arabic for "ordeal"), which brings together excerpts from chapters of the Koran with media reportage on Muslim violence and terrorism (http://www.liveleak.com/view?i=bc4_1206703296). Opening with the controversial Danish cartoons of the Prophet Mohammed, the film premiered on the Internet and garnered 1.2 million hits in just one hour. In spite of government warnings of potential violence, Wilders claimed his film was not "provocative," and told Nederlandse Omroep Stichting (NOS) television, "I think Islam and the Koran are a danger for freedom in the Netherlands in the long term, and I need to warn for that." As mentioned earlier, there are also groups of Internet-based intellectuals and activists who maintain blogs and websites that periodically recall these assassinations. An unintended consequence of their actions is that they keep the event in the public eye. An example can be found in the memorial celebration and events at the fifth anniversary of Van Gogh's murder.

On the fifth anniversary of his death, November 2, 2009, a number of memorial ceremonies and other activities took place. Amsterdam's mayor, Job Cohen, told Dutch radio, "We learned from it," while sociologist Jean Tillie said, "The problem in Dutch society is that there are groups of people who don't trust each other" (both cited on www.cbc.ca/arts/film/story/2009/11/02/theo-van-gogh-anniversary). Both of these statements reflect a particular perspective, that of the politician interested in managing crisis and that of the social scientist concerned with everyday attitudes and behaviors. The point is that the death of Theo van Gogh marked another turning point in an ongoing national debate about immigration policy, and more broadly, about what it means to be Dutch. The national self-image of a tolerant and caring nation was shattered by these two assassinations—what was now being negotiated was the meaning and limits of tolerance. The fifth anniversary celebrations featured a televised debate in which various intellectuals and politicians discussed the meaning of Van Gogh's death in light of the current political situation. One point of focus was the rise and significance of Geert Wilders in the future of Dutch politics. In the most recent national election (2010), Wilder's party gained 15 seats in parliament for a total of 24, whereas the PvdA, now headed by (the now former) Amsterdam mayor Job Cohen, failed by one seat to become the largest party in parliament. Although immigration was the central issue of the election campaign, it turned out not to be what decided the outcome itself. Since the election occurred in the midst of a global economic crisis, more traditional issues, such as unemployment, appear to have been the decisive factors.

Though immigration was not the deciding factor in this election, it remains the most vibrant and divisive issue on the national agenda, for it touches the very foundations of what it means to be Dutch. More like an open wound than a scar, the assassinations of Pim Fortuyn and Theo van Gogh will remain present in the collective consciousness and continue to be available for exploitation and mobilization as long as this issue is not resolved in some satisfactory way.

CHAPTER 6

CONCLUSION

THIS BOOK HAS BEEN CONCERNED WITH POLITICAL ASSASSINATION as traumatic occurrence and how, with the aid of mass-mediated representation, such an occurrence becomes an event that can set in motion a process of cultural trauma. Now, after the detailed presentation of six cases in three countries, we are prepared to address a central question: under what conditions does a political assassination lead to cultural trauma? One of the main theoretical contributions of this study I take to be this distinction between traumatic occurrence and cultural trauma. What I suggest, and believe to have shown, is that a political assassination is traumatic for those who feel themselves closely connected to the victim or victims, but that it is background conditions and the relative forcefulness and success of the narratives constructed by carrier groups that determine whether a traumatic occurrence will develop into a cultural trauma. To say this more systematically, there are several factors that condition the development of a cultural trauma from a political assassination: the timing of the occurrence; the political context; how authority is performed; the mass media representations—which include reference to and influence on collective memory; and finally, the presence of powerful carrier groups and their performance. In this conclusion, I will elaborate on these factors while drawing on the preceding chapters.

All six of the assassinations studied were traumatic, but not all resulted in, or contributed to, a process of cultural trauma: the assassinations of Pim Fortuyn and Theo van Gogh in the Netherlands and of Martin Luther King Jr. and Robert Kennedy in the United States did, whereas the assassinations of Olof Palme and Anna Lindh in Sweden did not. This means that I take a social constructivist point of view and oppose those who argue that occurrences are already events that can be considered traumatic in themselves. In this conclusion, I elaborate these points by drawing upon and comparing the six cases. Although much attention has been focused at the level of the nation, where the cultural trauma and the affected collective consciousness concerns "our society," one could also choose to focus on another level of analysis, such as that of a city or a group—something I will also elaborate on.

I have defined political assassination as a murderous act against an individual or individuals that engages a community. The victim or victims need not be elected officials—as was the case with Martin Luther King Jr., Pim Fortuyn, and Theo van Gogh; what is essential is that the victim is felt by others to represent something significant to their own identity, their foundational values, and their sense of belonging. This feeling of commonality and identification with the victim may well be emergent and constitutive, realized through the act of assassination and the collective emotion it evokes. This was the case, for example, for many in the Netherlands when Van Gogh and Fortuyn were murdered. These two figures alienated as many as they attracted while they were alive, but in death, especially when considering the manner in which they died, they united a wide collectivity—one with strong feelings of solidarity and collective belonging.

DEFINING A CULTURAL TRAUMA:
WHEN IS A CRISIS A TRAUMA?

Initially, I defined a cultural trauma as public discourse, carried out in a range of forums, where the foundations of collective identity are brought up for critical reflection. In this sense, a cultural trauma is a form of identity crisis, in which a collectivity loses the secure sense of itself and seems adrift in that liminal space that Emile Durkheim labeled *anomie*. But cultural trauma differs from crisis, not only in that it affects the foundations of collective identity, thus engaging the social whole and not only one or several institutions, but also in that it has outcomes with regard to longevity and long-term effect. Cultural trauma is an emotionally laden discursive process—a trauma drama—with long-term effects on memory and social practice. One can distinguish the process from the effects—in the way that one can distinguish a traumatic occurrence from a cultural trauma—through its long-term nature. The trauma process is an intense public discourse on collective foundations carried out in several arenas of society, and the effects can be located in collective memory as well as in altered social practice. An example of the latter would be changes in how members of a nation view each other, such as when the native Dutch began to distinguish themselves from "immigrants" and then "Muslims," affecting the narrative about "who we are."[1] Political assassinations are always shocking and can be said to be traumatic in the more conventional usage of the term, not only for the victim, but also for those who are present and feel themselves to be directly affected. This was so in all of the cases discussed—all of these assassinations set off a public discourse about the possible effects upon a collectivity that felt itself directly affected.

Yet, not all of them led to cultural trauma. In the Netherlands, the followers of Pim Fortuyn were dismayed and confused about how to proceed; political leaders and journalists worried about the effects on Dutch democracy. The same was the case in Sweden after the murders of Olof Palme and Anna Lindh. Although only a few years have passed since the murders of Fortuyn (2002) and Lindh (2003), I think one can make a different assessment concerning the long-term effects and the possibility of cultural trauma as opposed to a crisis that was spurred by a traumatic occurrence. The Netherlands is still (2011) in the midst of an ongoing public discourse about the meaning of Dutchness and the grounds for national identity, whereas in Sweden, this discussion remains muted and much less prominent, though signs exist that this might be changing. For the Dutch, aspects of this debate about national identity preceded the assassinations of Fortuyn and Van Gogh (Lechner 2008), but there is no denying that their deaths were significant emotional catalysts that widened and deepened that debate. I believe that one can speak of cultural trauma in the Netherlands, which was provoked by the cumulative effect of these two political assassinations. This is not the case in Sweden. Why? Lechner (2008) offers a partial explanation. He places the Dutch discourse on national identity within the wider framework of the expansion tendencies in the European Union (EU) and the ongoing effects of what he calls globalization. Current debates about what it means to be Dutch, he suggests, can be explained by the uneasy relation between national and cosmopolitan identity, spurred by the meaning and impact of a unified Europe and the economic and cultural effects of a globalizing world, which would include the population flows of migration and immigration. The underlying conditions Lechner describes are certainly important, but the same tensions are active in Sweden, and yet there is no comparable debate.

Why didn't the murder of the Swedish prime minister in 1986, and the foreign minister nearly two decades later, set off a debate about the foundations of national identity in Sweden, whereas the two murders in the Netherlands did? There are many possible and probable reasons, but I would like to put forward the argument that the manner in which these political assassinations were narrated and understood by significant segments of the population had a major impact. Several factors help to explain the difference. The countries are similar in that political violence is relatively rare, and whereas the Netherlands has a much greater population density, both have a comparable ratio of immigrants to the more settled population. Both are parliamentary democracies with a sitting and visible monarchy, though the Swedish royal family plays less of a political role than does the Dutch royal family, where the current queen is the formal head of state and officially proclaims any new government. One key difference, to my mind, lies in the timing of the assassinations. The assassination of Olof Palme came as a shock and seemingly out of nowhere; it was entirely unexpected (at least among the general population) and without apparent cause. The fact that the perpetrator was never identified only added to this mystery: why kill Olof Palme? And why now? The socialist vision that Palme represented was already in a precarious state. The long-term reign of the Social Democratic Party (SAP), where it could count on a majority in parliament and the undying loyalty of a weakening labor movement, was questionable. There was no obvious political motive or agent for his murder. In addition, the political transition was clear and immediate, with the new prime minister and party leader appearing on the same newspaper front page as the reportage on Palme's death. The assassination of Olof Palme was a shocking and traumatic event for the Swedish nation, but its long-term effects were most strongly registered in the SAP and the Swedish police corps. When another leading figure in the party, the sitting foreign minister, and in many eyes the heir-apparent, Anna Lindh, was murdered seventeen years later, there was an outpouring of collective grief, and the memory of Palme's assassination was immediately recalled. Again, however, the accumulated effect weighed most heavily on the SAP and the police corps. Though a "threat to Swedish democracy" and a "national trauma" were pronounced, there was no ensuing discourse about the foundations of national identity, no questioning of "who we are." This was facilitated by the highly effective manner in which those with political and judicial authority performed their roles, thus helping to manage the crisis. In Sweden, the two closely associated and unexpected assassinations were shocking and traumatic occurrences, but they did not result in cultural trauma. In the Netherlands, the timing was different. First, the assassinations occurred much closer to one another, and the link between them—not only in the temporal sense but also because the two victims could also be easily associated—could seem obvious, even to the politically uninterested. Second, the assassinations occurred in the midst of an ongoing debate about the nature of Dutch society and especially the role and place of an immigrant population within it. The two victims were key players in this debate, with Fortuyn embodying a central role in the more directly political debates and Van Gogh in the cultural issues. This meant that the assassinations could be more easily interpreted as political and thus used to mobilize certain groups and highlight certain issues. In short, the two assassinations in the Netherlands helped to ignite an already smoldering fire. This was also the case with the assassinations of Robert Kennedy and Martin Luther King Jr., as I will discuss below when I return to a more systematic comparison of the cases. Before that, let me offer some further reflections on the notion of cultural trauma.

The above example leads us to add a nuance to our definition of cultural trauma. As I use it here, cultural trauma refers to a critical and reflective public discourse on the foundations of collective identity, which emerges from or is spurred on by a shocking or traumatic occurrence. Following an earlier presentation (Eyerman 2008, see also Mast 2006), I distinguish between an occurrence and an event in order to highlight the difference between the real-time occurrence of a murder and its later representation, most specifically in and through mass media. It is through such framed representation or narration that an occurrence becomes an event. In a similar vein, I distinguish between a traumatic occurrence and a cultural trauma. Regarding political assassinations, one can speak of a range of reactions to shock and trauma. I understand a traumatic occurrence to be one that leaves those who experience it directly, or feel some immediate association and identification with the victim(s), with long-standing memory traces that affect their behavior in unexpected and often uncontrollable ways. A traumatic occurrence creates shock and dismay among those immediately present—either on the scene or in close proximity, spatially and/or emotionally—when it happens. A traumatic occurrence creates a biographical and historical watershed, a sense of before and after, which can shape not only individual, but group and generational consciousness as well. This draws on a more psychological notion of trauma, where individuals experience a strong emotional response to an incident which helps shape a collective association. To be more concrete, those present in the pantry of the Ambassador Hotel when Robert Kennedy was shot were greatly affected by their presence during that incident. It is possible to speak of a long-term emotional impact on these individuals, as well as a sense of shared experience that may bind them together (see Erikson 1995 on collective trauma emerging out of a shocking occurrence). The same could be said for those who learned about Robert Kennedy's death through contemporary mass media accounts and felt an attachment to the man, his cause, or his family, though they were not physically present. This use of trauma is different from that of cultural trauma, which refers to a discursive process and to collective, rather than individual, emotional response. Following the point made by several authors in Alexander et al. (2004), I would reiterate that cultural traumas are made, not born. Cultural trauma requires narration and representation, communication, and interested parties. As I use it here, the term refers to a conflict-laden discursive process, brought about through a traumatic occurrence, as part of the attempt to define its meaning, to designate who was responsible, to name the victims and the perpetrators, and in which the foundations of the collective are brought up for critical reflection (Alexander 2004).

THE CONSTRUCTION OF CULTURAL
TRAUMA: MAKING MEANING

My linking cultural trauma to strongly felt emotional experience is meant to address the issue raised in the opening chapter as to whether, given the power to represent, any occurrence or string of occurrences can be made "traumatic." Is cultural trauma simply a persuasive narrative (built around perpetrators and victims) that struggles to gain acceptance through forceful representation and/or which, once legitimated, gives positional status, such as that of "the victim" to those who seek it (see Laqueur 2010; Fassin and Rechtman 2009)? To put this in other terms—is cultural trauma a social construction that becomes a social fact through the concerted efforts of powerful interests to define the situation? This recalls a citation from Neil Smelser (2004:38) from Chapter 1, where a cultural trauma was defined as "an invasive and overwhelming event that is believed to undermine or overwhelm..." Although Smelser does reference an "event," it is the phrase "believed to undermine" that is crucial, because it raises the issue of how this belief might come about, how a group comes to believe that an event is overwhelming. Jeffrey Alexander (2004:10) makes a similar point when he writes, "Trauma is not the result of a group experiencing pain. It is the result of this discomfort entering into the core of the collectivity's sense of its own identity." Both Smelser and Alexander put emphasis on the *making* of trauma, its acceptance by a group and, more implicitly, on the efforts of social agents in this making. I agree—in order for a shocking event or traumatic occurrence to become cultural trauma, a process of social signification must occur, and the occurrence must be signified and become socially constructed and accepted as such (Demertzis 2009). What I would add and emphasize is the linking of this process to a traumatic occurrence.

In studying cultural trauma, one can focus on the process of construction, on the trauma drama, and on the agents and carrier groups that turn an occurrence into a cultural trauma—as was done in Eyerman et al. (2011). One can also ask the question raised at the very beginning of this book: can *any* shocking or traumatic occurrence be made into a cultural trauma, given powerful agents? Will *every* traumatic occurrence become a cultural trauma? Heins and Langerdahl (2011) have addressed the latter question with reference to the suffering of German citizens experienced at the time of the Allied bombings during World War II. They show that although individually traumatic, the bombing of German cities did not lead to any claims making or spur carrier groups to push the idea into the public realm in any sustained way. The suffering remained personal and private. In the same volume, Bartmanski and Eyerman (2011) reveal how the personal and private suffering of Polish citizens, after the 1940 murder of more than 15,000 members of the social elite (in what has come to be called the Katyn Massacre) was never permitted public discussion, and how this contributed to a cultural trauma process years later. Pinchevski and Liebes (2010) turn this question around and show how the live broadcast of the Eichmann trial in 1961 over Israeli radio was a catalyst for turning individual and private suffering into a collective one, but not into what I would call a cultural trauma.[2] Regarding the issue of whether or not any event can become a cultural trauma, given powerful forces who would make it so, one can speak of "invented" or imagined trauma, as in the case of Serbian nationalists who attempt to ground their movement on the defeat in Kosovo in 1389, an occurrence that might never have taken place, yet has been constructed as a powerful source of national identification (Spasic 2011). Rather than an actual event, one can speak of the power of its symbolic representation, or as Spasic writes, "of the symbolic, abstract meaning, not Kosovo as a real place." The movement from traumatic occurrence, real or imagined, to cultural trauma is thus complex and contingent, circumstances matter.

In this book, I have developed a constructivist position, arguing that certain occurrences—in this case, political assassinations—create conditions that are conducive to setting in motion processes of cultural trauma, but that not all such occurrences become cultural traumas. Cultural trauma will not happen without representation and without the aid of meaning-making forces, such as mass media and certain carrier groups, like intellectuals, who influence the formation and direction of the process. Because cultural traumas emerge through narration and representation, certain actors, what I call carrier groups, play a central role in the process. However, I do not believe that this is an arbitrary process, that any name or label can be made to fit any occurrence. Nor is it simply a matter of the power to define the situation. Certainly, there are a number of more or less successful cases of mobilization around "invented" or "chosen" traumas, such as the Serbian case mentioned above. But even here, some referent to a historical event is made, which can be contested. Would it matter to the cause of Serbian nationalism if the Battle of Kosovo could be shown never to have occurred in the way claimed? Probably not to true believers, but a case could at least be made against them; here, the norms of evidence and representation that guide the profession of history have an important place.[3] I agree with Sztompka (2004) that certain occurrences lend themselves to trauma construction, whereas others do not. However, even given what he calls the "trauma potential" of an occurrence, not all those exhibiting such potential will set a trauma process in motion. I have identified six cases of political assassination, each of which could be thought to have such potential, but not all of which resulted in cultural trauma. The attempts to label an occurrence a "trauma" might also fail, just as the application of any interpretative frame might be rejected by those to whom it is addressed.

Trauma narratives are about perpetrators and victims, with an asymmetrical relation between these two positions. Those designated to these positions might reject the label; for example, "victims" might reject the "weakness" or vulnerability associated with the term, preferring another label or narrative, even if there might be some potential gain involved in its acceptance. If we accept the idea of trauma as a narrated representation, then we must accept that as forms of communication and communicative action, the construction of narratives has a performative dimension, involving not only senders and receivers, but also actors and audiences. Narratives may be coded and weighted, but they require decoding and interpretation, something that implies a more active role for audiences than passive receivers. For communication to be successful, narratives must be constructed in recognizable and compelling ways. However unequal or asymmetrical the relation between sender and receiver might be, both sides—receivers and senders alike—are more than passive bearers of discursive structures performing their assigned and scripted roles. At the very least, actors in these "positions" must be acknowledged as capable of amending, rejecting, or challenging such structured identifications. All this points to the significance of the "successful" performances of carrier groups in re-presenting their message, and of political authorities in performing their role. Cultural trauma discourses are broader and deeper than trauma narratives, as there may be several competing narrative accounts within the cultural trauma discourse. They reach into the very core of collective identity and collective memory, as I demonstrated in a book about the formation of African American identity (Eyerman 2001). In my understanding, collective memory is more than a reservoir of images and meanings: it is an active agent in the making of cultural trauma.

Cultural traumas are not things, but processes of meaning making and attribution, a contentious contest in which various individuals and groups struggle to define a situation and to manage and control it. These forces cannot create trauma out of nothing—there is likely to be some powerful, shocking occurrence that creates the possibility, providing the opportunity to form and mobilize emotions and opinions; it is here that various narrative accounts compete to define the situation. It is also here that contextual factors and timing are essential, as will be elaborated on below. There are at least two dimensions in a cultural trauma, an emotional experience and an interpretive reaction. In a process where the foundations of individual and collective identity are shaken and called up for critical reflection, emotions that were triggered by a traumatic occurrence are worked through as attempts are made to heal the collective wound. All of which is to say that cultural traumas are more than a struggle between competing claims to define a situation, to distinguish perpetrator and victim, and to identify the nature of the pain. To assume this would be to see the process as dominated by strategic actors and action and to deny its communicative and interpretative aspects.

Analysis of cultural trauma may thus begin with a shocking or traumatic occurrence, a political assassination, for example, which has the potential to set in motion a trauma process. Such an occurrence has the power to both unify and divide, to create insiders and outsiders. One should always ask, as Giesen (2004) and Sztompka (2004) do, trauma for whom? The assassination of John F. Kennedy in 1963 was shocking to the vast majority of Americans and many others around the world; the same can be said with regard to Olof Palme's assassination in 1986. Both were shocking in part because they were so unexpected, seeming to come out of nowhere. Both were also traumatic in the more conventional, psychological sense, but neither resulted in cultural trauma, though in retrospect one can locate John F. Kennedy's assassination as a key incident in the cultural trauma process that developed shortly after, carried by a resurgent civil rights movement and the escalation of an increasingly unpopular war. The assassinations of Robert Kennedy and Martin Luther King Jr. in 1968 occurred within an already-polarizing and fragmenting American society, a national collective in the midst of redefining its foundations, though it might not have looked that way at the time. As traumatic occurrences, these assassinations struck more deeply within particular groups than throughout the nation as a whole. King's death, for instance, was most strongly felt among African Americans, triggering not only strong emotional reactions, such as shock, disbelief, and collective grief, but also unprecedented collective violence. At the same time, his death further catalyzed an ongoing internal debate among civil rights activists about the strategy and tactics of the struggle for racial equality. These were all part of the contest to define the situation and to frame and understand the meaning of that traumatic occurrence. Robert Kennedy's death was traumatic in different ways and for different groups. It was perhaps most strongly felt by his political supporters on the left-liberal wing of U.S. politics—they had lost a leader who had promised to end the war in Vietnam, to unite blacks and whites, and to "heal the divided nation." But his death was also powerfully felt because of the association with the Kennedy family, and most especially with his elder brother John. Widely felt emotions accumulated not only because of the close proximity to the assassination of Martin Luther King Jr. and the political links between them, but also because of a overarching sense of mourning for one of America's most-loved families—the nation had "lost another Kennedy" was an oft- repeated phrase. Although they might have struck more deeply into the consciousness of particular groups, both these assassinations, so close in proximity, strongly escalated an ongoing trauma process.

THE ROLE OF CARRIER GROUPS

Traumatic potential must be realized, emotions felt, meaning articulated, and blame attributed. This is both an individual and a collective process, but it is here that mass media play a determining role. First, they are crucial because they spread the "news" beyond those immediately present. Second, media representations provide interpretation, imposing a narrative structure that tells "the story" that frames the emotions evoked and acts as a contagion for their diffusion. This is done visually, orally, and through the written word, through dramatic photographs of the firsthand reactions of the general public, as well as through other specific media features such as sound and voice. Pinchevski and Liebes (2010) provide an analysis of the distinguishing features of radio in mediating private and public trauma, though television has now surely replaced it as the main bearer of drama and tragedy. In this sense, mass media actors are the first carrier group, parties with moral, professional, and commercial interest in portraying an occurrence and making it into an event. An occurrence gains significance as it is deemed newsworthy, codified, and disseminated to wide and widely diverse audiences. All of the political assassinations discussed in this book received the widest media attention, yet dissemination and interpretation differed. After the murder of Olof Palme, both Swedish and world media were more subdued. Coverage, which set a record for the number of Swedish households reached in the shortest possible time, focused largely on the man himself, his background and his accomplishments, as well as on the unexpected and shocking nature of his death. Collective grieving and moving forward were the most common themes, and the mass media played an important role in turning a negative incident into a more positive event by picturing a nation in grief and helping to create and transmit a sense of unity out of what could have been divisive. Following the murder of Anna Lindh, media attention focused on issues such as Swedish naiveté, the search for those responsible, and the security of public officials. As with Olof Palme, Lindh's personality and accomplishment were prominent themes, particularly her age, gender, family, and friendships. Again, national unity was portrayed, and even forged, one could say. Dutch coverage of the murders of Fortuyn and Van Gogh differed substantially, most especially concerning the death of the latter. Media coverage seemed to encourage public reaction. "We Are At War," screamed the headline of a respectable morning paper, quoting the words of the country's finance minister in responding to the presence of law enforcement and military personnel on the streets of the nation's capital (Eyerman 2008).[4] Having learned from the assassination of JFK, the U.S. media, most especially television, were extremely active in disseminating and constructing public reaction to the murders of Martin Luther King Jr. and Robert Kennedy, especially with reference to the latter. The death of "another Kennedy" was extremely newsworthy, though nothing like that of his older brother, after whose assasination television coverage was constant and continuous for four entire days, with hardly any commercial interruption.

If mass media represent the first carrier group, those who speak to and through the media from the outside are the second. These are the representative figures, the experts and authorities, who are called upon to explain and enlighten, who articulate various viewpoints in filling out the story as it is now being constructed. In all these cases, national and international political leaders were asked for their opinions in the immediate aftermath of the assassinations. Dutch politicians were canvassed by mass media, immediately following Pim Fortuyn's assassination, about its meaning and potential impact. British politicians Margaret Thatcher, Neil Kinnock, and David Owen all voiced their opinion in the first television coverage in the United Kingdom following the murder of Olof Palme. Academic experts on Islam and immigration were called forth to explain the process and potential of "radicalization" after the assassination of Theo van Gogh. President Lyndon Johnson established a commission to investigate the causes of violence and the meaning of assassination in the United States after the murders of Kennedy and King. These were all interested parties and members of carrier groups who helped to make and disseminate the meaning of these assassinations.

A third carrier group consists of those with more clear and direct connections to the occurrence—the friends, families, and supporters of those murdered. After the murder of Van Gogh, a small, but influential and media-savvy group calling itself "the friends of Theo van Gogh" organized themselves as an interest group in order to influence the interpretation and representation of his death. They were quick to counter what they felt were incorrect or false claims through the making of counter claims on television talk shows and in newspaper interviews and book reviews, while at the same time making public their own interpretations. As a well-known filmmaker as well as a friend and supporter, Theo van Gogh had actively attempted to influence the meaning of the assassination of Pim Fortuyn by making a popular film about it. It is part of the irony of his own death that he was killed while on his way to the studio where he was working on the film.[5] Friends and colleagues of Anna Lindh have published magazine articles and books about their relationships with the assassinated Swedish politician. In the United States, well-placed supporters and friends of Robert Kennedy wrote books and articles about the man and his mission. Nearly all of those in the inner circle surrounding Martin Luther King Jr. have published memoirs and autobiographies in which the fallen leader and the movement he represented play a prominent part.

Another carrier group (with less direct connection to the victims, but with clear personal and professional interests in shaping interpretation) comprises those authors, artists, and other intellectuals who write books and articles and make films and artworks with these assassinations as referents. There is an entire genre of thriller and crime fiction that has focused on political assassinations, including the ones discussed here. Tomas Ross, one of the "friends" of Theo van Gogh, has written a long counterfactual account of what could have happened had Pim Fortuyn only been wounded, rather than killed. The conditions surrounding the death of Olof Palme continue to be the subject of crime literature and nonfiction reportage both in Sweden and elsewhere. This unsolved murder is sometimes cited as the reason for the sudden emergence of Scandinavian crime fiction as a popular, nearly world-wide phenomenon, now reaching into the film world as well. The volume of literature, factual and imaginative, on the murder of Robert Kennedy and Martin Luther King Jr. is large and impressive. Beryl Bainbridge, a well-known British novelist, was reportedly working on a novel about Robert Kennedy's assassination called *The Girl in the Polka Dot Dress* just before she died in July 2010. A feature film called *Bobby*, marketed as "the story of the assassination of Robert Kennedy," appeared in 2006, with a cast of Hollywood stars. Although there have been many documentary accounts, to the best of my knowledge, no feature film has been produced about the assassination of Martin Luther King Jr. This might have to do with the sensitivity of the topic and the internal controversy and bickering still ongoing within the family and the inner circle of King's associates.

In addition to these individual and group efforts, collective actors, as diverse as foundations and social movements, act in similar ways to present the image and conserve the memory of these assassination victims. Those remaining organizations of the American civil rights movement are bearers of the memory of Martin Luther King Jr. in the same way as is his family. They not only bear his memory, but also claim the right to interpret the meaning of his activities. When the conservative "Tea Party Movement" held a rally at the Washington Mall in 2010, the site of King's famous "I have a dream" speech, and made claims about carrying on King's legacy, former civil-rights-movement activists were outraged and were quick to publicly denounce such claims.[6] The Robert Kennedy Center for Justice and Human Rights offers not only awards for books and article that "carry on the spirit of RFK," but also attempts to define what that spirit might be. There is also a European version of this organization.[7] The political party organized by Pim Fortuyn is still active in the preservation of his memory, and his supporters maintain a memorial in his name as well as organize conferences with the same aim. There is an Olof Palme memorial fund, along with foundation, that offers an annual prize in the field of human rights. Its Swedish website provides an answer to the question, "Who was Olof Palme?" (www.palmefonden.se). Similarly, a foundation and a prize exists in the name of Anna Lindh.[8]

Even long after the fact, such carrier groups accomplish at least two things, whether intentionally or not. They help to preserve and renew the memory of the victim at the same time as they offer another, varied and different, account of the assassination itself, contributing to the discourse around its meaning. Among these accounts are those that argue for or against an established or official version of these assassinations. Each of these six cases has promoted counterclaims, especially the one of Olof Palme, where the killer has yet to be identified. Even in cases—such as those of Pim Fortuyn, Theo van Gogh, Robert Kennedy, and Martin Luther King Jr.—where the perpetrator has been identified, tried, and convicted,—conspiracy theories abound. Such conspiracy theories include Van Gogh's own film on the Fortuyn murder, where a combination of U.S. political and defense industry interests, in collusion with Dutch counterparts, are depicted as involved with the assassination. Like Oliver Stone's 1991 film, *JFK*, Van Gogh's film makes use of actual news footage to make his case for conspiracy. As for Van Gogh's own assassination, a documentary account, produced by his friends and associates, makes similar claims about the complicity of the Dutch police (De Jong 2005). Blaming the Central Intelligency Agency (CIA), the Mafia, and the trade union movement is standard fare in American accounts of the murders of Robert Kennedy and Martin Luther King Jr.

MORAL FRAMEWORKS: MAKING SENSE
OF VICTIMS AND PERPETRATORS

The accounts of journalists, artists, and other intellectuals serve to keep the memory of the person and the circumstances of his or her death alive in the public mind at the same time as they argue from a particular point of view. In this sense, they are part of the meaning struggle, offering a partisan as well as a moral framework within which to interpret these assassinations. As such, they can be considered part of the emotional acting out and working through, which are essential aspects of the cultural trauma process. As Felman (2002:4) points out, trials can have much the same function, where the courtroom becomes a "theater of justice" and a social space for the reenactment of trauma. Significant factors in what does or does not become a cultural trauma are the more or less successful application and acceptance of these moral frameworks defining, for example, good and evil, which undergird the grounding myths or root paradigms that are present at any given time in a society. The taking of a human life is a crime in all societies; the taking of the life of a young public figure is more than a crime (though this is often a consideration in sentencing) because it robs both the person and the collectivity of their potentiality for greatness, their contribution to the common good. This makes the crime all the more horrible, turning death into tragedy. In the making of an event, modern mass media draw on deeply rooted sensibilities, structures of feeling, in their representations. Victims are pictured with families, in their youth and youthfulness, emphasizing their promise as well as their goodness. Perpetrators are depicted with different emphasis, as marginal, cunning, and ultimately evil individuals who threaten the common good. Such forms of representation contribute to the cultural trauma process, in the making of a traumatic occurrence into a dramatic event. Phrases like "national trauma" were commonly applied in the media accounts of these assassinations, but that is only part of the story. The moral frameworks that are taken for granted are even more telling in these constructions because they elicit seemingly spontaneous emotional reaction. In order to do this, words like "trauma," "victim," and "perpetrator" must be felt, as well as cognitively understood; they must resonate with deeply held beliefs, myths, and remembrances that evoke identification in an audience. Headlines like "We Are At War" have a surface as well as a deeply seated meaning. What is understood by such a phrase? Who are "we"? What does the word "war" evoke? To those who read that newspaper headline in the Netherlands after the death of Theo van Gogh, these terms probably had both an obvious and a not-so-obvious meaning that must have varied across that diverse readership. The Second World War was a common frame of reference for many in that audience, and it was referenced by Van Gogh himself, before he was killed, to make a point about what he saw as the impending danger of Muslim immigrants. He spoke of the "fifth column," the sound of marching boots, and "Islamic fascism." Such associations resonated with a particular audience because of emotions related to historical experience and to stories that had been heard or read, where evil Germans subjugated the good Dutch. This was a "war" with which many could identify, and such proclamations thus carried all the more emotional weight.

Consciously partisan or not, the application of a moral framework of good and evil or right and wrong highlights the cultural aspects that condition the emergence of a cultural trauma. This is another way of saying that those emotional reactions that cause shock and that define traumatic occurrences are shocking because they are filtered through this cultural framework or structure (Alexander 2004, Wagner-Pacifici 1986). The murder of a person in his or her prime—such as Anna Lindh, who to many represented (and was represented in media accounts as) a rising star and future prime minister as well as a "mother of two young children"—is shocking not only because of her political position but also because youthful potential and motherhood are foundational, taken-for-granted values that should not be violated. This makes her assassination feel "worse than Palme's," as one journalist expressed it. The same can be repeated with a slight modification for Robert Kennedy, the scion of a respected family, the father of young children, and the younger brother of a fallen noble leader. That both Lindh and Robert Kennedy (one could also add his brother John) were killed by "nobodies," insignificant and marginalized individuals, is difficult for many to swallow, given the stature of the victims. This in part explains why conspiracy theories abounded even after the trial and conviction of Sirhan Sirhan and the extensive investigation that supported the claim that Lee Harvey Oswald murdered John and Robert Kennedy, respectively. Or that James Earl Ray, a small-time criminal from a family of small-time criminals, could be solely responsible for the assassination of Martin Luther King Jr. It seems impossible to accept that noble figures could be killed by those so ignoble; it makes their deaths appear that much more meaningless and tragic. This theme was played up in media accounts, and those narrative frames that are "successful" are often those that link the incident with deeply rooted values and perspectives.

Such considerations help to explain why some assassinations catalyze and contribute to a cultural trauma process. Like Robert Kennedy, Anna Lindh was full of promise and potential, and her death was shocking to many, even those who did not share her political views, party affiliation, or nationality, because of that. She was also associated with a fallen leader, Olof Palme, and reference in the media was made immediately to her family, with her death made more tragic because of the effect on them.[9] Like Robert Kennedy's assassin, Lindh's was almost immediately apprehended, tried, and convicted, to the great relief of legal authorities who did not want "another Dallas" or "another Palme." There were similarities in the social position of the two perpetrators. Both were from immigrant families, young, single men who remained connected with their countries of origin. Both had vague political motivations for their actions. In neither case, however, were these political and cultural considerations long emphasized in media accounts. The fact that Sirhan Sirhan was a Palestinian refugee to the United States and that some of the attorneys who represented him did so for political reasons was not a significant factor in reportage, although it has since been made more important by conspiracy theorists (Ayton 2007 and Kaiser 2008, for example). Context and timing are significant here; had the murder occurred a few years later, when Palestinian activism was in full bloom, or today, during the "war on terror," this would have been front-page news and an important catalyst in a trauma drama. At the time, though, there was apparently enough drama around in the United States, hence there was no need for any more. The immigrant background and political interests of Anna Lindh's killer were mentioned briefly in Swedish media representations. But these soon took second place to a focus on his social marginality, mental health problems, and family hardship. Part of the blame for the perpetrator's actions was thus placed, implicitly more than explicitly, on Swedish society and the failure of the welfare state, of social services, and of mental health and police professionals to treat, protect, and prevent this occurrence. To be sure, the death of a young and promising female political representative was shocking because it violated fundamental values, and while it led to an outpouring of collective grief, it did not catalyze a discourse on the foundations of collective identity. The fact that the perpetrator was represented as a mentally unstable, lone individual contributed to that. Had Sweden been in the midst of a virulent and divisive debate about multiculturalism and the place of immigrants and immigration, as was the Netherlands at that time, or perhaps as Sweden is today, things might have been otherwise.

COLLECTIVE IDENTIFICATION AND MEMORY

Cultural traumas can only be named and known while in process and best studied in retrospect. It is only with the passing of time—how much exactly is uncertain—that we can know if the effect of a traumatic occurrence is still felt, still alive. In a study of reactions to the assassination of Olof Palme, Olof Johansson compared responses in surveys of Swedish citizens three weeks after the event to those four and six years later. He found that "the emotional effect of the assassination fades away fairly quickly and is replaced by a much more vague and unclear structural effect related to the total impact of the assassination seen as a dramatic event of national importance" (1995:265). I would interpret this to mean that lodged in collective memory, these emotions would reappear when a similar event occurred, that is, the assassination of Anna Lindh, as in Fassin and Rechtman's notion of trauma (mentioned above and elaborated below). In this sense, cultural trauma, as an intense public discourse around the foundations of collective identity, resembles the trauma experienced by individuals, where accumulated emotion can remain under the surface and become suddenly visible. The assassinations of Martin Luther King Jr. and Robert Kennedy occurred in the midst of a trauma process, a process, we can now say, that began with the assassination of John F. Kennedy and intensified with the increasing racial conflict and the escalation of the war in Vietnam. For all else, that assassination removed a leading political figure who might have been instrumental in mitigating the foundational racism in American society, smoldering beneath the surface since its constitution; it also eliminated someone who might have ended the "police action" in Vietnam before it became a full-fledged war. These were two of the significant factors leading up to the assassinations of Martin Luther King Jr. and Robert Kennedy, which took place in an extremely polarized and contentious society, during a period now enshrined as "The Sixties." The three assassinations, separated by a period of less than five years, were catalysts in a long-term cultural trauma that may have only received some closure with the election in 2008 of Barack Obama as the first African American president of the United States. One could ask what could have happened had only Martin Luther King Jr., and not Robert Kennedy been assassinated. How would that have affected the trauma process? King's assassination had already spurred Robert Kennedy in his quest for the presidency, and his public performances, in the wake of King's death, raised his stature as a viable candidate. Not only was Kennedy strongly opposed to the war in Vietnam, but he was the only one of the presidential contenders who showed any possibility of lessening racial tensions and quelling some of the civic unrest that was rampant in many urban centers across the country. These issues I have suggested were central to the ongoing cultural trauma. Had Kennedy not been assassinated, that process might well have taken another turn. His own assassination, just weeks after King's, further intensified the cultural trauma Although King's assassination may not have consciously and directly inspired the murderous actions of Sirhan Sirhan, the latter's killing of Robert Kennedy occurred in an atmosphere of frustration, violence, and cultural trauma, which made it seem both possible and logical to an angry and frustrated individual.

The assassinations of Pim Fortuyn and Theo van Gogh helped to catalyze an already ongoing contentious process about the meaning of Dutchness and the foundations of collective identity in the Netherlands. In retrospect, one can now see how long this process had actually been going on—at least since the 1980s—though it was not until the 1990s that these sentiments found a clear and articulate political voice and after 9/11 that they found a popular movement to broaden that debate beyond the realm of formal politics and public policy. Contentious emotions were building but not fully exposed until 2001 and the World Trade Center attacks, which helped put Pim Fortuyn in the center of public debate, marking him as a representative figure. Fortuyn was a central actor in turning the fears aroused in the Netherlands into a clear political and cultural issue. No comparable emotions were smoldering in Sweden; nothing so deeply rooted was exposed or revealed with the assassinations of Palme and Lindh, except, perhaps, some outmoded self-images about political leaders and fears of conspiration within the Swedish military and police corps. After the initial shock, these deaths resonated most strongly in two central Swedish institutions, the police corps and the Social Democratic Party (SAP), as mentioned earlier.

This can be connected with a methodological issue raised in the opening chapter: the relation between classical and cultural trauma. With the role of memory and collective identity in mind, one can ask: What is the role of traumatic occurrence in the cultural trauma process? In tracing the history of the concept of trauma in a professional and broader public discourse, Fassin and Rechtman (2009) reveal changing perspectives on the role of an event. In its first conceptualizations, they argue, a precipitating event, such as a railroad or workplace accident, was seen as a necessary cause for what were identified as traumatic symptoms: victims were traumatized as a result of some event, or what I call an occurrence. Early psychoanalytic theory altered this sequence by claiming that what was triggered by such an external incident were underlying internal (unconscious) fears and anxieties stemming from repressed childhood sexual fantasies. In this account, trauma preceded the triggering event, which was indeed a catalyst to symptoms, but ones whose roots lay deeply recessed in the victim's psyche, stemming from events further back in time. In other words, an event triggered memory and the unwanted recollection of past experiences.

In viewing political assassination through the lens of cultural trauma, I make use of both these accounts, at least as far as the relationship between occurrence and trauma is concerned. A major difference, however, stems from the fact that I am interested in cultural rather than individual trauma. I will return to this relation in a moment, but first let me elaborate on the role of an occurrence (for example, a political assassination) in cultural trauma. Cultural trauma is a process, a meaning struggle that is connected to a tear in the social fabric. One question, then, concerns the relation between the two—the tear and the process. Does one cause or precede the other? The answer is that such causality can be the case, but not necessarily so; it all depends on the context and the range of contingent factors mentioned in the opening paragraph of this chapter, namely, the timing of the occurrence; the political context; how well authority is performed; the mass-media representations and how well the narratives they create resonate; and finally, the presence of powerful carrier groups and their performance. The Palme assassination shook the nation, exposing its collective foundations for public reflection, but it did not tear the social fabric and spur a discourse on collective foundations. The assassinations of Martin Luther King Jr. and Robert Kennedy, on the other hand, shredded a fabric that was already exposed and worn. There is, in other words, no simple and direct relation between a political assassination as event and cultural trauma. A political assassination can be a trigger to already existing, but deeply hidden, traumas, but not necessarily to cultural trauma. Because it was an assassination, the murder of Martin Luther King Jr. triggered unprecedented civic violence as it was identified with, and thus exposed, the long history of racism and racial conflict in the United States. Because it was an assassination, the murder of Theo van Gogh became a catalyst to an outpouring of collective emotion, including violence, emotions that had accumulated since the murder of Pim Fortuyn, but that could also be traced to other historical events hidden deep within collective memory and the very idea of Dutchness itself. Most significant here were the lingering memories of the Second World War and the German occupation of the country; the significant loss of colonies, Indonesia, in particular; and its effect on the image and reality of the Dutch population (Eyerman 2008).

Mass-media narratives and the voices of various carrier groups, especially with reference to the Second World War, drew heavily on these memory strands. The assassination of Anna Lindh triggered an outpouring of collective grief along with memories of the Palme assassination. If it was a catalyst to anything more, it was the concentrated and concerted efforts on the part of responsible parties to manage this crisis and to resolve it as quickly and as efficiently as possible.[10]

We can now turn to the problematic relation between individual and collective in the theory of cultural trauma. Referencing the importance of the Holocaust in the development of trauma theory, Fassin and Rechtman write:

> The memory of the Holocaust is...a paradigm for trauma...in two ways. First it represents the most extreme reach of violence, and as such becomes an unavoidable reference point for any experience of pain, of suffering, and hence of trauma...Second, it developed after a period of silence, a fact that attests precisely to its traumatic nature. It is because of the delay between the event and its painful exposure to the public gaze that the process can be qualified as trauma. These two aspects establish the link between the collective and the individual...on the one hand, we have the foundational drama which is played out for the Jewish people and replayed for each individual within it [it could have been me], and on the other, the necessary delay before the appearance of the memory trace (in the group) and neurotic symptoms (in the individual). Thus in psychoanalysis the analogy between what is happening at the collective level and what is going on at the individual level establishes a connection between the culture and the psyche, a connection which lies at the heart of the politics of trauma: the collective event supplies the substance of trauma which will be articulated in individual experience; in return, individual suffering bears witness to the traumatic aspect of the collective drama. (Fassin and Rechtman 2009:18)

In speaking of cultural rather than psychological trauma, the relation between the individual and collective is quite different. To follow their example, in the case of the Holocaust, which, as Alexander (2009) has so elegantly shown, the wider social meaning and significance of this horrible event had to be socially constructed, communicated, and accepted before it could become the universal symbol that Fassin and Rechtman describe. This was apparently the case even for the individual victims themselves, as described above in reference to Israeli survivors (Pinchevski and Liebes 2010). A war crime had to become the Holocaust, a symbol of ultimate evil and universal suffering, where the signifier "it could have been me" is universalized to all human beings, and those who suffered are not only members of a particular ethnic or religious group, but any and all victims.

For individual Jews, however, even those far away in the United States, the identification with those who suffered directly could have been immediate: "It could have been me." Thus, it is bridging the gap between the individual and the collective through identification *as* (a Jew) and *with* (those who died because they were Jews).

In the case of cultural trauma, and with the example of political assassination as triggering incident, identification with the victim is not the same; there is no sense of "it could have been me." Rather, the victim must first be recognized and reconstructed as a representative figure, as "one of us," a symbol of something "we" fundamentally value: a fellow American, a Dutchman, a Swede. Or identification emerges through something more abstract, a principle that is valued, such as free speech, democratic society, the rights of women, and so on. There is, in other words, no "natural" identification, no direct (collective) "trauma," except through reflexive and mediated representation; although a case can be made for those immediately present on the scene and those directly related to the victim in some way. This, for example, could encompass those for whom Martin Luther King Jr. was a symbol of their "race," those who thought Pim Fortuyn was murdered because of his sexual orientation, or those who believed Anna Lindh was killed because she was a woman. But even such identification requires mediation. In all these assassinations, the grounds and the sense of identification, the sense of collective as well as individual suffering, emerges through the incident, through the victim, whose death becomes an event in part because it means something to a collectivity, often a collectivity it has helped constitute. The sense of collective belonging might have already been there, as potential, but was actualized through the act of identification, which is an interpretative act. This is, in part, what is meant by reflecting on the foundational values, which is at the heart of the definition of cultural trauma. The values that define the collective may be there, but they are largely taken for granted as part of collective memory. The assassination and the crisis that follows actualize that potential, providing the opportunity—not one sought after or desired and thus not ritualized—for collective realization, reflection, and debate concerning its grounding values. In modern society, the mass media are an essential means of this process. They not only mediate this reflection, but they also help to define and script it.

This identification is necessarily selective. Not all members of the nation, not all Swedes, or all Americans, or all the Dutch, identified with or reacted to these political assassinations in the same way. They were not "traumatized" in the psychological or psychoanalytic sense. Individually, they might not have experienced any long-term reactions or symptoms associated with trauma and being traumatized. Cultural trauma refers to a discursive process in which an event, or series of events, constructed from traumatic occurrences, leave memory traces on collective rather than individual memory (though the latter can and does also occur). Think of all those who remember exactly where they were and what they were doing when they heard about one of these six assassinations. This of course does not necessarily mean that they have long-term symptoms, though some do. A traumatic occurrence, in the sense I use it here, leaves a mark on collective memory, within a group, an institution, or a nation, which can emerge later as recollection and add to the collective reaction to another incident that is felt to be similar. Mass media again play a central role in drawing these connections, stimulating collective, rather than only individual, reaction. The relation between the individual and the collective in cultural trauma is a highly mediated and contingent one. There is no direct or necessary connection between an incident, or even an event, and an individual's reaction. This is exactly why the process can only be analyzed fully after a certain—again arbitrary—length of time has passed.

CULTURAL TRAUMA AS ANALYTIC FRAME

As an analytic framework, cultural trauma is a heuristic device that permits the historical reconstruction of the trauma process, the trauma drama, where the foundations that define a collective are brought up for reflection and debate. In addressing cultural issues and the question of "cultural" trauma, it is possible to speak of various levels of collective identity. It is also possible to speak of a cultural trauma more locally, such as within a city or a region, where a discourse on local identity is at stake. This was the case in San Francisco after the assassinations of Mayor George Moscone and City Supervisor Harvey Milk (Eyerman forthcoming). Whereas the assassination of John F. Kennedy can be said to have had a global impact, it left a distinctive mark on the city of Dallas, with officials, including those responsible for law enforcement, worried about the city's image for years after the occurrence. The same was the case for Memphis after the assassination of Martin Luther King Jr. No such local trauma can be identified in Stockholm, where both Olof Palme and Anna Lindh were murdered, or in Amsterdam or Hilversum, where the deaths of Van Gogh and Fortuyn occurred. In the Swedish case, the shock of these occurrences was immediately nationalized. These murders took place in the national capital of a highly centralized society, where, especially in political matters, issues of significance seem to emanate from Stockholm, moving from the center outward. Palme's murder temporarily unified a contentious and polarized political elite, just as it unified his own party. The nation came together with Stockholm as its center and the mass media as convener of the national assembly. As well as political tensions, regional differences were put aside as the nationally televised funeral focused full attention on what was occurring and what had occurred in Stockholm. The murder of Anna Lindh had a similar effect. Lindh was killed in the midst of a contentious battle over Sweden's entry into the European Economic Union (EEU), a battle that crisscrossed party lines. The nation came together to mourn, but Lindh's death did not influence the outcome of the national referendum in the way that many had predicted. A strong supporter of the "Yes" side, Lindh had been its poster figure, but, a few days after her death, the oppositional "No" side won a clear victory (56.2 percent against 41.8 percent, with a voter turnout of 81.2 percent). The Stockholm-based political elite lost this campaign and the nation an up-and-coming political figure, but the city suffered no ill effects from its association with either.

In comparison, the Netherlands is more decentered and the United States more multicentered. In the Netherlands, politics emanates from The Hague, whereas Amsterdam is a cultural center. Mass media are distributed from Hilversum, the site of the Fortuyn murder, but this geographical fact meant only that reportage was instantaneous, not that the image of the city was affected. It may have been of symbolic importance that Fortuyn, a media celebrity, was shot in the Hilversum Mediapark parking lot, and also that Van Gogh was murdered on a busy Amsterdam street in full public view, but neither had significant long-term impact at the city level.[11] One should perhaps modify this a bit, since Fortuyn was a Rotterdam-based politician as well as an emerging national figure, who won an astounding 35 percent of the votes in a municipal election in 2002 (Uitermark 2010:133). His funeral was held in Rotterdam, and monuments to his memory have been erected in that city; Fortuyn's Rotterdam home has become a shrine. However, this does not alter the fact that the impact of his death was not a local but a national event. There is also no escaping that Van Gogh was as much an *Amsterdammer* as he was a Dutchman. His carefully staged public persona—the overweight, obnoxious 'healthy smoker,' who said exactly what he thought to whomever he desired—was created and honed in a post-1960s Amsterdam subculture. Van Gogh's death, however, was felt and interpreted not so much as a blow against that subculture, but as a blow against the foundational Dutch values of tolerance and free speech. In death, Van Gogh became a symbol of what were represented as national values and virtues, not those of an urban subculture—something that he would probably have found ironic and hypocritical. The city of Amsterdam may have been the site of mass outpourings of anger and grief as well as of a monument placed in the vicinity of the murder scene, but anything more than this is not apparent. The monument itself is as much dedicated to free speech as it is to Van Gogh.

Although there are regional differences in the Netherlands, most clearly those between the predominantly Protestant North and the predominantly Catholic South, these differences were not as telling with regard to the assassinations as they were in the United States. The effects of the Civil War and the legacy of slavery are still felt in the United States, most clearly in the South, which, of all the regions of the country, still maintains a cultural and political distinctiveness. Especially in the 1960s and the high point of civil rights struggles, both Dallas and Memphis were Southern cities struggling with their image in the context of a widespread effort to recast a "New South," free from association with bigotry and racial violence. How others viewed these cities was something that generally concerned a number of local businesses, political leaders, and residents. Being the site of a highly visible political assassination did not help that image.

One can also speak, as Neil Smelser (2004) does, of institution-based "social trauma," where the shock waves of a traumatic occurrence leave traces on collective identity at the organizational level. Although the assassinations of Olof Palme and Anna Lindh may not have initiated a cultural trauma at the national level in Sweden, they clearly left strong legacies in the national police corps, the mass media, and, perhaps most especially, the SAP. As elaborated earlier, the memory of the failure to satisfactorily resolve the Palme assassination represented a heavy burden upon the collective memory of Swedish law enforcement representatives, especially in Stockholm. The SAP had lost a leader of international stature, an ideological figurehead, and it has never really recovered its sense of self as a political institution. Palme was the face of Swedish uniqueness, the embodiment of the "Third Way" between American capitalism and Soviet communism. After Palme's death, Anna Lindh was the first party representative to recapture some of that lost glory. She was a strong supporter of the EU and sought to use it as a basis for resurrecting something of Palme's vision, especially in international relations. Her death left the party once again seemingly adrift and in an ideological crisis. As part of their genealogy of the concept, Fassin and Rechtman (2009:16) define trauma as "the sudden emergence of memory at the moment of danger." This certainly is applicable in the case of the Swedish police corps in response to the Lindh assassination; the murder of Anna Lindh brought instant recall to police and judicial authorities. Swedish mass media, especially radio and television, were reshaped by the Palme murder and the surrounding investigation; whereas before the murder, these media had closed their news desks between 11:30 P.M. and 4:30 A.M., they have since been open around the clock (Weibull et al. 1987). The funeral was a media event, as the nation paused to watch the proceedings unfold in Stockholm (where the symbolic power of the SAP was resurrected) as its fallen leader was put to rest. As with the funerals of John and Robert Kennedy in the United States, the power of television to create a moment of national unity in grief was revealed for all to see. This profoundly influenced the way in which the Swedish mass media conceive of their social role.

The theory of cultural trauma provides a frame through which one can organize historical and empirical material in a structured and coherent way, allowing one to make sense of seemingly disparate occurrences. As a framework for analysis, a theory of cultural trauma allows one to study the struggle, to come to grips with traumatic occurrences, to locate the central actors in the meaning struggle, and to trace the process over long periods of time. In previous work, I have analyzed the meaning of slavery for the construction of African American identity in the United States (Eyerman 2001). In that book, I was interested in identifying the cultural mechanisms through which the experience of slavery became meaningful and significant for later generations of American blacks, who had no direct experience of slavery themselves. In other words, I wanted to understand how "slavery," as representation, became a symbol and a common ground for the establishment of a collective identity: the African American. In this current work, I have attempted something different: to identify the conditions under which a traumatic occurrence, a political assassination, can lead to a cultural trauma, a public discourse on the foundations of collective identity. The theory of cultural trauma has provided a frame through which I could reconstruct six political assassinations with the aim of showing how their meaning was constructed and the outcome varied. Through thick description, I have aimed at thick explanation: to reveal why this was the case. What, in summary, accounts for this difference? The assassinations of Olof Palme and Anna Lindh in Sweden, traumatic occurrences both, did not result in cultural trauma, primarily because there were no underlying and ongoing tensions and conflicts about national identity and no significant carrier group to orchestrate these assassinations to promote an identity crisis. These assassinations were traumatic occurrences that did not tear the social fabric. To be sure, they caused crises, collective pain, and anxiety, but they could at the time be managed rather well by those in authority. At the same time, however, these assassinations have left a trace on the collective memory, a wound that could very well be reopened. Sweden is currently in the midst of a relatively subdued debate about the aims and limits of nonEuropean immigration, and a new political party has emerged with this issue as its prime concern. At this point, its influence, though being felt primarily at the local and regional level, they have now entered the national parliament. Should another traumatic occurrence take place, which could in some way be associated with this issue, a cultural trauma could very well result.

In contrast, the assassinations of Pim Fortuyn and Theo van Gogh were significant catalyzing incidents in an already ongoing debate in the Netherlands about the meaning of Dutchness and the foundations of national identity. Not only were there significant carrier groups to orchestrate this struggle, but there were unresolved tensions and deep-seated emotions stemming from relatively recent historical events—the German occupation during the Second World War; the treatment of Dutch Jews and the loss of colonies, especially Indonesia and its effect on the makeup of the Dutch population—that were rekindled through these assassinations. This is not to say that there exists nothing similar in Sweden—underlying class and ethnic tensions did and do exist—but these were not exploited during the crises created by these assassinations. In the Dutch case, the main actors in contributing to the development of cultural trauma out of the traumatic occurrences were the mass media, the political parties and social movements, as well as the collective response of various religious and ethnic groups for whom these assassinations had conflicting meanings.

The assassinations of Martin Luther King Jr. and Robert Kennedy in the United States occurred in a period of even greater societal polarization, where collective protest and violence were everyday occurrences and where these assassinations were both cause and effect. They were a contributing cause to cultural trauma in that they raised the levels of frustration and anger to new heights. They were effects in the sense that both of the victims were representative figures of underlying tensions and hopeful possibilities in the American debate about its collective foundations. Key actors in conditioning the emergence and development of cultural trauma were the two main political parties, themselves radically divided internally, and the social movements, the movement against the war in Vietnam and the civil rights movement, which articulated opposing visions of what it meant to be an American and what its founding values meant. The mass media of course itself became a significant agent in the entire process by helping to articulate, orchestrate, and disperse these polarized visions across the nation and the world. One significant factor in the American case, largely missing from the others, was a rising distrust in established leadership and basic societal institutions, most particularly the political establishment, the military, and those responsible for law and order. The reports of government commissions to investigate the causes of violence in general, and political assassinations in particular, were met with great skepticism. On the one side, the police were part of the problem and on the other, the main solution. This general distrust and suspicion of those in authority was a major contributing factor in the cultural trauma process, for it severely limited the ability of legitimate authority to manage the ongoing and escalating crisis.

As an intense public discourse over the foundations of collective identity, which is initiated or spurred along by a traumatic occurrence with long-term effects, cultural trauma connotes something negative, even dangerous, for a collectivity. A traumatic occurrence, such as a political assassination, is clearly so. However, the trauma process itself, though intense and contentious, need not necessarily have only negative consequences. The process may eventually lead to reconciliation and social repair, being a process of working through, as much as of acting out. New, more stable foundations might well be the outcome of a cultural trauma process, leaving the collective with a different and perhaps more positive sense of itself. This was the case with (West) Germany after the cultural trauma of the post–Second World War, when national identity had to be rethought on new foundations (Giesen 2004). This is clearly the intent of truth and reconciliation commissions, trials of responsible parties, official apologies, and memorial ceremonies. Whether or not the United States is a society with a better sense of itself for having gone through the cultural trauma of the 1960s remains an open, politically charged question. Whether the Netherlands will emerge from its ongoing cultural trauma with a fortified sense of itself also remains to be seen. Nations learn from crises, or suffer them.

NOTES

1 THE PRIMAL SCENE

1. My account here builds on the one provided by Vincent Bugliosi (2007), which is based on the premise that a lone gunman, Lee Harvey Oswald, shot and killed John Kennedy. There remains a controversy as to whether or not there was more than one shooter at the scene. For the purposes of my argument that is irrelevant, as I am interested in the effect of the assassination, not who committed the actual act. These controversies are important, however, in the struggle to determine the meaning of an assassination, and I will discuss this and other conspiracy theories in a later chapter. My account of the media coverage is based on the following sources: Newseum, *President Kennedy has been Shot* Naperville, IL: Sourcebooks, 2003); "The Lost JFK Tapes" National Geographic 2009; and *Four Days in November* (New York: St. Martin's Press, 2003), which is a compilation of the coverage in the *New York Times*.

2 POLITICAL ASSASSINATION, TRAUMA, AND NARRATION

1. For an erudite discussion of ways of defining and understanding political assassination, see Ben-Yehuda 1993, especially chapters 1–2. Ben-Yehuda prefers to speak of political assassination events, rather than of political assassinations, and develops a topology toward that end.

2. A more recent study carried out by the Institute for Peace and Conflict at Uppsala University recorded 93 murders of heads of state and foreign ministers around the world during the period 1946–2007 (*Dagens Nyheter* 14 September 2008, p.5).This study was apparently commissioned after the murders of Palme and Lindh, in much the same way as was the Commission—after the deaths of Kennedy and King—although there was no direct governmental involvement. As in the U.S. study, one of the main concerns was with prediction and prevention. The report considered the murders of Palme and Lindh to be impulse killings carried out by lone individuals and thus difficult to prevent, given Sweden's open society. In labeling the murders "impulsive," the report called them "a uniquely Swedish phenomenon," and recommended strengthening the security around Swedish officials as the only reliable way of prevention.

3. During an early stage of their investigation into the murder of Anna Lindh, the Swedish police made use of a special task force composed of various professionals, including psychologists, law enforcement professionals, and lawyers. This group used

profiling techniques that were first developed in the United States in the 1950s, but are now in common usage around the world. Of the four basic categories, one profile was of special interest in this case: the reflective criminal. This category was broken down into two basic types—those who act out their personal fantasies through criminal acts and those who want to communicate something to others through such acts. It was this latter category that best seemed to fit Lindh's assailant.

4. It is possible, I think, to say that certain books by Adorno, Bauman, and Freud were written in connection to working through personal trauma.

5. This is a different way of speaking about "radical constructivism" than LaCapra (2001:8), who uses it in the context of the line between history-writing and fiction. In LaCapra's sense, those like Hayden White—who argue that on the formal level there is no fundamental difference between writing history and writing fiction because both necessarily make use of narration—are radical constructivists.

6. A parallel might well be the Marxian idea of class consciousness and the distinction between class-in-itself and class-for-itself.

7. Although not in the Habermasian sense—see footnote 15 in Chapter 3—for more on this.

8. Zelizer (1992:4) writes similarly of American journalism after the assassination of John Kennedy: "It was a turning point in the evolution of American journalistic practice not only because it called for the rapid relay of information during a time of crisis, but also because it legitimated televised journalism as a mediator of national public experience."

3   REMEMBERING THE 1960S: THE ASSASSINATIONS OF MARTIN LUTHER KING JR. AND ROBERT KENNEDY

1. Jeff Zeleny, "In Painful Past, Hushed Worry about Obama, *New York Times* February 25, 2008, www.nytimes.com/2008/02/25/us/politics/25memo.html

2. Here, one could also add the assassinations of Malcolm X in 1965 and Medgar Evers in 1963, as well as the prior attempts on Martin Luther King.

3. *New York Times* August 30, 1968:1.

4. The character played by Sean Penn in the film *The Assassination of Richard Nixon* (DVD 2005) calls Nixon "the greatest salesman ever" as he watches actual newsreel footage of the president. He explains that judgment while commenting on the disparity between the promises made in the inaugural address and what Nixon actually did. The film is loosely based on real events. In 1974, Samuel Byck committed suicide after being wounded by police aboard a commercial airliner that he had boarded in an attempt to hijack and to crash it into the White House.

5. About the strike and what occurred after King's assassination, Pat Watters reports: "The sanitation worker's strike...was settled in a way obvious from the beginning—by mediation. This was achieved through the services of an undersecretary of labor with orders from the President to do in the aftermath of tragedy what might have been done to avoid it. The union won small pay increases, grievance procedures, a dues check-off system. And it won the simple symbol of dignity that the black men in it had sought all along, so small a thing, mere recognition in an official City Council resolution of the right of the union to negotiate with the city" (Watters 1969:8–9).

6. The report would soon become an object of disdain for politicians running "law and order" campaigns, because of one of its conclusions, namely, that aggressive police tactics served only to provoke further violence. This only strengthened their claim that a 'permissive culture' was at the root of the troubles facing American society.

7. Jackson's role in the whole affair is full of ambiguity. Immediately after King's assassination, Jackson made the false claim to the mass media that King had died in his arms on the balcony of the Lorraine motel. Although present at the scene, Jackson was not on the balcony, and it was actually Ralph Abernathy who was the closest to King. In recounting Jackson's role Hampton Sides (2010:190) writes: "Perhaps the stress of the tragedy was getting the better of him, or perhaps he sensed an opportunity, but at this point [as he was being interviewed by the press immediately after the shooting] Jackson began to spin a small fiction that would grow in the days ahead, one in which he imagined himself playing the approximate role that Abernathy had in fact played on the balcony." This claim of Jackson's was strongly challenged and resented by others close to King and was seen by some as part of the infighting in connection with determining his replacement as head of the Southern Christian Leadership Conference (SCLC). Soon after the assassination, Jackson returned to Chicago, where he gave a televised interview where, dressed in a bloodstained shirt, he repeated the same story about cradling the dying King in his arms. As Sides (2010:235) writes, "Jackson failed to mention the odd way the blood got there. He then left for a busy itinerary of other interviews and public appearances, wearing his bloody shirt through the day." For whatever reason, Jackson appears to have been taking a cue from Jacqueline Kennedy's bloodstained dress.

8. With the memory of the John Kennedy assassination so close at hand, police and the medical authorities took special care with the autopsy of the body of MLK. Remembering the continuing controversy about the path of the bullets and the confusion that surrounded the autopsy of the slain president, the doctor in charge in Memphis worked with federal and local police officers who observed his every move.

9. Another possible motive is, of course, money. Racist groups throughout the country had placed a bounty for the murder of Martin Luther King; one of these, for 50,000 dollars, came from someone in Ray's hometown. After his arrest, many groups and individuals came forward with offers to fund his defense. These included the United Klans of America and The Patriotic Legal Fund of the National States Rights Party, which were connected with J. B. Stoner (Sides 2010:378). Ray boasted that money was never an issue and that "I can make a half-million dollars...I can raise a lot of money, write books, go on television (Sides 2010:380).

10. Richard Lentz (1990) offers a substantial analysis of the "crisis." Martin Luther King posed for newsweeklies (*Time, Newsweek,* and *U.S. News and World Report*) when his politics shifted from reform to radicalism.

11. The leadership of the SCLC is still shrouded in controversy. A *New York Times* (www.nytimes.com/aponline/2010/06/03/us) Internet bulletin from June 3, 2010, is headlined "SCLC Back in Court" to determine who is in charge of the organization. The current head, the Reverend Bernice King, the daughter of Martin Luther King, who was an infant when he was murdered, is part of a controversy concerning the spending of campaign funds.

12. Celebrating the day of King's death would mean taking into account his violent death and thus open commemoration to what Vinitzky-Seroussi (2001) calls a "narrative of violence." She analyzes the attempts to incorporate an account of the assassination of Israeli Prime Minister Yitzhak Rabin into school textbooks. The fact that Rabin was killed by a politically motivated person in the context of a radically divided polity created a problem for how to describe the event in a way that would accommodate vastly opposing interpretations of the meaning and motivation for his death. Her account of the process of negotiation builds upon that of Wagner-Pacifici and

Schwartz (1991), which analyzes the controversy surrounding the Vietnam Veterans Memorial.

13. The first police radio broadcast described the suspect as "...a male Latin, 25 to 26, 5-5, light build, dark bushy hair and dark eyes. Wearing blue Levis, blue jacket, blue tennis shoes." In the police car after his arrest, one the officers later recalled, "I was looking at him, and I thought maybe he was Mexican or Hispanic. I'm Mexican, and I speak Spanish. I asked him, 'Habla Ingles?' He wouldn't say anything" (cited in Moldea 1995:51). There were several other descriptions broadcast by the police, something that would later fuel conspiracy theories. One listed the suspect as a "male Caucasian, 20 to 22, 6' to 6' 2", built thin, blond curly hair, wearing brown pants and light brown shirt..." Another broadcast around the same time said, "No.1, male Latin, 30 to 35, 5' 9 1/2", stocky, wearing a wool hunter's hat with a small brim. No. 2, described as female Caucasian."

14. The Ramparts Division would later become the site of one of the largest police misconduct scandals in American history, as well as the subject of many popular television shows and feature films focusing on police drama, gang activity, and rap music. The Ramparts Division covers the areas west and northwest of downtown LA, one of the most densely populated regions of that city and also of the nation.

15. One of the psychiatrists involved in the trial theorized that this repeating of phrases was a form of self-conditioning and programming. By writing over and over that "RFK must die," Sirhan, he surmised, was preparing himself for the deed (see Kaiser 2008:373). Recent theory suggests that this is not uncommon with murderers, and that they mentally prepare themselves for a violent crime in the days before actually carrying it out, thus making it possible that the act itself becomes more or less automatic and that they may not even remember or be aware during the act itself. This may have been the case with Sirhan, and Robert Kaiser—who was employed by the defense team during the trail—continues to believe that someone indeed did "program" Sirhan. Kaiser continues to believe in the so-called Manchurian Candidate conspiracy, as opposed to Moldea, who became convinced that Sirhan was the lone killer after earlier believing that there were two shooters that day. *The Manchurian Candidate* is the name of a novel made into a well-known Hollywood film in which a former American soldier and prisoner of war is programmed by North Koreans to assassinate the American president. Ironically, John Frankenheimer, the director of the 1962 film, hosted the exhausted RFK the night before his death, and it was Frankenheimer who drove the Senator to the Ambassador Hotel on June 5, 1968.

16. Later conspiracy theories would claim that this defense hindered a deeper probe into the possibility that others, a "second shooter" might also have been involved, and that it meant leaving unexamined the obvious discrepancies, such as the claims of several eyewitnesses that Sirhan was no closer that three feet away when he fired his shots and the coroner's testimony that the powder burns on the body of the victim suggested shots at point blank range (see Moldea 1995, Turner and Christian 2006, Kaiser 2008). The diminished capacity defense was also crucial to the defense attorneys in the case of Dan White in 1979. White was accused of killing San Francisco mayor George Moscone and city supervisor Harvey Milk. He was convicted of voluntary manslaughter, rather than murder, largely through the so-called "Twinkie defense" (Twinkies being a popular cake at the time)—the claim that he suffered from diminished mental capacity after eating too much junk food. This case created such a stir that the diminished capacity defense was eliminated from the California statues in 1982, after a referendum.

17. NBC news interviewed a witness on camera directly after the shooting who claimed to have seen a woman running down a fire escape at the Ambassador Hotel, shouting, "We killed him, we killed him" (Kaiser 2008:25). This led eventually to theories about co-conspirators, one of whom wore a polka-dot dress, as described by this witness.

4 THE END OF INNOCENCE: THE MURDERS OF OLOF PALME AND ANNA LINDH

1. This was reported in an interview in *Sydsvenska Dagbladet*, November 16, 2008:A17. The headline read, "Nobel Prize winner—Almost a Fundamentalist Swedish Social Democratic" (Nobelpristagaren—Nästan Som en Svensk Betongsosse).

2. This account builds on official government documents, especially SOU 1988:88.

3. Weibull et al. 1987, give an account of the issues and delays in media coverage and news diffusion of the Palme murder. They show, for example, that most Swedes did not hear of the assassination until the next morning and that only two-thirds of Swedish morning newspapers managed to print something about the murder that day. All this had to do with the structure of the mass media at the time and the actual time of the murder.

4. According to later accounts, one reason for Holmer's appearance was that he had been away the previous night when the murder occurred and had to rush back to Stockholm to take charge of the investigation. He had apparently been on his way to an annual skiing event in the far north of the country and was reached in a hotel room he shared with his mistress. Holmer's marital problems were to become part of the story line.

5. By then there was a suspect in custody, though Holmer, like some social democratic leaders, thought there was a political conspiracy behind the murder. In custody was Viktor Gunnarsson, whom Swedish newspapers referred to as "the 33-year-old," since they were forbidden by law to give the name. Gunnersson was later released before he was formerly charged with the murder when Holmer's case against him unraveled in an embarrassing sequence of false and uncertain testimony (for details see Bundeson 2005).

6. Ingvar Carlsson (1999:50) recounts those with whom he conferred directly after the formal ceremonies: the United Nations secretary-general, the French president, ministers from the Soviet Union and the United States, the Indian and Israeli prime ministers, the chairman of the socialist international, the former president of Tanzania, and leaders from the Nordic countries.

7. In his memoirs, Carlsson (1999:49) proudly recounts the swiftness of this political succession and how efficiently the system worked. The entire process, from the murder of Palme to his own assumption of power, took less than two weeks.

8. In making his claim for an alternative to the dominant view that Christer Pettersson was guilty of the murder, Borgnäs recounts a number of occasions where Swedes had conspired to murder prominent figures. One of the most telling was the murder of Swedish King Gustav III in 1792. Borgnäs uses this example also to point to the difference in police work in both cases. In 1792, Swedish police worked very effectively to capture those responsible, whereas in 1986, they did not.

9. Östberg (2010) argues that in Palme's case, this was more rhetoric than reality. Though proclaiming political neutrality, the Swedish military was always closely tied to the United States and NATO. In 1991, Prime Minister Ingvar Carlsson informed

Parliament that membership in the EU was compatible with Sweden's neutrality (Hadenius 2000:196).

10. Gunnar Wall (1996:34) lists the changes in SAP orientation that began in the aftermath of Palme's death: being less critical of American foreign policy; a new campaign to join the EU; closing of the gap with the liberals and conservatives regarding economic policy; and abandoning not only the plan for employee funds, but also the entire idea of worker codetermination at the workplace.

11. Ungsgaard (2005:122) reports that Anna Lindh could very well have died at the scene if not for the first aid administered there by doctors who happened to be in the mall. There were three doctors who responded to the loudspeaker call for help, one of whom was the doctor at Anna Lindh's children's school.

12. Some Swedish newspapers regularly feature a page for unsolicited articles on topics of current interest. These are frequently authored by academics and politicians.

13. Democracy and the parliamentary system came relatively late to Sweden, not being firmly established until the beginning of the 1920s. Led by the SAP, the labor movement and several other *folkrörelser* played a central role in this.

14. There were two other fatal attacks that occurred at around the same time. Sweden had recently changed its policy regarding the institutionalization of the mentally ill, and there was concern that an increasing number of potentially violent individuals were on the streets. The first announcements of a possible suspect in television news reports mentioned the likelihood of the perpetrator being a homeless or mentally ill person.

15. Sweden does not have a jury system; instead, trials are heard before a standing board of community representatives.

16. Social theorists will immediately think of Jürgen Habermas and his theory of communicative action. Communicative action is the highest form of human action in this account, where a subject views her opposite also as a subject in an interaction, as both sides attempt to reach a mutual understanding. This assumes not only a symmetrical relation between the two parties, but also an underlying agreement about the meaning of interaction. The expressive or communicative offender also views his audience as subjects and intends to convince them of the rightness of his position, to say through actions exactly how he or she feels. There is no attempt at dialogue, however. The communicative action here is an acting out of a form of attention getting, which is not compatible with Habermas's subjects seeking mutual understanding.

17. Rönnegård (2008) argues that it was budget considerations that account for the lack of bodyguards watching over Anna Lindh during her shopping trip. Others, including Lindh herself, make this a gender issue. Lindh had once said, when asked about this, that it was perhaps easier for her male counterparts to have bodyguards.

18. This is a matter of strong dispute, as Jennekvist in his account claims that such a command center was set up immediately.

5   THE END OF TOLERANCE: THE MURDERS OF PIM FORTUYN AND THEO VAN GOGH

1. This interview has since been recast with an anti-European and anti-German message, complete with a Wagner soundtrack by opponents to the EU and posted on the Internet (see "Theo van Gogh and Pim Fortuyn on the E.U." posted by crixus on January 13, 2008, http://www.youtube.com/watch?v=bv8CiW6xX3U. The video

ends with photographs of the bodies of Fortuyn and Van Gogh, which were taken immediately after their respective murders.

2. According to Margry (2003:106), this was the first political murder since the Netherlands became a kingdom in 1813. He writes, "In the Republic of the Netherlands which preceded this, there were indeed political murders, the most famous being those of Prince William of Orange (William the Silent) at Delft on July 10, 1584, and of Grand Pensionary Johan de Witt and his brother Cornelis in The Hague, on August 20, 1672."

3. See 'Pim Fortuyn: "If Something Were to Happen..." posted by pimsghost on February 6, 2007 http://www.youtube.com/watch?v=B4Sl4CvmjfE.

4. Uitermark (2010:79–81) shows how public support for Fortuyn jumped significantly with each television appearance, especially as the election approached.

5. My account of Fortuyn's assassination builds upon Faber (2008).

6. *Rotterdams Dagblad* (May 8, 2002:713) reported that a special showing of Oliver Stone's film JFK would be made as a way of commemorating Fortuyn's murder. *De Telegraaf,* May 7, 2002 (Martin Koolhoven byline) ran the headline, "His Mother Was For Years Afraid of an Attack 'Like That Against Kennedy.'" A commemorative book written after his death bears the title *Professor Pim The Life of the Dutch Kennedy* (Santegoeds 2002).

7. This marks a difference from Harvey Milk—the struggle for homosexual rights were part of the political left in the 1960s—whereas with Fortuyn, there is a shift to the Right, and many traditional political parties have made this part of their platform. Moreover, many of those seen protesting in front of the parliament in The Hague appear to be those who would not normally support gays and lesbians; in fact, they seem to be the opposite, something that makes Fortuyn rather unique.

8. Pantti and Wieten (2005:304) point this out as part of a media strategy and the attempt to turn something negative and potentially dangerous into something positive by constructing a progressive narrative. They also provide data on the extensive and extraordinary television coverage of the Fortuyn murder and funeral.

9. One must be a little careful to draw conclusions from dress and appearance. In some parts of Europe, Sweden for example, shaved heads, boots, and Lonsdale shirts are also the uniform of left-oriented young males, though this style of dress has, by now, largely been appropriated by the neo-Nazi extreme right.

10. A video posted on YouTube showing television coverage of the funeral procession has a recording of "You'll Never Walk Alone" as its sound track.

11. The American writer and syndicated conservative columnist Daniel Pipes provided commentary on the trial and on Van Gogh's murder (www.sullivan-county.com/wcva/van_gogh1.htm). Pipes was a featured speaker at the Pim Fortuyn Memorial Conference in The Hague, in 2006.

12. Justus Uitermark (2010:82) suggests that while he was alive, Fortuyn revolutionized Dutch politics. He writes, "Fortuyn redefined the logic of politics through a style that could mobilize an electorate cynical of established parties and anxious about social transformations, including the growing presence of minorities and Muslims...he pioneered a particular form of political organization. Rather than a political bureaucracy...the party functioned as a marketing bureau that organized events and campaigns around its one and only brand." This would provide a model for other breakaway politicians like Geert Wilders, who inherited not only some of the issues Fortuyn championed, but also a particular way of conducting politics.

13. Several commentators later viewed these attacks as a "rehearsal" for the assassination. These included Peter Siebelt, who would write a book about an alleged conspiracy

regarding Forutyn's murder (Siebelt 2004). In his analysis of the Dutch immigration debate, which includes a discourse analysis of the Dutch media, Uitermark (2010:81) argues that there is little evidence of such "demonization."

14. Ahmed Hamdi was arrested the evening of the murder at Bouyeri's apartment. The two were alleged to be members of the so-called Hofstad Group (a name given to a number of Dutch-Moroccan young men and women who had been under police surveillance). Several other alleged members were arrested several days later. After the murder of Theo van Gogh and Bouyeri's conviction, another trial that focused on the activities of this group was held. Although several alleged members received prison sentences for infractions such as the illegal possession of weapons (including hand grenades) and the attempted murder of Dutch police officers, no truly conclusive evidence of any conspiracy with regard to the murder of Theo van Gogh was presented. An appeals court later ruled (2008) that they did not constitute a terrorist organization. A new trial began in July 2010.

15. On the same day, in the United States, National Public Radio (NPR) broadcast an interview, "All Things Considered," with a Dutch radio reporter on its 5:00 P.M. news program. With the six-hour time difference, this would be 11:00 P.M. in the Netherlands. The Dutch reporter included an eyewitness account of the perpetrator as wearing a traditional Moroccan *jaballa* (long gown). This later proved to be incorrect. Citing another eyewitness, England's *Birmingham Post* (November 3, 2004, www.lexusnexis.com/us/Inacademic) described the murderer as "wearing a long beard and Islamic garb," something that was also false. News of the murder was broadcast across the globe, and stories appeared the same day in all major metropolitan centers.

16. These translated quotes are taken from Bloomgaarden and de Vreese (2007:7).

17. The issue of whether or not a nonbeliever like Van Gogh could be a legitimate target of a religiously motivated assassination is an interesting question, as is the issue of whether or not Mohammed B. sought and received the proper permission from religious authorities for carrying out his act.

18. My account builds on my previous book on this assassination, Eyerman (2008).

19. Her application for political asylum would eventually come back to haunt Ali. In 2006, she was forced to resign from parliament after a television program revealed that she had used a false name when filling in her application in 1992. A long and emotional debate ensued, in which the possibility that she might lose her citizenship was raised. The political turmoil surrounding Ali's status and the role of government ministers in the issue resulted in the fall of the reigning political coalition. Two days later, it was announced that Ali could retain her Dutch citizenship. She currently resides in the United States.

20. Although Bouyeri was raised in a Muslim household and apparently followed the rituals associated with Islam, his identification with his religion could be called thin, in that it was multilayered. Sometime in 2003, he moved toward a much thicker identification with Islam and with a particular radical or politicized version.

21. This highly publicized event occurred in June 2004. Dressed in a white gown, head covering, and a false beard, Van Gogh spoke on the theme "How radical Islam has changed Amsterdam." He ridiculed those who might be attracted to this ideology and movement. In a typically self-deprecating way, he began his remarks: "After the questions was put to me on this stage how Amsterdam has changed, I immediately thought of myself. As a result of my disappointing experience with the weaker sex, I went looking for a belief in which a woman knows her place." He then went on to

ridicule Mayor Cohen when listing other "advantages" of this belief: "...the biggest advantage is that the Mayor of Amsterdam is a useful idiot who continually seeks a 'dialogue' with us." In the guise of an imam, Van Gogh then "threatened" Hirsi Ali: "We will deal with the Hirsi Ali problem soon enough, despite the body guards... it is only a question of time when there will be a nice funeral, just like the one for that other heathen, Pim Fortuyn" (for a translation of the entire performance, see www. militantislammonitor.org/pf.php?id=333).

22. Another "friend" of Van Gogh, the author Theodor Holman, reports in his recent book on Van Gogh that Fortuyn had asked Van Gogh to become minister of culture in his eventual government(www.nu.nl/politiek/2113592/fortuyn-vroeg-van-gogh-als-minister.html).

6 CONCLUSION

1. Here we can distinguish between discourse and narrative as I use the terms. By discourse I mean a structured, rule-bound public discussion about topics of general concern. By narrative I mean the frames and forms that structure accounts and stories. In this sense, discourses are wider and broader and can contain many narratives.

2. This insightful article also reveals how Holocaust survivors, who up to the point of the Eichmann trial, had been stigmatized and marginalized within an Israeli society oriented toward a progressive future and wanting to forget its past, could now find a collective voice (see also Alexander and Dromi 2011). A similar phenomenon can be seen in contemporary Argentina, where left-wing survivors of the military junta, that is, those who had not "disappeared," have moved from being stigmatized to playing a central role as witnesses in the ongoing legal procedures against members of the military regime.

3. There is a long academic discussion about the relation between history and memory, as well as about what has been called "traumatic memory." See, for example, LaCapra 2001. The so-called historians' dispute (which took place in Germany during the 1980s) about the historical interpretation of the Holocaust also focused on the relation between historical facts and their representation (see, for example, Habermas 1990).

4. In their analysis of Dutch media coverage of Fortuyn's funeral, Pantti and Wieten (2005) argue the opposite—that the media was concerned with creating unity out of a very dangerous and divisive situation, similar to the manner in which the Swedish press had conducted itself after the assassination of Anna Lindh.

5. The DVD version of *006* contains a running diary, recorded after each day of filming, in which Van Gogh recounts the day's activities and what he seeks to portray about the murder of Fortuyn. Since the film was released posthumously and we are aware of the protagonist's fate, it is quite moving to view these recorded sessions, which reveal a thoughtful and subdued artist at work on material that he clearly loves.

6. Historian Taylor Branch, author of a three-volume history of Martin Luther King and the civil rights movement, was called upon by the *New York Times* (September 5, 2010:9, Sunday Opinion) to mediate the controversy. He concluded his rather favorable remarks about this new march on Washington by stating, "Our political health, in the spirit of Dr. King's march, requires thoughtful and bold initiatives from all quarters."

7. The building of a number of new schools, called the Robert F. Kennedy Community Schools, on the site where the Ambassador Hotel once stood was the subject of great

controversy in 2010. This was the case not because of the name or the location, but because of what some saw as the extravagant expense and design of the project (*New York Times* September 5, 2010:14). In defending the schools, Paul Schrade, himself the victim of one of the bullets aimed at Robert Kennedy, said, "This is a wonderful tribute to him. This is what he wanted."

8. The Palme assassination is also part of a course in crisis management at the Swedish National Defense College, which has also published a report on the incident (www.crismart.org).

9. Mervi Pantti (2005:366) makes a similar case in her study of the coverage of the murders of Palme and Lindh in the Finnish press. She uncovers several formulas used by the media to make possible "more extensive possibilities for identification and consequently for emotional engagement" (p 366). She writes, for example, "Both Palme and Lindh were described as great human beings, 'the best of us', but also ordinary. Their stories were identical. Palme was one of us because he wanted to walk back home from work…In Anna Lindh's case, it was her rucksack that was elevated to a symbol of ordinariness: she was a successful yet down-to-earth woman."

10. For an analysis of those acts of crisis management, see Hansen (2000).

11. In their study of the diffusion of the news of Olof Palme's death, Weibull et al. (1987) show how the time and place of the murder influenced knowledge about it. Because Palme was killed around midnight in a country where radio and television shut down early, most people in Sweden knew nothing about the murder until the following morning. If Palme had been assassinated during the day, they write, things would have been very different.

REFERENCES

Abrams, Philip (1982) *Historical Sociology*. Ithaca: Cornell University Press.

Alderman, Derek (2006) "Street Names as Memorial Arenas," in Romano and Raiford 2006, pp. 67–95.

Alexander, Jeffrey (2004) "Toward A Theory of Cultural Trauma," in Alexander et al. 2004.

———— (2009) *Remembering the Holocaust: A Debate*. New York: Oxford University Press.

Alexander, Jeffrey and Elizabeth Breese (2011) "Introduction" in Eyerman et al. (eds.) 2011. *Narrating Trauma: On the Impact of Collective Suffering*. Boulder, CO: Paradigm Publishers.

Alexander, Jeffrey, and Shai Dromi (2011) "Trauma Construction and Moral Restriction: The Ambiguity of the Holocaust for Israel," in Eyerman et al. 2011.

Alexander, Jeffrey, Ron Eyerman, Bernard Giesen, Neil Smelser, and Piotr Sztompka (eds.) (2004) *Cultural Trauma and Collective Identity*. Berkeley: University of California Press.

Alexander, Jeffrey, Bernhard Giesen, and Jason Mast (eds.) 2006. *Social Performance*. Cambridge: Cambridge University Press.

Ali, Ayaan Hirsi (2004) *Submission*. Amsterdam: Augustus.

Anthony, Andrew (2010) "Göran Lindberg and Sweden's Dark Side," *The Observer* (www.guardian.co.uk/world/2010/aug/01/goran-lindberg-sweden-crime-palme).

Arendt, Hannah (1961) "Truth and Politics," in *Between Past and Future: Six Exercises in Political Thought*. New York: Viking.

Åsard, Erik (2006) *Det Dunkelt Tänkta* (Dark Thoughts). Stockholm: Ordfront.

Ayton, Mel (2005) *A Racial Crime*. Las Vagas, N.V.: ArcheBooks.

———— (2007) *The Forgotten Terrorist: Sirhan Sirhan and the Assassination of Robert F. Kennedy*. Dulles, VA: Potomac Books.

Bartmanski, Dominik, and Ron Eyerman (2011) "The Worst was the Silence: The Unfinished Drama of the Katyn Massacre" in Eyerman et al. 2011.

Bauman, Zygmunt (1989) *Modernity and the Holocaust*. Ithaca, NY: Cornell University Press.

Bell, J. Bowyer (2005) *Assassin*. New Brunswick, NJ.: Transaction.

Ben-Yehuda, Nachman (1993) *Political Assassinations by Jews*. Albany: State University of New York Press.

Bloomgaarden, Hajo, and Claes de Vreese (2007) "Dramatic Real-World Events and Public Opinion Dynamics. Media Coverage and its Impact on Public Opinion to an Assassination. Evidence from a Quasi-Experimental Panel Study." *International Journal of Public Opinion Research* 19, no. 3:354–66, www.Oxfordjournals.org.

Borgnäs, Lars (2006) *En Iskall Vind Drog genom Sverige* (An Icy Wind Swept Through Sweden). Stockholm: Norstedts.

Bonjean, Charles, Richard Hill, and Harry Martin (1965) "Reactions to the Assassination in Dallas," in Greenberg and Parker 1965, pp. 178–198.

Brown, Elaine (1992) *Taste of Power*. New York: Pantheon.

Bugliosi, Vincent (2007) *Four Days in November: The Assassination of President John F. Kennedy*. New York: W.W. Norton & Company.

Bundeson, Jan (2005) *Blood on the Snow*. Ithaca, NY: Cornell University Press.

Carlsson, Ingvar (1999) *Ur Skuggan av Olof Palme* (Out from Olof Palme's Shadow). Stockholm: Hjalmarsson and Högberg.

Caruth, Cathy (ed.) (1995) *Trauma: Explorations in Memory*. Baltimore: Johns Hopkins University Press.

——— (1996) *Unclaimed Experience*. Baltimore: Johns Hopkins University Press.

Chorus, Jutta, and Menno de Galan (2002) *in de ban van Fortuyn* (Under Fortuyn's Spell). Amsterdam: Mets and Schilt.

Chappell, David (no year) "Dream: The Battle over Martin Luther King's Legacy," unpublished manuscript.

Clarke, Thurston (2008) *The Last Campaign: Robert F. Kennedy and 82 Days That Inspired America*. New York: Henry Holt.

Cleaver, Eldridge (1968) *Soul on Ice*. New York: Delta.

Dayan, Daniel, and Elihu Katz (1992) *Media Events*. Cambridge, MA: Harvard University Press.

Daynes, Gary (1997) *Making Villains, Making Heroes*. New York: Garland Publishing.

De Jong, Stan (2005) *Prettig Weekend* (Pleasant Weekend). Amsterdam: Column Xtra.

Demertzis, Nicolas (2009) "Mediatizing Traumas in the Risk Society. A Sociology of Emotions Approach," in Hopkins et al. 2009.

Dyson, Michael (2008) *April 4, 1968: Martin Luther King Jr.'s Death and How it Changed America*. New York: Basic Books.

Eissler, K.R. (1986) *Freud as Expert Witness*. Madison, CT: International Universities Press.

Eppridge, Bill (2008) *A Time It Was: Bobby Kennedy in the Sixties*. New York: Abrams.

Erikson, Kai (1978) *Everything in its Path*. New York: Simon and Schuster.

——— (1995) "Notes on Trauma and Community," in Caruth 1995.

Eyerman, Ron (2002) *Cultural Trauma Slavery and the Formation of African American Identity*. Cambridge: Cambridge University Press.

——— (2008) *The Assassination of Theo van Gogh*. Durham, NC: Duke University Press.

——— (forthcoming) "Harvey Milk and the Trauma of Assassination" *Cultural Sociology*.

Eyerman, Ron, Jeffrey Alexander, and Elizabeth Breese (eds.) (2011) *Narrating Trauma: On the Impact of Collective Suffering*. Boulder, CO: Paradigm Publishers.

Faber, Johan (2008) *Wat Bezielde Volkert Van Der G.* (What Possessed Volkert Van Der G.). Amsterdam: Nijgh and Van Ditmar.

Fassin, Didier, and Richard Rechtman (2009) *The Empire of Trauma: An Inquiry into the Condition of Victimhood*. Princeton, NJ: Princeton University Press.

Felman, Shoshana (2002) *The Juridical Unconscious: Trials and Traumas in the Twentieth Century*. Cambridge, MA: Harvard University Press.

Felman, Shoshana, and Dori Laub (1992) *Testimony: Crises of Witnessing in Literature, Psychoanalysis, and History*. New York: Routledge.

Ford, Franklin (1985) *Political Murder*. Cambridge, MA: Harvard University Press.

Franchell, Eva (2009) *Väninnan* (A Friend). Stockholm: Bonniers.

Frank, Gerold (1972) *An American Death*. New York: Doubleday.

Freyd, Jennifer (1997) *Betrayal Trauma: The Logic of Forgetting Childhood Abuse*. Cambridge, MA: Harvard University Press.

Giesen, Bernhard (2004) "The Trauma of the Perpetrators: The Holocaust as the Traumatic Reference of German National Identity," in Alexander et al. 2004, pp. 112–154.

Greenberg, Bradley, and Edwin Parker (eds.) (1965) *The Kennedy Assassination and the American Public.* Stanford, CA: Stanford University Press.

Habermas, Jurgen (1975) *Legitimation Crisis.* Boston, MA: Beacon Press.

———— (1990) *The New Conservatism: Cultural Criticism and the Historians' Debate.* Cambridge: MIT Press.

Hadenius, Stig (2000) *Svensk politik under 1900-talet* (Swedish Politics in the 20th Century). Stockholm: Hjalmarsson and Högberg.

Hamill, Pete (2008) "The Last Campaign," in Bill Eppridge, *A Time it Was: Bobby Kennedy in the Sixties.* New York: Abrams.

Hansen, Dan (2000) *The Crisis Management of the Murder of Olof Palme.* Stockholm: Crismart.

Hartman, Geoffrey (1996) *The Longest Shadow.* New York: Palgrave Macmillan.

Heins, Volker, and Andreas Langenohl (2011) "A Fire That Doesn't Burn? The Allied Bombing of Germany and the Cultural Politics of Trauma," in Eyerman et al. 2011.

Higgonnet, Margaret (2002) "Authenticity and Art in Trauma Narratives of World War 1" *Modernism/modernity* 9, no. 1: 91–107.

Holmberg, Sören, and Lennart Weibull (2004) *Lyckan kommer och lyckan går* (Good Times Come and Go) SOM Report 36 (Society, Opinion, Mass Media). Gothenberg: Gothenberg University Press.

Hopkins D., J. Kleres, H. Flam, and H. Kuzmia (eds.) (2009). *Theorizing Emotions.* Frankfurt: Campus.

Horkheimer, Max, and Theodor Adorno (2002) *Dialectic of Enlightenment.* Stanford, CA: Stanford University Press.

Horowitz, Irvin (1972) *Assassination.* New York: Harper and Row.

Jennekvist, Leif (2005) *Mordet på Anna Lindh* (The Murder of Anna Lindh). Stockholm: Bonniers.

Johansson, Olof (1995) "Swedish Reaction to the Assassination of the Swedish Prime Minister Olof Palme." *Scandinavian Political Studies* 18, no. 4: 265–83.

Kaiser, Robert (2008) *R.F.K. Must Die.* New York: The Overlook Press.

Kansteiner, Wulf (2004) "Genealogy of a Category Mistake: A Critical Intellectual History of the Cultural Trauma Metaphor." *Rethinking History* 8, no. 2: 193–221.

Kaplan, E. Ann (2005) *Trauma Culture.* Piscataway, NJ: Rutgers University Press.

Kantorowicz, Ernst (1957) *The King's Two Bodies.* Princeton, NJ: Princeton University Press.

Kaplan, E. Ann, and Ben Wang (2004) *Trauma and Cinema.* Hong Kong: Hong Kong University Press.

Kirkham, James, Sheldon Levy, and William Crotty (2002) *Assassination and Political Violence: A Report of the National Commission on the Causes and Prevention of Violence.* Honolulu, HI: University Press of the Pacific.

LaCapra, Dominick (2001) *Writing History, Writing Trauma.* Baltimore: Johns Hopkins University Press.

Laqueur, Thomas (2010) "We Are All Victims Now." *London Review of Books* 32, no. 13.

Lechner, Frank (2008) *The Netherlands.* New York: Routledge.

Lentz, Richard (1990) *Symbols, The News Magazines, and Martin Luther King.* Baton Rouge: Louisiana State University Press.

Mannheim, Karl (1952) "The Problem of Generations," in *Essays in the Sociology of Knowledge.* London: Routledge and Kegan Paul.

Margry, Peter Jan (2003) "The Murder of Pim Fortuyn and Collective Emotions, Hype, Hysteria and Holiness in The Netherlands?" *Ethnofoor: antropologisch tijdschrift* 16:106–131.

Mast, Jason (2006) "The Cultural Pragmatics of Eventness: the Clinton/Lewinsky Affair," in Alexander et al. 2006.

Moldea, Dan (1995) *The Killing of Robert F. Kennedy.* New York: W.W. Norton and Company.

Monahan, Brian (2010) *The Shock of the News.* New York: NYU Press.

Morgan, Edward P. (2006) "The Good, the Bad, and the Forgotten" in Romano and Raiford 2006.

Mossman, B.C. and M.W. Stark (1991) *The Last Salute: Civil and Military Funerals 1921–1969.* Washington, D.C.: Department of the Army.

National Geographic (2009) *The Lost JFK Tapes.* DVD

Newseum (2003) *President Kennedy Has Been Shot.* Naperville, IL: Sourcebooks.

Nilsson, Karl Alvar (2001) *Ondskan, Hatet, Mordet* (Evil, Hate, Murder). Stockholm: Hjalmarsson and Högberg.

Östberg, Kjell (2010) *När Vinden Vände* (When the Wind Changes). Stockholm: Leopard.

Pantti, Mervi (2005) "Masculine Tears, Feminine Tears and Crocodile Tears: Mourning Olof Palme and Anna Lindh in Finnish Newspapers." *Journalism* 6, no. 3: 357–77.

Pantti, Mervi, and Jan Wieten (2005) "Mourning Becomes the Nation: Television Coverage of the Murder of Pim Fortuyn." *Journalism Studies* 6, no. 3: 301–13.

Pels, Dick (2003) *De geest van Pim* (Pim's Spirit). Amsterdam: Anthos.

Peri, Yoram (ed.) (2000) *The Assassination of Yitzhak Rabin.* Stanford: Stanford University Press.

Perlstein, Rick (2008) *Nixonland.* New York: Schribner.

Pinchevski, Amit, and Tamar Liebes (2010) "Severed Voices: Radio and the Mediation of Trauma in the Eichmann Trial." *Public Culture* 22, no.2: 265–91.

Polletta, Francesca (1998) "Legacies and Liabilities of an Insurgent Past." *Social Science History* 22, no. 4: 479–512.

Ray, James Earl (1992) *Who Killed Martin Luther King Jr.?* New York: Marlowe and Company.

Risen, Clay (2009) *A Nation on Fire.* Hoboken, NJ: Wiley.

Romano, Renee, and Leigh Raiford (eds.) (2006) *The Civil Rights Movement in American Memory.* Athens: University of Georgia Press.

Rönnegård, Eric (2008) *Kris I ledningen för svensk polis* (Leadership Crisis in the Swedish Police). Stockholm: Jure.

Schlesinger, Arthur (1978) *Robert Kennedy and His Times.* New York: Ballantine Books.

Schwartz, Barry (2000) *Abraham Lincoln and the Forge of National Memory.* Chicago: University of Chicago Press.

Sewell, William (1992) "A Theory of Structure: Duality, Agency and Transformation." *American Journal of Sociology* 98, no. 1: 1–29.

Sewell, Mike (1996) "British Responses to Martin Luther King Jr and the Civil Rights Movement, 1954–68," in Ward and Badger 1996.

Sides, Hampton (2010) *Hellhound on His Trail.* New York: Doubleday.

Smelser, Neil (2004) "Psychological and Cultural Trauma," in Alexander et al. 2004.

Siebelt, Peter (2003) *Econostra.* Soesterberg: Aspekt.

SOU (1988, 1999) *Rapport av Parlamentariska kommissionen med anledningen av mordet på Olof Palme* (Report of the Parliamentary Commission into the murder of Olof Palme). Stockholm: Justitiedepartmentet.

Spasic, Ivana (2011) "The Trauma of Kosovo in Serbian National Narratives," in Eyerman et al. 2011.

Steers, Edward (2001) *Blood on the Moon: The Assassination of Abraham Lincoln.* Louisville: University of Kentucky Press.

Stern, Steve (2004) *Battling for Hearts and Minds: Memory Struggles in Pinochet's Chile.* Durham, NC: Duke University Press.

Sztompka, Piotr (2004) "The Trauma of Social Change: A Case of Postcommunist Societies," in Alexander, et al. (eds.) *Cultural Trauma and Collective Identity.* University of California Press, Berkeley.

Uitermark, Justus (2010) "Dynamics of Power in Dutch Integration Politics" PhD thesis, University of Amsterdam.

Unsgaard, Edvard (2005) *Mijailovic.* Stockholm: Norstedts.

Verdery, Kathrine (2000) *The Political Lives of Dead Bodies.* New York: Columbia University Press.

Vinitzky Seroussi, Vered (2009) *Yitzhak Rabin's Assassination.* Albany: SUNY Press.

Volkan, Vamik (2001) "Transgenerational Transmissions and Chosen Traumas: An Aspect of Large-Group Identity." *Group Analysis* 34, no. 2: 79–97.

Robin Wagner-Pacifici (1986) *The Moro Morality Play.* Chicago: University of Chicago Press.

——— (2010) "Theorizing the Restlessness of Events." *American Journal of Sociology* 115, no. 5: 1351–86.

Wall, Gunnar (1996) *Mörkläggning* (Cover-up). Gothenberg: Kärret.

Ward, Brian, and Tony Badger (1996) (eds.) *The Making of Martin Luther King and the Civil Rights Movement.* London: Macmillan.

Watters, Pat (1969) "In Memphis: One Year Later." Atlanta: The Southern Regional Council In Cooperation with the Tennessee Council on Human Relations.

Weibull, Lennart, Rutger Lindahl, and Karl Erik Rosengren (1987) "News Diffusion in Sweden: The Role of Media." *European Journal of Communication* 2, no. 3: 143–70.

White, Hayden (2008) "The Historical Event." *Differences: A Journal of Feminist Cultural Studies* 19, no. 2: 9–34.

Wilkinson, Doris (ed.) (1976) *Social Structure and Assassination Behavior: The Sociology of Political Murder.* Cambridge, MA.: Schenkman.

Zertal, Idith (2005) *Israel's Holocaust and the Politics of Nationhood.* Cambridge: Cambridge University Press.

Zelizer, Barbie (1992) *Covering the Body.* Chicago: University of Chicago Press.

——— (2000) "The Past in Our Present: The Assassinations of Yitzhak Rabin and John F. Kennedy" in Peri 2000.

Index